RC 480.55 .C68 2010
Coren, Alex.
Short-term psychotherapy

SHORT-TERM PSYCHOTHERAPY MHCC WITHDRAWN

D0223127

BASIC TEXTS IN COUNSELLING AND PSYCHOTHERAPY

Series editor: Stephen Frosh

This series introduces readers to the theory and practice of counselling and psychotherapy across a wide range of topic areas. The books appeal to anyone wishing to use counselling and psychotherapeutic skills and are particularly relevant to workers in health, education, social work and related settings. The books are unusual in being rooted in psychodynamic and systemic ideas, yet being written at an accessible, readable and introductory level. Each text offers theoretical background and guidance for practice, with creative use of clinical examples.

Published

Jenny Altschuler
WORKING WITH CHRONIC ILLNESS

Bill Barnes, Sheila Ernst and Keith Hyde
AN INTRODUCTION TO GROUPWORK

Stephen Briggs
WORKING WITH ADOLESCENTS AND YOUNG ADULTS 2nd edition

Alex Coren
SHORT-TERM PSYCHOTHERAPY 2nd edition

Jim Crawley and Jan Grant
COUPLE THERAPY

Emilia Dowling and Gill Gorell Barnes
WORKING WITH CHILDREN AND PARENTS
THROUGH SEPARATION AND DIVORCE

Loretta Franklin
AN INTRODUCTION TO WORKPLACE COUNSELLING

Gill Gorell Barnes
FAMILY THERAPY IN CHANGING TIMES 2nd edition

Fran Hedges
AN INTRODUCTION TO SYSTEMATIC THERAPY WITH INDIVIDUALS

Sally Hodges
COUNSELLING ADULTS WITH LEARNING DISABILITIES

Linda Hopper
COUNSELLING AND PSYCHOTHERAPY WITH CHILDREN AND
ADOLESCENTS

A McFayden
WORKING WITH CHILDREN WITH LEARNING DIFFICULTIES

Ravi Rana
COUNSELLING STUDENTS

Tricia Scott
INTEGRATIVE PSYCHOTHERAPY IN HEALTHCARE

Geraldine Shipton
WORKING WITH EATING DISORDERS

Laurence Spurling
AN INTRODUCTION TO PSYCHODYNAMIC COUNSELLING 2nd edition

Paul Terry
COUNSELLING AND PSYCHOTHERAPY WITH OLDER PEOPLE 2nd edition

Jan Wiener and Mannie Sher
COUNSELLING AND PSYCHOTHERAPY IN PRIMARY HEALTH CARE

Shula Wilson
DISABILITY, COUNSELLING AND PSYCHOTHERAPY

Steven Walker
CULTURALLY COMPETENT THERAPY

Invitation to authors

The Series Editor welcomes proposals for new books within the Basic Texts in Counselling and Psychotherapy series. These should be sent to Stephen Frosh at the School of Psychology, Birkbeck College, Malet Street, London, WC1E 7HX (e-mail s.frosh@bbk.ac.uk)

Basic Texts in Counselling and Psychotherapy
Series Standing Order ISBN 0–333–69330–2
(outside North America only)

You can receive future titles in this series as they are published by placing a standing order. Please contact your bookseller or, in the case of difficulty, write to us at the address below with your name and address, the title of the series and the ISBN quoted above.

Customer Services Department, Macmillan Distribution Ltd
Houndmills, Basingstoke, Hampshire RG21 6XS, England

SHORT-TERM PSYCHOTHERAPY

A PSYCHODYNAMIC APPROACH

2nd Edition

ALEX COREN

DIRECTOR OF PSYCHODYNAMIC STUDIES,
UNIVERSITY OF OXFORD

© Alex Coren 2001, 2010

All rights reserved. No reproduction, copy or transmission of this publication may be made without written permission.

No portion of this publication may be reproduced, copied or transmitted save with written permission or in accordance with the provisions of the Copyright, Designs and Patents Act 1988, or under the terms of any licence permitting limited copying issued by the Copyright Licensing Agency, Saffron House, 6–10 Kirby Street, London EC1N 8TS.

Any person who does any unauthorized act in relation to this publication may be liable to criminal prosecution and civil claims for damages.

The author has asserted his right to be identified as the author of this work in accordance with the Copyright, Designs and Patents Act 1988.

First edition published 2001
Second edition published 2010
First published 2001 by
PALGRAVE MACMILLAN

Palgrave Macmillan in the UK is an imprint of Macmillan Publishers Limited, registered in England, company number 785998, of Houndmills, Basingstoke, Hampshire RG21 6XS.

Palgrave Macmillan in the US is a division of St Martin's Press LLC, 175 Fifth Avenue, New York, NY 10010.

Palgrave Macmillan is the global academic imprint of the above companies and has companies and representatives throughout the world.

Palgrave® and Macmillan® are registered trademarks in the United States, the United Kingdom, Europe and other countries.

978–0–230–55157–2

This book is printed on paper suitable for recycling and made from fully managed and sustained forest sources. Logging, pulping and manufacturing processes are expected to conform to the environmental regulations of the country of origin.

A catalogue record for this book is available from the British Library.

A catalog record for this book is available from the Library of Congress.

10 9 8 7 6 5 4 3 2 1
19 18 17 16 15 14 13 12 11 10

Printed in China

'Look,' Aileen said. 'Forget Prozac. Forget Freud's abandonment of the seduction theory. Forget Jeffrey Masson – or is it Jackie Mason? The only thing that is going to revolutionize this profession is Bidding the Job.'

'I specialise in Christmas,' said the psychotherapist, a man named Sydney Poe, who wore an argyle sweater vest, a crisp bow tie, shiny black oxfords, and no socks. 'Christmas specials. You feel better by Christmas or your last sessions free.'

'I like the sound of that,' said Aileen. It was already December first. 'I like the sound of that a lot.'

(Lorrie Moore, 'Birds of America')

CONTENTS

INTRODUCTION TO
SECOND EDITION

Compared to the vast amount of neurotic misery there is in the world, and perhaps need not be, the quantity we can do away with is almost negligible ... at some point or other the conscience of society will awake and remind it that the poor man should have just as much right to assistance for his mind as he now has for the life-saving help offered by surgery; and that the neurosis threaten public health no less than tuberculosis ... we shall then be faced by the task of adapting our techniques to the new conditions. (Freud, 'Lines of Advance in Psychoanalytic Therapy', *Standard Edition*, vol. 17, 1919)

The new conditions have clearly arrived; some would say they have been apparent for some considerable time.

When the first edition of this book appeared, short-term therapy, particularly within the psychodynamic tradition, was viewed as an upstart, or interloper on a form of open-ended therapy that was seen as the gold standard of the clinical firmament. This is less the case today where a variety of brief interventions are competing for the limited resources in public sector mental health settings, and short-term interventions, of one form or another, have become the norm. The question now is 'Why does this person need open-ended therapy?' rather than 'Why does this person need a short-term intervention?' Short-term therapy has, in the parlance of our time, become the default option. This radical reconfiguration of clinical practice, while welcome to many, needs to be seen in the context of some confusion as to whether this development has come about for clinical, managerial or financial reasons. Cost containment issues should not obscure the very real advantages of planned short-term interventions. This edition attempts to address this question as well as offering readers an updated review of both the field of contemporary clinical short-term practice and, more specifically, additional material on issues of clinical practice which, I hope, are practical, easily accessible and will provoke further thought on how short-term psychodynamic practice can develop.

Arguably, today's short-term interventions are by design rather than, as was the case at the time of the first edition, by default, where the clients tended to vote with their feet, or drop out before the therapist was (or believed his client was) ready to finish. Therapy by default is unplanned, where clinicians do not work with the issue of time or within a short-term mindset which has 'time sensitive' or 'time aware' as its central organising feature.

Clinical practice suggests that short-term therapy is what most clients receive and that this forms an increasingly large part of a clinician's workload. It is arguably the case that while this is the reality of the contemporary consulting room experience, many clinicians still view open-ended or time-unlimited therapy as the framework from which 'brief therapies' are viewed and evaluated. Indeed, to call time-limited therapies 'brief' already begs the question that there is something which is the opposite of brief and therefore is, by definition, all that 'brief' is not: relaxed, leisurely, thorough, and timeless. It is for this reason that I have attempted, as in the first edition, to avoid the use of the word 'brief' in this book. Wherever possible, I have continued to use the terms 'short-term', 'focal', or 'time-limited therapy' (TLT) which are more able to transcend the evaluative, and, for many clinicians, emotionally laden, term 'brief therapy'.

Many time-limited therapies are not particularly 'brief', however that is defined (see below), but what distinguishes them is the open acknowledgement that the therapeutic frame needs to incorporate and use time as a therapeutic resource. To deny this is to deny our own relationship with – or 'transference' to – mortality and the fact that, as human beings, our time is finite. The limitation on time gives therapies a definite beginning, middle and end – resembling life itself – and, again like life, has the effect of avoiding therapies becoming aimless and drifting towards unclear, and often unsatisfactory, ends.

While it remains the case that the psychodynamic tradition has struggled to incorporate more focal or time-limited approaches, today there is a range of dynamic interventions that are speaking to the contemporary therapeutic climate without losing that which is essentially psychodynamic. Many have been included in this edition and offer guidance on how to develop, use and expedite the therapeutic process of focal therapies. The understanding of issues such as transference/counter-transference, the therapeutic alliance, unconscious and pre-conscious metaphors, developmental theory and the use of self in the therapeutic dyad, can be helpful in applying a time-limited therapeutic framework. It is the contention of this book that therapeutic relationships have the capacity to be transformational and that this is not related to length of therapy but to the ability to establish, understand and use a therapeutic relationship which places primacy on the 'here and now' therapeutic process of the consulting room.

What is meant by short-term therapy? In a sense, there are as many definitions of what time-limited therapy is as there are therapists and clients. 'Short-term' work can range from a one-off consultation to over a year's weekly work; the definition is often dependent on the therapist's own professional training, theoretical orientation and background. As we shall see, there is a wide variation in the length of therapies among time-limited therapists, who differ not only from open-ended therapists, but also between themselves, on a whole range of issues. My own preference is to distinguish between what we could call a focal consultation, or conversation, which may be in the region of four to six sessions, and planned focal therapy which can involve treatments whose length can stretch over some months. What characterises short-term psychodynamic therapy are high levels (within the context of the psychodynamic school) of therapist activity, and the attempt to work within a psychodynamic focus which links presenting problem, past conflict or trauma and the relationship with the therapist, the 'here and now' of the therapeutic process.

As we move into a world where economic factors, third party financial providers of therapeutic help and most importantly the preference of the 'consumers' of therapy themselves, are influencing the parameters of therapeutic work, it behoves us as clinicians to seriously take stock of what we offer and attempt to evaluate and articulate what it is we do and why we attempt it. This edition continues to highlight the advantages, as well as the limitations and dangers, of time-limited therapy.

This edition updates the historical survey of the psychodynamic school of practice and looks at what is psychodynamic in contemporary short-term approaches. I have continued to use *italics* to draw attention to core themes in relation to modern short-term therapies as they occur in the text.

What forms the central focus of this edition is the articulation of a short-term psychodynamic model, incorporating new and varied clinical examples of focal interventions and more material on the 'how to' aspects of short-term work with particular emphasis on current practice and work settings. The additional practical component includes new material on how to establish a short-term therapeutic relationship, the importance of a therapeutic focus (with material on how that might be achieved), working with differing clinical populations (especially those deemed borderline or presenting with personality disorders) as well as new material on the increasing evidence base for short-term dynamic interventions.

Chapter 1 updates the first two chapters of the first edition in tracing the development of focal therapies highlighting the features which are of contemporary importance. This includes the strengths, and difficulties, of the various models and links these to current practice.

Chapter 2 provides an updated critical overview of the current field and outlines what I consider to be the major current clinical therapeutic orientations. Given the plethora of treatments available, I have, as in the first edition, made subjective decisions as to what to include and used as my guide either those therapies which are widely practised or those that have some links – however peripheral they might initially appear – to psychodynamic theories.

Chapter 3 follows the previous chapter in articulating, and describing, a model of focal therapy which incorporates new developments in, among others, attachment theory, affect regulation, self-reflection and the importance of affects within the therapeutic dyad and their relation to both transference and counter-transference. Concepts of therapeutic process, the use of the therapeutic frame, transferential metaphors and symbols, narrative beliefs about the self, are all used to develop the concept of idiom in the therapeutic discourse with examples of how this can be understood and used in focal interventions. New material describes how these concepts can be used to effect a flexible clinical framework for time-limited therapies.

Chapter 4 discusses the somewhat controversial area of assessment for short-term interventions with a particular focus on Oedipal and pre-Oedipal stages of development and states of mind. This includes a discussion of how these, often misunderstood, concepts can be applied to working with a variety of clinical populations presenting with complex and long-standing difficulties. Various strategies and techniques, including the difference between a dynamically supportive and a dynamically expressive framework, are described in speaking to the differing clinical presentations in contemporary practice.

Chapter 5, while looking at the differences in therapeutic technique and practice between longer-and shorter-term therapies, describes the key principles of psychodynamic short-term therapy. It highlights and discusses some technical difficulties which are likely to be problematic for clinicians coming from open-ended frameworks. Particular attention is paid to the therapeutic alliance, therapeutic activity, realistic treatment aims and goals and the relationship to time. Key to this is how to establish, keep to and develop, a therapeutic focus. Focus formulation, and the importance of developing this as a collaboration within the therapeutic dyad, are described and a therapeutic stance, which is ideally both conversational and collaborative, is highlighted.

Chapter 6 addresses the training and supervisory needs of the time-limited focal therapist and presents a model of supervisory practice. The implications for training in the changing nature of clinical practice are highlighted with reference to the professional and personal competencies required by clinicians in using a short-term dynamic framework.

Chapter 7 looks at the clinical application of a time-limited model in various contexts and discusses how short-term therapy is practised, and how it can affect the therapeutic task, process, aims and goals. Of particular importance is the issue of working with difference in the domains of culture, religion and ethnicity.

Every clinical encounter involves engaging with difference. It is intrinsic (rather than extrinsic) to the model of short-term therapy articulated in this book, that the discovery of the client's idiom, central to working briefly, involves engaging with cultural, religious and ethnic difference. The discovery of a mutually shared language and therapeutic idiom involves engaging with cultural frames of reference, social networks and belief systems very different from one's own. Concepts of psychological distress or unease, the notion of a private self, or of privileging ideas of individual self-realisation, may not exist in some cultures or may be perceived and expressed in very different ways and have differing meanings. The short-term therapist will learn from their clients the particular emotional vocabulary, cultural, ethnic or religious significance which they accord to their lives and put this to the service of a shared therapeutic formulation and goal. Western philosophical and literary traditions – with their emphasis on forms of individual introspection and a capacity to reflect – which underline many therapeutic frameworks, need to be considered in relation to the client's own framework for understanding their distress. This is the foundation of the model of short-term therapy described in this book which may make it more acceptable to ethnic, social, cultural or religious minorities than more traditional open-ended psychodynamically informed interventions which emphasize Western philosophical and cultural traditions. We need to allow our clients to teach us their culturally specific idioms.

Chapter 8 looks at the current evidence base for short-term psychodynamic interventions and addresses the challenges, and potential problems, both for the clinician and client, of time-limited therapies. This includes some discussion of the wider social and ethical implications of the increasing use of focal therapies in an age of managed care, which can be perceived, and experienced by clinicians, as attempts by non-clinicians to set the framework for treatments. The dangers of psychological therapies becoming a form of social engineering, as opposed to personal liberation, are highlighted. More specifically, this chapter explores how to work with the clinicians' own feelings and clinical judgement in these contexts.

In conclusion, I hope this second edition offers the reader a useful, concise and intelligent explanation of short-term therapy, its uses and application in the twenty-first century.

Alex Coren
Oxford

1

IN THE BEGINNING: THE HISTORY OF SHORT-TERM THERAPY IN THE DEVELOPMENT OF PSYCHOANALYSIS

Freud was the original brief therapist. If symptoms, as originally suggested, were caused by traumatic memories which were repressed – or forgotten – it followed that if these memories could be recalled, and the feelings associated with them experienced, the symptoms would abate. Hypnosis was the preferred mode of treatment beginning with Breuer's treatment of Anna O. (Freud 1955). This was thought to be efficacious since recovery depended on the patient remembering something which was excluded from conscious thought or experience. Freud, noticing that not all patients could be hypnotised, developed the 'cathartic' method where the patient would lie on the couch and, often with the aid of gentle pressure on the forehead and the therapist's active urging, 'forgotten' memories and feelings were recalled. These techniques were to become the forerunners of psychoanalysis. However, these early and experimental treatments were brief, symptom-focused, and relied heavily on the active intervention of the therapist. In this they are very similar to modern focal therapies where brevity, therapeutic activity and a central organising focus are central themes.

The legacy of Freud

Freud suggested that the patients who would benefit from psychoanalysis included those who were highly motivated, reasonably intelligent, and showed a 'positive attitude' towards therapy and the

therapist. Motivation was important since Freud stressed the resistance which would surface once the patient becomes aware of 'the
direction in which the treatment is going'. The therapist had to be
firm in encouraging and insisting on the patient's ability to
remember while at the same time allowing himself to be appropriately supportive and 'educative' both in terms of talking about the
process of treatment and in making the 'unconscious conscious'.
This would enlist the patient as a 'collaborator' rather than condemn
the patient to being a passive and dependent receptacle of the therapist's wisdom. Transference only became the central feature of the
treatment much later although even at this time Breuer and Freud
recognised that 'material may be considered *either in the transference
or in the memories of the past*' (Flegenheimer 1982).

Freud believed that psychoanalysis was not applicable to the
'most serious' cases and could only be used for the milder ones.
Ironically today the reverse is claimed by the proponents of psychoanalysis and the more lengthy open-ended therapies: more intensive therapy is applicable for more serious pathology, less so for
minor developmental problems. This debate, as we shall see, is one
which is current among contemporary time-limited therapists.

Freud's early treatments only lasted a few weeks or months. Given
the nature of his theories at the time – that a combination of interpretation and insight would lead to recovery – the therapist need only
make the correct interpretations and the client accept them for symptoms to abate. If the client resisted, the therapist would make every
effort to convince the client of the correctness of the interpretation.
Early analysis, including Freud's self-analysis, was very brief. Gustav
Mahler's treatment consisted of one 4-hour session while an initially
sceptical Bruno Walter was successfully treated in five to six interviews spread over a period of time (Walter 1947). Lucy R. was seen
regularly over a nine-week period, a therapeutic frame which would
be seen as standard by many modern time-limited therapists, while
Katharina (Freud 1955) was seen once. Katharina's consultation is of
particular interest since it resembles many of the theoretical and
clinical applications of contemporary short-term therapies.

Freud was walking in the Hohe Tauern mountain range 'so that
for a while I may forget medicine and more particularly the neurosis',
when he was approached by Katharina, enquiring whether he was a
doctor. Freud, surprised and interested to 'find that neurosis could
flourish in this way at a height of over 6,000 feet' entered into what
he called a '*conversation*' (rather than a consultation) with her.
Katharina complained of periods of being 'out of breath' and, after

enquiring about the context in which these episodes occurred and their associations, Freud was able to *reframe the symptom* within a psychological framework. Freud was sure that the episodes of breathlessness were anxiety attacks; 'she was choosing shortness of breath out of the complex of sensations arising out of anxiety'. By questioning her on the exact nature of the symptom (*start where the client is* and do not be afraid to be active in asking questions and taking control), he was able to explore possible formulations for Katharina's difficulties. Freud's account of his meeting with Katharina is worth quoting in some detail. (Italics highlight the similarities between early Freud and modern time-limited therapies particularly in the areas of brevity, focus and therapist activity.)

> Was I to make an attempt at analysis? I could not venture to trans-plant hypnosis to this altitude but perhaps I might succeed with *simple talk*. I should have to try a *lucky guess*. I had found often enough that in girls anxiety was a consequence of the horror by which a virginal mind is overcome when it is faced for the first time with the world of sexuality. So I said '*If you don't know, I'll tell you how I think you got your attacks.*' [This can be seen as a tentative and humble reconstructive formulation similar to modern focal approaches.] 'At that time, two years ago [the time of the initial attack], you must have seen or heard something that very much embarrassed you, and that you had rather not have seen.

Katharina goes onto relate seeing her 'uncle' ('discretion' led to Freud only subsequently revealing that 'uncle' was actually Katharina's father) in a sexually compromising position with her cousin which led to the break-up of the 'uncle's' marriage. Katharina blamed herself for this and goes onto recall 'uncle's' attempts to seduce her. Freud ends by saying:

> If someone were to assert that the present case history is not so much an analysed case of hysteria as a case solved by *guessing* [this raises the interesting issue of the use of intuition in therapy which will be discussed in Chapter 6], I should have nothing to say against him … I hope this girl, whose sexual sensibility had been injured at such an early age, derived some benefit from our conversation. I have not seen her since.

While Freud can be accused of 'leading the witness' as a result of his activity, questioning and focus (which as we shall see is a common criticism of contemporary short-term therapists) and appears to place reliance on what he terms 'guesswork', he is perhaps unnecessarily defensive about this since his interventions are based on both his clinical experience and theory of neurosis. Freud was left not knowing the outcome of his conversation with Katharina, leaving us, and possibly him too, curious; an outcome common to many contemporary focal therapists. As Groves (1996, p. 447) points out:

> [Katharina] shows [Freud's] willingness to *adapt the therapeutic frame* to the temporal situation of the 'patient' … it is equally remarkable for the artistic tension and narrative force that survive translation and partly explain Freud's being nominated in the late 1920's for the Nobel Prize – not in medicine but in literature.

Freud eventually replaced the cathartic method with 'free association' which required therapeutic passivity and increased the likelihood that patients would regress and become more dependent on the process of therapy. They were also more likely to form a transference neurosis (a specific illusion of the therapeutic relationship) which would take longer to analyse and treat. Trauma theory was supplanted by the Oedipus complex. Issues of resistance, 'character' analysis, working through, and difficulties over termination can all be seen to be a consequence of the new analytic technique of free association and ensured that therapies were destined to take longer. Therapists became less active, challenging or supportive, and interpretations, both in relation to the therapist (i.e. transference) and in relation to the patient's early history (i.e. reconstruction) became central to the treatment and to therapeutic change. Therapeutic grandiosity, in the belief (and hope) that all aspects of mental life could and should be analysed, led to therapies developing a sense of timelessness which therapists, in thrall to the new 'science', did nothing to dissuade. With the loss of any sense of finite time, there was consequently no need for a focus and a reduced urgency for symptom relief or symptomatic attention. If therapies were becoming longer, they had almost by definition to become more rigorous; what other rationale could there be for the increasing length of time clients spent in the consulting room? 'Rigour' and 'depth' still remain contentious issues in contemporary debates about 'long-term or short-term' treatments. In psychoanalysis and psychoanalytic psychotherapy, increasing knowledge has led to the inevitable belief that treatments need to be longer; we could, however, infer that knowing more about them should make them shorter and it is this – and the increasing evidence base for short-term treatments – which in part fuel the development of briefer treatments among contemporary psychodynamic practitioners.

The fact that many of the early cases treated by the cathartic method improved, while others treated by free association showed less progress did nothing to dampen psychoanalytic zeal. Therapies became longer and longer and, as in many fundamentalist sects, anything that deviated from the true faith was rejected and ostracised. This may go some way to explaining why psychoanalytic clinicians have become so suspicious, uncomfortable and uneasy with the idea of time-limited therapy (TLP), and are tempted to regard it as somehow an inferior and diluted version of the 'real thing' (Coren 1996).

However, therapeutic passivity was not the only option for Freud at the time. Some believe he took the wrong turn. Malan (1992) views the choice that Freud made in reacting to increased resistance on behalf of the client with increased passivity on the part of the therapist as disastrous for the development of the psychodynamic therapies.

There is a long and honourable tradition of brief psychoanalytic psychotherapy and it is to its original proponents that we now turn.

Otto Rank and birth trauma

Freud had proposed a theory which was increasingly dominated by the ideas and philosophy of medicine. The 'drive–structural theory', as it was called, relied heavily on the belief that there were instincts/drives which were seeking release and which were confronted by an 'ego' or sense of self, which mediated between the individual and his environment. Essentially an intra-psychic, one-person, theory, it paid relatively little attention to the involvement of other people. As a consequence its clinical applications viewed the therapist as a detached observer or, if intervention was required, a guide. Many of Freud's contemporaries became uncomfortable with these ideas and began to posit clinical approaches which were more based on relational, that is two-person, concepts. Among the earliest dissenters were Otto Rank and Sandor Ferenczi.

Rank, emphasising the trauma of biological birth, drew attention to this event as a metaphor for separation, individuation and development for all individuals. Rather than view anxiety as a consequence of the individual's struggle to contain impulses, more especially sexual and aggressive drives, Rank saw it as a response to a 'primal fear, which manifests itself now as a fear of life, another time as a fear of death' (Rank 1929). Implicit in his view is the belief that therapy, like life, would need one day to end and that in every therapeutic hour issues of separation and individuation would be in evidence. Rank saw the patient as being in a relationship with the therapist which must end one day and the acceptance of this became the core ingredient of any successful therapy. The patient was encouraged to individuate and separate from the therapeutic process, and, since this involves similar issues to those experienced in the original birth trauma and its metaphoric equivalents, it is this element of therapy which is curative. Rank thought patients needed to be actively empowered to express their 'will' and thought the danger of Freudian therapy was that the patient would passively capitulate to the therapists' 'new explanation' for their behaviour or feelings. Along with this, he was the first to express concern that long-term, open-ended therapies, while enabling the therapist to learn more about psychological and psychic functioning, were unlikely to cure, or help, the patient as quickly as possible. Rank was among the first to espouse a developmental model for psychoanalysis rather than one circumscribed by ideas of 'medical cure'. These ideas continue to inform some of the contemporary 'lifetime models' of short-term therapy. Rank advocated:

- an emphasis on present experiences and relationships;
- emphasis on transference, especially in relation to the primary attachment to the mother, rather than any sexual or aggressive manifestations of drives or instincts;
- setting a termination date for therapy;
- open exploration of feelings and thoughts – and their clinical resistances – in relation to the therapeutic dyad.

Termination dates were set according to when Rank thought the patient was 'struggling with the will to individuate' (Messer and Warren 1995). For Rank, the patient is always aware that the treatment must one day finish. Not surprisingly, given Rank's belief in the trauma of birth and intrauterine life, he believed most patients would choose a period between seven and nine months in treatment, repeating the original maternal separation. Issues of dependency, separation and relatedness were central to any therapy, and needed to be incorporated into the therapeutic frame. Individuation, the fundamental goal of therapy, could best be addressed through acknowledging and working with limited time. His views on this are similar to those held today by James Mann: setting a time limit assists the patient in accepting the reality of finite time. The theory of the birth trauma and time limits led to treatments often only a few months long and heralded the ending of Rank's relationship with Freud in 1926.

Sandor Ferenczi, mutuality and the theory of trauma

Ferenczi, like his early collaborator, Rank (Ferenczi and Rank 1925), was concerned about the increasing therapeutic passivity, intellectualisation (a fear that psychoanalysis was becoming an academic and pedagogic discipline) and the increasing lack of any affective contact between patient and therapist which was being sacrificed to the increasing 'scientific approach' of Freud's developing practice. Believing that by placing paramount importance on the emotional experience of therapy, shorter therapies would result, Ferenczi experimented in increasing the emotional content of sessions, challenging the belief that the therapist should be a blank screen, and raised issues, alive today, about therapeutic neutrality which was becoming a cornerstone of psychoanalysis. Uneasy with the increasing academic preoccupation of psychoanalysis in its desire to become a profession allied to science and medicine, Ferenczi believed that psychoanalysis had become confused as to whether it was an academic, intellectual discipline or a clinical treatment aimed at curing distressed people. Believing that Freud had lost interest in the therapeutic aspects of psychoanalysis (that is, in essence, a relationship between two people centred around curing the patient's 'pain'), Ferenczi advocated 'active' involvement with patients during the therapy. While therapeutic passivity and inactivity were justified by those claiming scientific objectivity and neutrality for psychoanalysis, Ferenczi believed that vulnerable patients needed interpretations and scientific integrity less than support, encouragement and therapeutic 'nourishment' (Stanton 1990).

Together with Rank, Ferenczi held that childhood deprivation and conflict led to neurosis. As a consequence, he believed that deeply distressed or disturbed patients needed sometimes to be held and physically comforted and that to withhold this would be cruel, if not sadistic. Ferenczi suggested that therapeutic activity could redress the earlier parental failures that the patient had experienced and had brought them into therapy. Freud dismissed this by calling it 'the kissing technique', an accusation from which

Ferenzci's reputation in mainstream psychoanalysis never fully recovered, but in retrospect we can see how Ferenzci was attempting to stress the importance of process (i.e. the therapeutic relationship), rather than intellectual understanding, in therapy, as he comments in a letter to Freud dated 17 January 1930:

> I do not share ... your view that the therapeutic process is negligible or unimportant, and that simply because it appears less interesting to us we should ignore it. (quoted in Dupont 1995)

Rejecting the 'rigidity of analysis', Ferenczi advocated active and flexible interventions. Believing that Freud was becoming a pedagogue, teaching his patients what their symptoms meant and represented, Ferenczi wanted to establish a new cooperative therapeutic relationship and thereby empower his patients. Uncomfortable with what he viewed as the hypocrisy and conceit of certain analytic stances, he linked the 'trauma of the powerless child' in the face of the adult world with the trauma of the patient faced with an overbearing analyst:

> Ferenczi draws parallels among the child traumatised by the hypocrisy of adults, the mentally ill person traumatised by the hypocrisy of society and the patient, whose trauma is revived and exacerbated by the professional hypocrisy and technical rigidity of the analyst. (Dupont 1995)

Ferenczi believed that patients suffered from childhood deprivations and believed that rigid therapies were likely to revive and repeat the childhood traumas which they were attempting to cure. Inflexible therapies, and by implication therapists, could damage your health by subjecting you to a further trauma. This then becomes merely a repetition (as opposed to repairing or healing) of previous traumas. Uneasy with a theory which was increasingly becoming transformed into a rigid dogma, he was concerned that patients who were excluded from the increasingly rigid criteria of analysability were being effectively denied any therapeutic help. This was in itself traumatising. Ferenczi believed that all patients who asked for help should receive it and it was up to the therapist to decide and devise the most appropriate therapeutic response. The treatment needed to fit the patient, rather than the other way round.

At the time, these were radical ideas. They can be seen to predate modern concepts of the multi-disciplinary team – or triage – where clients are allocated to the treatment which most suits their needs rather than having to adapt to a single, possibly inappropriately rigid, therapy. This issue is also of central significance when assessing for time-limited therapies.

Ferenczi's view about trauma included a belief that therapists were often defensive about their own feelings and experiences in a manner which was unhelpful, and often harmful, to their patients. His response to this was the idea of 'mutual analysis'. When the therapist found himself struggling to help or provide support, he was encouraged

> [To] acquaint [the patient], as sincerely, as he can, with his own weaknesses and feelings. The analyst thus allows his patients to know better where they stand with him, even if in that way the patients must confront and assimilate some painful realities, they will cope better with these than with feigned friendliness. (Dupont 1995)

This raised the interesting issue of the therapist's self-disclosure – still a contentious topic – which will be discussed in Chapter 6. Ferenczi undertook these early experiments in the use of what we now call counter-transference by having double sessions, or alternating sessions – one for the therapist and one for the patient. This clearly became extremely problematic, not least in respect of boundaries and confidentiality, but was designed to address the power imbalance in therapy as well as enable both therapist and patient to 'place themselves in relation to the other with greater assurance'. Ferenczi's experiments in 'mutual analysis' failed, not least since they led to the roles of patient and therapist becoming blurred. Ferenczi eventually recognised the difficulties in this method but 'mutual analysis' can be seen as an early way of understanding and using counter-transference interpretations especially in relation to the therapist's 'blind spots'. This has particular relevance to short-term therapy.

Alfred Adler

Mention should be made in this section of Alfred Adler with particular reference to his contribution to the development of time-limited therapies. Taking up the issue of power in relationships, Adler saw this sense of powerlessness as rooted in the child's earliest reality. He proposed that the child has a primary wish to achieve mastery and this was rooted in social reality. Believing Freud was wrong to pay so little attention to reality factors in the child's (and, by definition, the adult's) development, Adler's thinking extended into social and educational areas. Adler believed that psychopathology arose

> [because of] a mistake in the whole style of life, in the way in which the mind has *interpreted its experiences*, in the meaning it has given to life, and in the actions with which it has answered the impressions received from the body and its environment, ... these *mistaken impressions* are acquired in early childhood. (Adler 1958; my italics)

In striving for unattainable personal goals and the pursuit of personal superiority, the individual was in danger of losing sight of his relatedness to others. This has a particularly contemporary relevance. While Adler was one of the first analysts to place the individual in a social and relational context, it is his therapeutic techniques which are of interest to us. Adler helped the patient to understand and recognise *'faulty beliefs'* which were not necessarily in the realm of consciousness. The patient had the 'courage' to do so as a result of his relationship with the therapist. Adler's approach took the form of *'discussions'* around the patient's misconceptions and how they related to his life. His therapeutic technique, while empathic and intuitive, also included *'guessings'* which were tentative suggestions and hypothesis which could be confirmed, negated or changed by subsequent material. He was also attentive to physical appearance, manner, posture and the symptom in giving clues to the faulty maladaptive beliefs which caused the patient difficulties. As we shall see, these are themes that recur in contemporary short-term therapies.

Ferenczi, Rank and Adler had become concerned at the increasing amount of time that analyses were appearing to take and the clinical application of theories that they thought were becoming increasingly impersonal. They emphasise how the patient's early deprivation or conflicts are repeated in the therapeutic relationship, advocate a more active therapeutic stance, rather than the purely interpretative, and in their belief in focusing on the symptom and its relationship to earlier deprivations or traumas, can be seen to be advocating a form of treatment which mainstream psychoanalysis found difficult to incorporate. Due to this they were in time condemned to 'the psychoanalytic Gulag; the world of not psychoanalysis' (Mitchell 1997).

Alexander and French

Alexander and French (1946) considered their work an extension of the more relational models of Ferenczi and Rank. They shared Ferenzci and Rank's belief that problems were related to previous deficiencies in environmental provision and parenting and their treatments reflected this in having an explicitly reparative aim. Alexander and French challenged the importance of facilitating the expression of repressed memories, historical reconstruction and interpretations. What was mutative in therapy they believed was the patient's emotional experience, rather than the correct interpretation. Therapy needed to be both an emotionally intense and short experience. Like Ferenczi and Rank, Alexander believed that long therapies often drifted into intellectualisation and consequently became less emotionally involving:

> An extreme generosity with interviews is not only uneconomical but, in many cases, makes the analysis less penetrating. Daily interviews often tend to reduce the patient's emotional participation in the therapy; they become routine, and prevent the development of strong emotions. (Alexander, in Barton, 1971)

Intensive treatment thus has the opposite outcome from what was intended. The 'corrective emotional experience', as it became known, was based on the new experience of an old conflict. Moreover, the repetition of previous experiences in the therapeutic relationship (although anticipated in that the client would seek, consciously or unconsciously, to repeat previous patterns) needed to be met by a new and different therapeutic response. It was these differences which were seen to be therapeutic. An example would be of a client who, subject to hostile and rejecting parenting, would expect the same, or a similar, response from the therapist only to be met with the opposite, i.e. a therapist who could be both accepting and nurturing. This is what was held to be curative.

> Because the therapist's attitude is different from that of the authoritative person of the past, he gives the client an opportunity to face again and again, under more favourable circumstances, those emotional situations which were formerly unbearable and to deal with them in a manner differently from the old. (Alexander, in Barton, 1971, p. 67)

What was required was the *'principle of flexibility'*. Alexander believed that therapists had tended to select their clients to fit their technique or theoretical base and that few had attempted 'to adapt the procedure to the diversity of cases they had encountered'. Consequently, he advocated the principle of clinical flexibility to ensure that the therapist – or therapy – can adapt the technique to the needs of the client rather than the other way round.

He was aware of the danger of dependency and advocated that treatment be interrupted for periods so that clients could actively work on their real-life problems without the therapist. Alexander made the point that many analyses had been revitalised by an unexpected absence or change on the part of the analyst which he believed could precipitate more 'relevant' material than the weekly or daily routine. Believing that 'the analytic process is not confined to the analytic interview', what clients did between sessions was as important as what happened in them. Sessions were then arranged 'flexibly' which aided the independence of the client and acknowledged real-life events outside the consulting room.

Clients were encouraged to focus on current life problems rather than the past which was only seen as relevant if it was in any way related to the current problem:

> The nearer the analyst can keep the [client] to his actual life problems, the more intensive and effective the therapeutic process is. From the point of view of ... research it might be advisable to encourage the patient to wander back into ... his early youth. *Therapeutically, however, such a retreat is valuable only insofar as it sheds light on the present.* Memory material must always be correlated with the present life situation, and the patient must never be allowed to forget that he came to the physician not for an academic understanding of the aetiology of his condition, but for help in solving his actual life problems. (Alexander, in Barton 1971)

Alexander also cautioned against what he termed 'transference gratification'. Alexander was aware that Freud had struggled with the possibility that the gratifications that the transference relationship may offer might outweigh, or replace, 'the desire to be cured'. Freud had remarked that transference 'impasses' had, in the early years of his practice, led to difficulty in persuading the patient to continue, while in his later years it had led to his difficulty in inducing them to finish. The notion of the 'impasse', and the need to focus actively on it, are important in short-term therapies. For Alexander, the transference relationship ran in parallel with real-life experience; it was less a repetition than a rehearsal and in essence must be orientated towards the present and future. Therapy must be in the service of life, not the other way around.

Transference can also provoke compliance. Having discovered the analyst's 'predilections', the patient may 'bring interesting material and give the impression of deepening insight and steady progress' and while 'the analyst may believe they are engaged in a thorough "working through", in reality the procedure has become a farce ... procrastination on behalf of the patient' (Alexander, in Barton 1971).

Regression, seen in psychoanalysis as the means by which early conflicts became accessible, was thought by Alexander less as evidence of the depth of an analysis, than 'a neurotic withdrawal from a difficult life situation back to childhood longings for dependence, gratifiable only in fantasy'. Thus, regression can be a defence which needed to be interpreted. The principle of flexibility ensured that regressions, where untherapeutic, were avoided. Alexander stressed that it was more important to work on *'transference patterns of behaviour'* rather than allowing/encouraging a regressive transference neurosis to develop.

Alexander's concept of the corrective emotional experience was criticised as a 'manipulation' of the transference not least by attempting to provide a therapeutic response diametrically opposite to the one the patient would expect. In response to this, and accusations that the concept of flexibility was artificial, Alexander countered that it was less a manipulation than analytic neutrality and the emotional non-participation of the traditional analytic approach.

Commenting that Freud himself had come to the conclusion that the time comes when the analyst must encourage the patient to 'engage in those activities he avoided in the past', Alexander believed that 'curbing the patient's tendency to procrastinate and to substitute analytic experience for reality (by careful manipulation of the transference relationship, by timely directives and encouragement) is one of the most effective means of shortening treatment' (Alexander, in Barton 1971).

It is perhaps ironic that these issues have become contentious again in contemporary psychoanalysis not least in relation to Lacan who found 5-minute sessions more effective than the standard 50-minute analytic hour.

The work of Alexander, together with Ferenczi and Rank, not only offered a coherent blueprint for how psychoanalytic concepts could be used in shorter therapies but also presaged a shift from the one-person drive/structural/instincts/defence model to modern object relations theory which recognised a therapeutic relationship in which both parties were constantly relating and influencing each other. The therapeutic relationship was now becoming the central feature of therapeutic improvement or change, no longer merely a blank screen for the projection of the patient's fantasies. However, in their time, brief treatments and their exponents were severely attacked by the psychoanalytic establishment and suffered a period of often malign neglect. Psychoanalysis believed – and some would say continues to believe – that notions of brevity and relationship are incompatible. It was the work of Michael Balint and his colleagues which led to time-limited therapies being rediscovered.

Michael Balint

Balint had been analysed by Ferenczi and shared with him the belief that patients attempt to obtain the unconditional love in therapy which had been denied them in childhood. This he came to term the 'search for the primary love object'. Like Ferenczi, he recognised that the increasing length of psychoanalytic treatments were actually providing new 'obstacles to cure'.

The work of Balint and his colleagues (Balint et al. 1972) implicitly recognised that previous attempts at describing briefer therapies had foundered on issues of therapeutic 'activity' and 'manipulation'. They had been rejected by the psychoanalytic establishment because of their apparent disregard of the value of transference interpretations. Since psychoanalysis had not been able to incorporate these new techniques, Balint attempted, through stressing the importance of interpretation, to place focal therapy back onto a continuum with psychoanalysis. Balint's initial attempts at 'focal therapy' foundered, perhaps not surprisingly, because of familiar concerns among his colleagues over whether the new techniques and methods might challenge and endanger pure psychoanalysis. Balint, however, persevered and a 'focal therapy workshop' was set up at the Tavistock Clinic from which Balint and colleagues (Ornstein and Enid Balint) wrote up a single case study: a Mr Baker, who presented with episodic paranoid jealousy. He was seen by Balint for 27 sessions over a 15-month period and followed up for a further four and a half years. The case study makes interesting reading for modern brief therapists for the light it throws on Balint's attempts to apply psychoanalytic concepts to focal therapy while still placing importance on central psychoanalytic tenets such as interpretation and instinct theory. Balint's 'Focal Therapy' can be seen to develop themes outlined by both Ferenczi and Alexander. Primacy was placed on the developing relationship between the patient and the therapist. The psychopathology of Mr Baker – which most analysts would have considered severe and at times during the treatment led to the possibility of hospitalisation – was of less importance than the developing therapeutic relationship and interaction between Balint and his client. Primacy was placed on viewing treatment as a *process* between two people.

In the account of Mr Baker's treatment, the workshop pioneered the use of an assessment form which placed emphasis on the specific quality of the doctor–patient relationship, salient features (i.e. *important moments*) of the initial interview, and the importance of having *focal aims*. Mr Baker's treatment roughly followed the two focal aims which were set in the initial interview.

Having a well-defined focal aim brought up the issue of *selective attention and selective neglect* specifically in relation to interpretations. The focal therapist could not pay equal attention to all material and only those aspects of the client's material that enhance the work of the chosen focus are interpreted.

This is not to say that whatever appears unrelated to the focus is ignored but that the therapist has to choose what to 'name and respond to'. In this way, the therapist chooses what to interpret and influences the direction and process of the therapy. This was a very new concept of interpretation.

Balint believed attention had to be paid to material within the orbit of the focal aim. He acknowledged that interpretations can be manipulative but are tentatively offered and confirmed or rejected by the client's ensuing material. They assist in defining the focus and are amenable to change and development.

Therapeutic flexibility included seeing Mr Baker with his wife – and occasionally only seeing his wife – as well as on occasion seeing Mr Baker's friends which Balint termed 'milieu therapy'. Recognition is paid to the work that goes on outside the therapy and that this might be as important as the work done in sessions. In a letter to Balint, Mr Baker says 'You, Dr. Balint, started something very important and I was able to finish it' (Balint et al. 1972, p. 121). This is very similar to what has been termed the 'ripple effect' in modern short-term therapies. In addition, for psychoanalytic practitioners, the notion that therapies may be incomplete and yet beneficial was radical and new.

The 'Focal Workshop' led to early attempts to delineate criteria for those who may benefit from shorter therapies. These included:

- a willingness/ability to explore feelings;
- a willingness to work within a therapeutic relationship based upon interpretation;
- the therapist's ability to understand the client in dynamic terms;
- the therapist's ability to formulate some kind of circumscribed treatment plan. (Malan 1963)

Balint viewed therapeutic change as a three-stage process. The therapist had to 'accept' what the client offered, 'understand' it, and then 'interpret' it at the appropriate moment. Consequently, focal therapy could be seen as being a form of applied psychoanalysis; the interpretation of unconscious and pre-conscious material was still seen as being central and mutative. In this way, Balint hoped to bridge the gap between the early brief therapists who were seen as challenging, and being a threat to, psychoanalysis, and the psychoanalytic profession. Central to this was a clear therapeutic aim, a focus which enabled the aim to be achieved and the necessity not to be 'sidetracked' by the wealth of analytic material. Balint applied these new techniques when offering a consultancy service to family doctors.

We now move on to look at how concepts highlighted by the early brief therapists have developed over time, who, by placing emphasis on interpretation, insight and the transference relationship can be seen to continue in the mainstream of analytic tradition.

Generalisations are problematic since contemporary short-term therapies differ not only from long-term therapies but also among themselves particularly in relation to therapeutic activity, focus, what constitutes brevity and the selection criteria. There are, however, increasingly areas of similarity and overlap. We shall begin with Sifneos, Davanloo and Malan.

Peter Sifneos: anxiety-suppressive and anxiety-provoking therapies

Peter Sifneos (Sifneos 1972, 1979) distinguished between anxiety-suppressive and anxiety-provoking short-term treatments. His anxiety-provoking technique is based upon careful selection criteria, early and active use of transference interpretations, and confrontation. Relatively little attention is paid to termination.

Sifneos places a high emphasis on the first meeting with a new client, seeing it as a microcosm of therapy. Active himself as a therapist, he expects the same response from his clients. Anxiety-provoking therapy is applicable to clients with well-circumscribed neurotic symptoms and aims at limited dynamic change, emphasising problem solving and crisis intervention. Anxiety-suppressive therapy is aimed at more disturbed clients and is more supportive in nature.

In *anxiety-provoking therapy*, Sifneos only included clients who could be seen to have problems at an Oedipal level of functioning. Clinical assessment required some evidence that the client's difficulties originated from the Oedipal stage of development which were seen to be a legacy of three-person relationships. Clients who were thought to evidence pre-Oedipal problems, a result of faulty or disturbed dyadic relationships, were thought to be unsuitable for anxiety-provoking therapy since they would have difficulties establishing the basic trust fundamental to the forging of a working therapeutic alliance and terminating treatment. This continues to be an important distinguishing criterion used by some contemporary time-limited therapists.

Treatment is seen as 'anxiety-provoking' since it directly confronts the client's defences rather than attempting to 'interpret the meaning or function of the defences' (Flegenheimer 1982). Transference is interpreted rigorously as is any form of resistance. This bears similarities to contemporary emotionally expressive short-term therapies (see ISTDT and AET below).

Sifneos does not use the framework of a definite termination date. No time limit is set but the client is informed from the outset that the treatment will only last 'several months', and is encouraged to share responsibility for the decision of when to terminate. Termination is, in part, the client's responsibility which decreases the client's dependence and passivity. What assists termination is 'the diligent avoidance of all pregenital issues throughout the treatment process' (Flegenheimer 1982). What this means is that issues around separation anxiety, and the development of an unhelpful transference neurosis, are kept to a minimum. Sifneos suggests that these problems can be avoided by stringent selection, the client sharing responsibility for the treatment, and the 'selective neglect' of all pre-Oedipal material. Sifneos' anxiety-provoking therapy has a maximum of 20 sessions with most lasting between 12 and 16 sessions.

His selection criteria are carefully drawn up and include:

- ability of the client to present with a circumscribed complaint;
- evidence of a 'meaningful' relationship during childhood;
- capacity to relate to therapist in the first meeting and to be open in expressing feelings;
- psychological sophistication and intelligence;
- motivation for change over and above symptom relief;
- ability to see symptoms as having a psychological dimension;
- 'emotional honesty' and capacity for introspection;
- ability to 'participate actively' in treatment;
- curiosity;
- a realistic view of what can be achieved in therapy and a willingness to make the 'necessary sacrifices'.

The focus of this therapy is extremely narrow: 'the failure to grieve a death, inability to finish a project because of success, fear, triangular futile love relationships – the standard grist of the analytic mill – these high level neurotic conflicts are the province of anxiety-provoking therapy' (in Groves 1996).

One of the objections that Sifneos himself acknowledged was that the selection criteria mainly included clients who 'were so healthy that they do not require any treatment at all'.

Sifneos contrasts anxiety-provoking therapy with *anxiety-suppressive therapy*. This is aimed at less healthy clients who might be discomforted by the more confrontational stance of anxiety provoking therapy. It is aimed at more disturbed, by implication, pre-Oedipal, clients and is more supportive in nature and includes environmental manipulation, reassurance and, if necessary, medication. Crisis support could last up to two months, brief therapy could last from two months to one year while, for clients with long-standing psychological difficulties and a history of poor interpersonal relationships, longer-term therapy may be indicated. However, similar selection criteria to the anxiety-provoking therapies applied. Clients receiving anxiety-provoking therapy were seen weekly over a period of time, anxiety-suppressive clients frequently were seen more intensively, often a number of times a week, but sometimes only for a few minutes. This reflects the more crisis-oriented and supportive direction of the therapy.

These two types of therapy are offered to different clinical populations and recognise that treatment needs to be tailored to the client's presenting problem and psychopathology. However, insight and interpretation are still seen as central to progress and cure and the 'one-person psychology' of the drive/structural model predominates.

David Malan and the triangle of insight

David Malan had worked with Michael Balint in the Focal Workshop at the Tavistock Clinic. Having initially thought that they would attempt to apply analytic techniques to relatively healthy clients who presented with acute problems they 'found none ... [so] we were then forced to take on any patient who came for treatment' (Malan 1979). Believing at first that they would need to use 'superficial techniques', they were surprised to find that clients responded well to 'deeper interpretations'. Attempting to avoid transference interpretations, they found that as psychoanalysts they were 'conditioned' to respond to transference material with transference interpretations. As a result, they 'stumbled' on a surprising and unexpected finding: even clients with long-standing difficulties appeared to achieve both symptomatic and dynamic relief in a brief time scale using a 'deep' technique (transference interpretations). Particularly therapeutic appeared to be interpretations linking the current interaction with the therapist with significant figures from the client's past.

In the initial interview, a *focus* was sought and a *trial interpretation* attempted. This gauged the client's initial suitability for brief work and became the cornerstone of their assessment process. The focus tended to be relatively narrow and defined by the therapist. Trial interpretations were seen as important not only in estimating the client's suitability to work with interpretations in the therapy, but also enabling a therapeutic alliance to be formed. If the interpretation was helpful in the first session, then therapeutic work could start. Care would be taken before making one since the therapist has to have some confidence that the client will be able to make constructive use of it rather than experience it as persecutory. The interpretation should be linked to the area of the focus and serves to find – or reformulate – a tentative focus. If the focus is correct, the client is likely to become more intensely engaged, more committed to the treatment and produce more material. The therapist's formulation of the focus is done on the basis of the triangle of insight. Assurance is sought that the focus is acceptable to the client. This is done by gauging the response to trial interpretations, the ease with which the client talks about feelings and problems, and the extent to which he displays positive motivation to engage in the treatment and consider change.

Brief intensive psychotherapy is then indicated, providing the following factors are not in evidence:

- prediction (on the therapist's part) that issues are too involved, complex or deep-seated;
- severe dependence and 'other unfavourable' transference manifestations;
- depressive or psychotic decompensation;
- the threat of suicide;
- uncontrollable acting out.

The client needed to be able to make substantive contact with the therapist, and to be motivated for change. Recognising that difficulties in termination were likely to pose problems in briefer work, clients who appeared to have 'complex or deep-seated issues' in this area were deemed inappropriate since 'there [seemed] little hope of working [these] through in a short time' (Malan 1976). Inevitably these selection criteria included some clients who presented with pre-Oedipal problems but Malan increasingly came to believe that this was not necessarily a contraindication for brief intensive therapy. Of more importance was the *capacity to have formed previous meaningful relationships*. This was highly correlated with good outcomes and a positive indicator as to how the client would respond to the therapist.

Central to the technique was clarification and interpretation of the *triangle of insight* or *persons*. This is the three-way link between the here and now relationship with the therapist, similar feelings which have been directed toward significant people in the client's past, and the problem as it manifests itself in the client's current relationships. The *current* conflict is frequently associated with the precipitating factor which brought the client into treatment and is observable in the therapeutic relationship. The *historical* – or *nuclear* – conflict can be a result of 'early traumatic experiences ... family constellations or *repetitive patterns*'. The closer the current and nuclear conflicts, the better the prognosis. In Malan's example of 'The Man with the Headaches', who presented with anxiety symptoms and chest pains precipitated by the cardiac illness of his father, the current and nuclear conflict were virtually the same, which ensured that 'the therapy will sort of roll out in front of you automatically'. The client will always be talking about his core conflict and the therapist will merely have to make focal interpretations.

The triangle of insight links with another psychoanalytic triangle: that of *impulse*, the resultant *defence* and consequent *anxiety*. This was in keeping with the Freudian belief that it is censored desire which causes symptoms. In therapy, it is the clarification of this in relation to the triangle of insight which is helpful.

Initially no time limit was set at the beginning of treatment. Clients were told that they would be seen for a matter of months and if further treatment was indicated, they would be referred for longer-term therapy. However, as confidence in the new technique grew, a time limit was set from the start. Malan eventually set a time limit of between 20 to 30 sessions from the outset of treatment and went on to recommend 'twenty sessions for an ordinary (straight-forward) patient with an experienced therapist' and 30 sessions for 'an ordinary patient with an inexperienced therapist' (Malan 1992). According to Malan:

> [Time limits] give therapy a definite beginning, middle, and end – like the opening, middle and end game in chess – and help to concentrate both the patient's material and the therapist's work, and to prevent therapy becoming diffuse and aimless and drifting into long-term involvement. It enables the prospect of termination to be brought in quite naturally as the time for this approaches; and often this enables a therapy that had been in danger of becoming diffuse of becoming clear and focal again. To adapt Dr. Johnson, being under sentence of termination doth most marvellously concentrate the material.

Malan went on to believe the setting of a termination date, as opposed to a specific number of sessions, was preferable, since it dealt with the 'chore' of keeping track of missed sessions and the possible ambiguity as to whether they counted towards the total. Despite the time limit, the client is given to understand that he can see the therapist on an ad hoc basis after the therapy is finished. In contrast to other approaches, Malan does not believe that this compromises the emotional impact of termination.

Malan believed that the need for therapeutic activity stemmed from the need to keep the therapy in focus given the wealth of material that can be produced. Activity includes *'selective interpretation, selective attention, and selective neglect'* (Malan 1976). Material is selected according to its proximity to the focus.

Malan acknowledges that termination may need specific attention in short-term therapy, particularly with clients where separation factors are paramount. In clients where the focus is more on Oedipal issues, termination may not be central but in extending briefer therapies into his work with pre-Oedipal clients, he recognised that endings are crucial and must be incorporated into the treatment. Malan, however, used the standard techniques of psychoanalysis; interpretation of the transference, of defences and of the 'nuclear' or 'core' conflict. At pains to stress the technical similarities between psychoanalysis and brief intensive psychotherapy, Malan believed '[I]nterpretations used differ in no way in any form of psychoanalytic therapy … interpretations of resistance, fantasies, and above all, forms of transference' (in Davanloo 1978).

Using techniques which are not dissimilar to open-ended analytic treatments, Malan's outcomes suggested that the beneficial effects went well beyond mere symptom relief. Rather than being superficial, Malan's brief intensive psychotherapy included an understanding of the underlying dynamic conflicts and their origin.

Unlocking the unconscious: Habib Davanloo

Habib Davanloo's Intensive Short-Term Dynamic Psychotherapy (ISTDP) includes many of the clinical techniques of Sifneos and Malan, including the use of trial interpretations to test the client's motivation and the capacity or willingness to work briefly in an intensively analytic way. Davanloo suggests that the client's response to a period of 'trial therapy' is the best indicator of a client's suitability for the treatment. Other criteria considered important include:

- some evidence of reciprocity ('give and take') in relationships, particularly in relation to the therapist;
- access to specific feelings or affects and whether they can be tolerated (e.g. anger);
- affective, rather than intellectual, response to interpretation;
- flexible defences;
- transference and counter-transference reactions.

Davanloo initially believed motivation, especially if increased after interpretations, to be an important criteria, but more recently has viewed the need for client motivation to be 'a criterion created by therapists who cannot treat highly resistant, complex patients' (in Groves 1996).

Contraindications include those clients who show 'intense reliance on projection, massive denial, major reliance on acting out in dealing with conflicts, acting out combined with projections, or a few rigid persistently used ego defence mechanisms' (Davanloo 1978).

Davanloo (1990) has described the trial therapy as serving to 'unlock the unconscious'. The most important aspect of this period of trial therapy is to acknowledge and confront the client's resistance (often evidenced by passivity, withdrawal and vagueness), especially in relation to its manifestations in the transference. This frequently mobilises anger which is then defended against but produces more material in relation to the client's central conflict. A similar triangular link is then made between the client's material in relation to the therapist (T), significant figures in the client's current life (C) and significant people in the past, e.g. a parent who 'may have taught such (relational) patterns in the first place' (P). Davanloo terms this the *triangle of persons* (TCP). As with Malan, this is seen in relation to a further therapeutic triangle, *the triangle of conflict*. The triangle of conflict is similar to Malan's impulse, defence, anxiety triangle. Davanloo terms this the *DAI triangle* – defence, affect and impulse. The closer the congruity between these two triangles, the more effective the treatment is likely to be. The earlier that interpretations in the triangle of persons can be made, the shorter the likely treatment. It follows that feelings (which may be denied or defended against by passivity or vagueness) towards the therapist or treatment, need to be addressed from the beginning of the trial therapy. We shall return to these triangles in Chapter 3. Davanloo also makes use of what he calls '*subtly loaded words*' in order to speak to some fundamental, often unconscious, trait in the client, a theme we shall return to when discussing technique. The therapist formulates the presenting problem in relation to the therapeutic triangles which enables the client and the therapist to agree on the focus for treatment at the end of the period of trial therapy

Davanloo's technique is aimed not only at Oedipal or neurotic problems but is also described as benefiting clients who may evidence personality problems of long duration. What is most apparent in Davanloo's work is the direct, and some would say, relentless, attack on the client's passivity, withdrawal or vagueness. These are seen as defensive *choices* on the part of the client. The 'gentle but relentless' confrontations are particularly designed to elicit feelings of anger or resistance. The client's powerful emotions, particularly towards the therapist, are defended against, but the therapist's constant interpretation of these leads to their expression in the therapy. The acceptance of these uncomfortable feelings, without any negative consequences in the therapy, further strengthens the therapeutic alliance and increases client motivation. The client shares responsibility for the treatment and warded off feelings and behaviour in the therapy are actively pointed out to the client. While no definite time limits are set, treatments appear to last between two to forty sessions depending on the client's psychopathology and the complexity of the focus. Davanloo (1978; 1994) sees short-term therapies on a continuum depending on the 'central structure of the patient's conflict'. Oedipal problems are treated in 'two to fifteen' sessions while 'deeper problems produce excellent results in twenty-five to thirty-five, or an upper limit of forty, sessions'. Treatment is ended when there is evidence of improvement – or change – in one or more areas of the triangles described above.

The assault on defences and the concentration on the client's anger and resistance make this a potentially problematic technique. Davanloo's method demands the utmost therapeutic neutrality and control on behalf of the therapist and an ability to pick up and focus on the early, and frequently slight, manifestations of resistance. However, neutrality does not mean a passive therapist. For Davanloo, activity does not mean having to be directive; one can be extremely active yet non-directive. There is no place for a passive therapist in this treatment since 'we cannot wait for the material to bubble up'. Resistance is dealt with by relentless questioning:

> Interpretation of the negative transference is highly essential. I would also emphasize the importance of early and repeated interpretation of resistance and ambivalence ... which are of great importance in maintaining the therapeutic alliance. (1994, p. 344)

Termination is not viewed as a major issue and with less disturbed clients can be dealt with in one session while in treatments with multiple foci or with more disturbed clients, termination is addressed in the last two to six sessions.

What can be seen as potentially disquieting is the frequent repetition of an interpretation until the client is ground into submission and agrees with the therapist. Paradoxically, these 'bulldozer' techniques make Davanloo's therapy potentially helpful to obsessive and phobic clients, who had been thought to be unresponsive to briefer treatments, by addressing the split between their feelings and intellect (Flegenheimer 1982).

Sifneos, Malan and Davanloo closely follow in the psychoanalytic tradition by placing great emphasis on interpretation, transference and the importance of insight. The drive/structural model of the mind of id, ego, superego and impulse, defence, and anxiety is central to their frameworks. Allowing for modifications of psychoanalytic technique, change is based on those factors found in psychoanalysis: deep interpretations, aimed at the unconscious, which make distinctive emotional contact and lead to insight. They assume that any assessment for short-term therapy would essentially be along these modified psychoanalytic lines and that the establishment of a focus is achieved within this context. If a focus cannot be determined within the first few interviews, brief intensive therapy is not indicated. Central to Malan's approach is selective listening and selective interpreting in the context of the focus. Davanloo concentrates on repeated confrontation of the client's defences in order to expose the hidden feelings and conflicts while Sifneos confronts the client's 'impulses as well as teaching patients about their psychodynamic' (Messer and Warren 1995, p. 92).

What we can see here are the attempts to place brief therapies within the context of psychoanalysis. Unlike Alexander and Ferenczi, who were viewed, perhaps somewhat erroneously, as proposing a heretical and threatening model of analysis, these writers, by using basic psychoanalytic techniques, were not seen as a challenge to psychoanalysis. Thus they were able to present themselves as following in the mainstream psychoanalytic tradition and, if somewhat uneasily, to be incorporated within the psychoanalytic fold. However, this did not mean the acceptance of brief therapies but led to a renewed debate on their efficacy and whether they constituted a treatment that could be called analytic. These debates led to the notion that brief dynamic therapies might be 'different' from psychoanalysis while still making use of fundamental analytic ideas in clinical practice. What we also begin to see, in the importance placed on the client's interaction with the therapist, is a move towards the 'object relational' model of therapy where the client's use of the therapist as a microcosm of relationships in the real world, gradually replaces the emphasis placed on the drive–instinct, observer–observed, model of early psychoanalysis. The idea of a two-person psychology is introduced which liberates the therapist from the stance of passive observer. Therapist and client can potentially be part of a dyad that constantly interacts and it is this recognition that enabled focal therapies to further develop with the therapeutic relationship increasingly being the agent of change.

Experiential short-term therapy

This is most apparent in the more recent developments in focal therapies where the work of Malan and Davanloo have increasingly coalesced in a range of expressive/experiential short-term treatments (Fosha, 2000; Della Selva, 2004; Malan and Della Selva, 2006). Fosha's Accelerated Empathic Dynamic Psychotherapy (AEDP) is closely linked to the Intensive Experiential/Expressive Short-term Dynamic Therapies (IESTDP). What these approaches (Davanloo's Intensive Short-term Dynamic Psychotherapy, Accelerated Empathic Psychotherapy (AET) (Foote 1992; Alpert 1992), Accelerated Experiential Dynamic Psychotherapy (Fosha 2000] share and stress is the primacy of the experiential component of therapies. It is the experience of the previously defended against affect in *the here and now of the client–therapist relationship* which is the central agent of change. These therapies feature a high level of therapeutic activity, selective focusing, an active therapist and client engaging in a collaborative endeavour, focus on the here and now of client–therapist interaction, attention to minute somatic/bodily fluctuations during sessions and a belief in the experiential element of therapies to facilitate change. In their development, they are also less manifestly adversarial/confrontational than the original ISTDP, viewing the treatment as 'radical empathy and emotional engagement through attunement, resonance, affect sharing, affirmation and self disclosure' (Fosha 2000, p. 3).

These treatments view themselves as within the psychoanalytic tradition (symptoms arise from feelings which have become unconscious because they are too painful) but place central importance on asking the client what he feels rather than interpreting what he feels (which can be used defensively by both client and therapist) so that the affect, often experienced somatically, can be experienced directly in the session. Following from Frieda Fromm-Reichman's (1950) comment that the patient is in 'need of an experience not an explanation', the initial phase of treatment – where clients are asked what they feel rather than told via interpretations – leads to what is termed the *central dynamic sequence* between therapist and client which would include the client's 'tactical defences' to avoid painful affect. These are not interpreted but the client is encouraged to experience the painful affect which they are blocking via their defences, and to verbalise or visualise (we see here how even contemporary psychodynamic brief therapists tend to use a variety of interventions drawn from many therapeutic traditions) previously hidden impulses in the session. This is facilitated by the increasing emotional engagement with the therapist. What is of interest is that these therapies are making much use of attachment theory, reflective self-function and affect regulation which we shall discuss in Chapter 5. It is a reflection of their confidence in the efficacy of their treatment, and the psychodynamic foundation of their interventions, that they have been able to move beyond the holy grail of interpretation as the agent of therapeutic change.

Termination (and the time frame) tend not to be major issues since the treatment ends when the client has 'got what he came for' although it is noted that characterological problems take longer than developmental ones and that clients in crisis are particularly open to shorter treatment times. Extensive use is made of follow-up sessions.

Summary

Early psychoanalysis was symptom-focused and active. As we have seen, resistance and the transference neurosis led to therapy becoming longer, unfocused and passive. It is possible that the embarrassment felt by the analytic profession towards hypnosis and the cathartic method of the early Freud have contributed to the vehement response with which short-term therapies have been subjected by the analytic community. For psychoanalysis, focal time-limited therapy is nothing less than the return of the repressed. The interest now shown by the analytic community in shorter therapies is a recognition that analysis is going back to its origins. However, as we have seen in this chapter, this has not been achieved without considerable ambivalence and resistance which has led to the unease which is felt towards short-term dynamic therapy within the psychoanalytic tradition. This historical legacy continues to exert considerable influence on the development of dynamic time-limited therapies. This chapter has traced the development of psychoanalytically informed short-term therapies from the early Freud to contemporary experiential treatments based on analytically informed practice. We now consider how contemporary time-limited therapies are widely influenced by psychodynamic theory and practice before articulating a model of short-term dynamic interventions.

2

APPLICATION OF PSYCHOANALYTIC THEORY AND PRACTICE IN CONTEMPORARY TIME-LIMITED THERAPIES

Men are troubled not so much by things as by their perception of things. (Epictetus)

Psychoanalytic theory, and by implication clinical practice, has struggled to embrace two competing views. The drive model with primacy given to instincts, drives and desire, and the object relations model which stresses the individual's interactive relationship with others. This is the faultline which has been apparent in psychoanalytic theory and practice since the days of Freud and his followers. This parallels contemporary debates about nature versus nurture. It follows that short-term therapies based upon the former will be occupied with the interpretation of drives and their defences and will place primacy on classical techniques of interpretation and insight. As psychoanalysis and its applications have become more 'relational and less drive orientated' (Aron 1990), more emphasis has been placed on the therapeutic relationship of transference and counter-transference, especially the 'here and now' interactional components of the therapeutic relationship. Less attention is paid to unconscious conflicts than to attempts to master real-life daily experience; consequently, the focus has moved to maladaptive relationships and their consequences rather than pathological factors within any given individual. There is now widespread recognition that both members of the therapeutic dyad influence each other and that this mutual subjectivity has become the focus of many relational focal therapies. Relationships to others, and the impact these have on the sense of self, are the central feature of the brief therapies in this section. There is always an 'other' with whom one is interacting although that 'other' may be an internal template or construct of one's own making. It is the *mental representation* of our interactions with others that is of primary concern.

As a consequence, these theories place less emphasis on a single organising focus for their work. The focus can be more diverse, couched in terms of personality traits or character, and the therapeutic emphasis is more on here and now interactional experience both in the consulting room and in the real world. Less emphasis is placed on specific selection criteria. As one would anticipate from a theory that places relationships at its centre, less importance is placed on individual client characteristics, while greater importance is given to the personal qualities brought by both client and therapist to the therapeutic encounter.

These theories also highlight a different understanding of the transference. Rather than viewing transference as neurotic templates from the past which need interpreting, there is more emphasis on the 'here and now/in the room' transference. The therapist is not a blank screen and a receptacle for the client's projections. Transference is viewed as an expression of the interpersonal reality of the client which has been shaped by his personal experience, background and development. These internalised relationships, which constitute the object relational transference, 'consist of ideas or beliefs about the self, others and [the] interaction between self and others' (Messer and Warren 1995). How this is manifested in the consulting room and its relation to the interactional focus are the source of transference interpretations. In order for this to be successful, the therapist needs to be aware of his own counter-transference and how it impacts on the therapeutic dyad.

Some of these theories also bear a passing resemblance to the work of Alexander and the 'corrective emotional experience' by stressing the importance of a new experience in the therapeutic relationship where insight and interpretation are of less importance than the affective quality of the relationship between the client and the therapist. The therapeutic relationship is a metaphor for the client's interpersonal and intrapsychic problems and is the laboratory where these are repeated and enacted.

A variety of contemporary therapies have been developed which lend themselves to a limited time frame and have drawn on psychoanalytic object relations theory in viewing problems as interpersonal and linking this with the intrapsychic in a two-person psychology.

The Vanderbilt Group

The cyclical maladaptive pattern of the Vanderbilt Group (Binder and Strupp 1991; Strupp and Binder 1984; Levenson 1995), although initially not specifically directed towards time-limited therapy, has led to the articulation of a time-limited dynamic psychotherapy (TLDT) which stresses the interactional model of the contemporary practice.

The central assumption of TLDT is that the client's difficulties stem from disturbed interpersonal relationships. These were learned in the past and are maintained in the present. The client, with the therapist as a participant observer, re-enacts these difficulties in the therapy. The focus can be wide, i.e. a personality trait, although it is assumed that there is one primary and identifiable relationship pattern.

Central to this is the *Cyclical Maladaptive Pattern* (CMP). This is a working model of behaviour and action originally outlined by Peterfreund (1983) and defined as:

> a central or salient pattern of interpersonal roles in which the patients *unconsciously* cast themselves; the complementary roles in which they cast others; and the maladaptive interactional sequences, self-defeating expectations, negative self appraisals, and unpleasant affects that result. (1983, p. 140)

These categories, together with the therapist's counter-transference, will provide a picture of the client's primary interpersonal way of relating. Formulating the client's difficulty will be done in the context of the CMP. Of particular importance are the internal representations of self and others, the interactions with others and the effect that these have on the client's beliefs about the self.

TLDP focuses on repeated interactional traits and views the transference as a reflection of interactional experiences and beliefs. Primacy is given to a new experience in the therapeutic relationship (where the therapist is part of the process) rather than interpretation and insight. Proponents of TLDP suggest twenty to thirty sessions. However, emphasis is less on the exact number of sessions (which are related to the ease and clarity which a treatment focus is established) than the cultivation of a time-limited attitude on behalf of both therapist and client.

The framework of the therapy is psychodynamic with particular reference to object relations and self-psychological theories. In looking at, and encouraging thinking about, the interaction between self-concepts and how they affect relationships with other people, it also takes in some cognitive-behavioural ideas (Binder 2004).

Stress response system

The stress response system is a twelve-session therapy (Horowitz 1991) which is a phase in specific, interpersonal therapy of particular relevance to traumatic loss. In this treatment the focus is on loss and mourning and is based on a relational view of personality development. Central to the treatment focus is what is termed 'person schemas', which are 'internalized representations of self, others and relationships' (Groves 1996). Traumatic events are perceived, experienced and processed through 'personal schemas' which in effect are personal mental structures which help us to organise and give meaning to experience. An example Horowitz gives is that of a young woman's reaction to the sudden death of her father. After dealing with the acute phase of mourning the loss, the remainder of the twelve sessions was spent looking at her conviction of herself as weak and flawed with a corresponding belief that her father had disliked and rejected her since she had not lived up to his ideals. These are what Horowitz terms personal schemas, or schematic representations, which underlie our reactions to sudden traumatic events and need to be central to therapy. Therapy is exactly twelve sessions and the issues, which both client and therapist need to focus on in each session, are outlined in advance. (For an outline of the prescribed treatment phases, see Horowitz 1986, p. 31.)

Using the well-observed responses to traumatic stress, a distinction is made between responses of

- *intrusion and repetition* where the therapist needs to be supportive in enabling the client to reduce and manage overwhelming anxiety:
- *denial/numbing* where there is active encouragement by the therapist on the emotional expressions of feelings that have been denied or have been feared to be too frightening and consequently avoided or repressed.

While this is similar to more recent aspects of cognitive behavioural therapy (see below), what is interesting is the attempt to link personality traits with specific clinical techniques and therapeutic aims. Hysterical personalities tend to be overwhelmed by global anxiety and need help in clarifying and binding emotions, while the obsessive compulsive personality, preoccupied with details as a way of warding off emotion, needs to be assisted in tolerating emotions and helped to 'hold on' to the source of the anxiety. Horowitz thereby attempts to draw attention to the differing responses to what can be a similar situation by two personality traits or types, which have different clinical implications.

Although the treatment is aimed at a narrow and relatively healthy population, it is an interesting and helpful approach to Post Traumatic Stress Disorders (PTSD) (Horowitz 1997).

Of particular relevance is the importance placed on the relational aspects of coping with sudden loss or trauma.

IDE therapy

Interpersonal, developmental and existential therapy (IDE, Budman and Gurman 1998) attempts to integrate interpersonal, developmental and existential conflicts into a therapeutic framework which is time-sensitive and highly focused. Taking issue with long-term therapies which they see as inevitably leading to therapeutic drift, the major feature if IDE is the belief that most therapeutic benefit occurs early in treatment. The law of diminishing returns applies. Consequently a flexible use of time is suggested with more intensive work for four to eight visits, then spreading out the remaining sessions to reduce dependency and enhance the client's capacity to manage on their own. Combining developmental, existential and interpersonal paradigms, IDE is based on the premise that during the client's early development there has been some 'faulty learning'. This can be either conscious or unconscious but importantly becomes 'a *template* for future behaviour and relationships'. It is this template which influences feelings, behaviour and relationships. The key question is 'Why has this person come for help now?' and is viewed from both an environmental and developmental (an 'obsessive fear of death is rather different at age 25 than it is at age 75') perspective. The focus is then related directly to the client's life stage. There is a flexible attitude to time. Therapy appears to be between twenty to forty sessions in length and includes the variable spacing of sessions. Rather than 'the more therapy the better', therapy is seen as the springboard for change which happens outside or after the completion of therapy.

The use made of the time can be a major therapeutic variable and an important intervention which needs to be acknowledged for each individual client. However, the flexible use of time, which in IDE includes follow-up appointments and further courses of therapy when a developmental obstacle is encountered, is very different from using time as a central organising framework for therapy.

The work of James Mann

James Mann's time-limited psychotherapy (1973, 1992) deals explicitly with the therapeutic use of time. The central therapeutic issue is the relationship to time; time is always running out. Mann believes the limitless time of longer-term therapies functions to deny the reality of finite time. Symbolically it functions against acknowledging our own ending – death. For Mann, the link between time and reality is insoluble. In offering precisely twelve sessions, there is no ambivalence in relation to time and the limited time frame is used to influence the therapeutic process and is the major therapeutic variable. Mann is interesting in his description of time as gendered ('father' time and 'limitless' maternal time), developmental, ('child' versus 'adult' time), and the importance placed on the literalness of time. His therapeutic hour is 60 as opposed to the more usual 50 minutes. By calling an hour 50 minutes, Mann believes the therapist is denying the reality and the true nature of time which functions as a denial of our mortality.

Therapy revolves around issues of separation and individuation and focuses on what Mann terms the *chronically endured pain* which is a generalised, often relational, difficulty which leads to negative feelings which the client harbours towards himself. The 'pain' has been recurrent over time and linked to features in the past which continue to be active in the present. Particular attention is paid to the way (and the time in the session) in which the central issue is conveyed, be it through words, actions, feelings or behaviour. Mann (1992) describes a phase-specific twelve-session treatment which, with its emphasis on separation and individuation, lends itself particularly well to developmental difficulties in these areas.

The suggestion that the way in which we give meaning and relate to time is inseparably related to our own mortality and issues of loss and separation has also been highlighted by other psychodynamic authors interested in short-term therapies (Molnos 1995). In this light, the difficulty that the therapeutic profession has in relation to shorter therapies can be seen as evidence of a denial of the finiteness of time and our own mortality. As Mann points out, all therapies evoke this whether therapists are aware of it, and choose to use it to facilitate therapy, or not.

Mann's approach, dominated as it is by the single theme of separation–individuation, may not be applicable to all clients, although, as it is a ubiquitous human developmental task, one could argue that the majority of people seeking help are likely to present with issues in this general area. Shefler (2001) has developed Mann's work with reference to contemporary therapeutic issues.

Psychodynamic interpersonal therapy (PIT)

Hobson's (1982) conversational model of therapy which places emphasis on the nature of the therapeutic relationship, or the way attempts at forming that relationship are negotiated, has provided the framework for working within a time limit with clients with severe and chronic difficulties who have had considerable experience of unsuccessful previous treatments (Guthrie et al. 1999). The model was originally termed the 'conversational model' and is derived from psychodynamic principles but also incorporates humanistic and interpersonal concepts. A conversation develops and deepens through tentative but intuitive *'guesses'* by the therapist who seeks corrections and modifications from the client. In this sense, therapy is an evolving process. Believing that engagement tends to be taken for granted in many therapies, this model of interpersonal short-term therapy places the issue of trust at the centre of working with very damaged people. The relationship is entered into with a particular focus on issues of intimacy and trust and, using the model of conversational therapy, attempts to understand how a conversation is developed rather than the content of what is discussed. With these very damaged and suspicious clients, being able to hold a conversation at all, be it verbal or emotional (or even of regular attendance) is a major therapeutic advance. Client and therapist together attempt to develop a 'mutual feeling language'. Tentative links are made (rather than interpretations) about the therapeutic relationship, involving the use of metaphor to generalise to other areas of the client's life. Focusing on ten basic skills (frame maintenance, making tentative statements as opposed to asking questions or making interpretations, making 'I' rather than 'We' comments, negotiation, picking up verbal and non-verbal cues, a focus on feelings (often associated with somatic pain, not unlike ISTDT), working in the 'here and now' relationship rather than the 'there and then', and using amplification, hypothesis and metaphor), PIT is able to use a number of therapeutic traditions in working with the therapeutic relationship.

PIT, which has a manual although is not manualised, is relatively straightforward for both experienced and less experienced clinicians to learn and has an increasing evidence base with varied clinical populations (Guthrie et al. 1991, cited in Creed et al. 2002; Guthrie et al. 1999, 2001, 2003; Barkham et al. 1999; Creed et al. 2003; Shapiro 1987; Stiles et al. 2006). Many of these studies were with clients with complex problems where PIT was found to be as effective as cognitive behavioural therapy (CBT).

Interpersonal therapy

The specific issue of loss is addressed in the interpersonal therapy of depression (IPT). The work of Klerman (Klerman et al. 1994), based on his treatment of depressed clients, is predicated on the assumption that depression occurs in an interpersonal context. This follows in a direct tradition from Freud who had indicated as early as Mourning and Melancholia (1917) that depression is related to loss. For Freud, depression and grief were related to the loss of a person (or object); Klerman links depression with attachment theory. Current relationships are based upon the nature of early childhood attachments which are refined rather than repeated in adolescent and adult experiences. IPT takes its starting point from the belief that close and satisfactory attachment relationships are a protective factor against depression and that when these attachments are disturbed or disrupted, depression is more likely to occur. Treatment focuses on present, rather than past, functioning in relationships and concentrates on interpersonal phenomena such as changes in a person's role vis-à-vis others or what are termed 'role transitions' which involve life events necessitating the move from one social role to another. IPT focuses on four problem areas that may be relevant for a given client: grief, role disputes, role transitions, or interpersonal deficits. Therapy uses specific techniques depending on which of the four areas are chosen as foci. Between twelve and sixteen weekly sessions are suggested with the more severe problems (in the interpersonal deficits domain) lasting up to a year. IPT describes phases of treatment and the tasks to be completed at each phase, and has become attractive to purchasers of mental health services as it is manual led and can easily be learnt by lay people (Wilkinson 2008).

While IPT appears to have little in common with the more dynamic therapies, the importance it places on attachment and current relationships (especially the issue of transition and development as a result of current relationships) warrants its inclusion. We now move on to discuss therapies which have a more cognitive and behavioural approach. These are not necessarily psychodynamic in orientation and tend not to view the use of the limited time framework as a central part of the therapeutic process. However, they do share some common features with focal dynamic therapies which we shall discuss in the next chapter.

Behavioural approaches and cognitive behavioural therapy (CBT)

Behavioural approaches focus primarily on changing current behaviour, and de-emphasise internal events and subjective experience. They are based on the premise that human behaviour, including various patterns of psychopathology, is learned and thus can be modified by new learning, or relearning of old patterns of behaviour. Assessment aims to understand the cues or antecedents that elicit behaviour, and the consequences or 'rewards' that follow it. Some of the core principles and strategies of these approaches, for example, that of reinforcement, role playing, extinction and modelling are commonly used, even by those whose predominant orientation is not behavioural, and feature in some of the more structured short-term therapies.

Cognitive therapies focus on how individual emotions are influenced by cognitive processes and structures. Their basic premises include:

- Behaviour and affect are mediated by cognitive processes.
- Maladaptive behaviour and affect are correlated with maladaptive cognitions.
- The task of the clinician is to identify these cognitions and modify them through an active and experiential treatment.

Cognitions are defined increasingly widely and are seen to include thoughts, attitudes, assumptions, abstract beliefs, values, fantasy, dreams and imagery. At the centre of cognitive therapy is the *cognitive triangle* which is represented as consisting of the event, emotions and cognition. This can also be represented as the interrelationship between thoughts, moods, physical reactions and behaviour. By changing thoughts, one can change feelings and vice versa.

Beck (1979) traces these ideas back to Adler, who, as we have seen, believed clients suffered from 'mistaken opinions' and 'faulty beliefs' which are mediated and corrected through the relationship with the therapist. Ellis' rational-emotive therapy (1973) started from the standpoint of an individual's 'core irrational ideas' which included the prescriptive, and potentially personally harmful 'shoulds, oughts and musts'. Rational emotive therapy was described as a treatment lasting up to twenty sessions following the ABC method: A is the 'Activating experience', B the individual's Belief system, and C the emotional Consequence of A and B. Treatment proceeds until it reaches point D where the therapist Disputes the irrational beliefs with empirical evidence and logical reasoning.

Beck, who had trained as a psychoanalyst, suggested that events are processed by fleeting and barely conscious 'automatic thoughts' which mediate between an event and the perception, feeling and behaviour associated with it. These automatic thoughts, in effect, the individual's unique and personal interpretation of events in the world, help identify an individual's central belief system. In essence, these automatic thoughts are predicated on how people see themselves in the world. The assumption is made that people are less troubled by disturbing events themselves than beliefs and meanings which they ascribe to them. The subjective meaning of the event is as important as the event itself.

Automatic thoughts are related to the individual's *core beliefs* which operate as a set of key assumptions about ourselves, others, and ways of being in the world. The internal dialogues that people have with themselves ('self-talk') are reflections of the individual's core beliefs which are central to their self-concept and self-esteem. These core beliefs about the self and the world are in some ways similar to how psychoanalysis views internal objects and part objects. This is how meaning becomes assigned to specific events.

Beck's original cognitive therapy was brief, problem and solution-focused, involving homework, suggested reading ('bibliotherapy') and role play. It challenged negative automatic thoughts and helped practise new behaviour. Initially developed in treating depression, contemporary CBT is now used to treat a variety of problems including those with high degrees of severity (Hawton et al. 1989; Salkovskis, 1996; Sanders 1996; Clarke and Fairburn 1997).

CBT is based on a collaborative partnership between therapist and client. The assumptions of the cognitive model are explained to the client and he is introduced to the ideas of 'automatic thoughts' and 'negative cognitions'. This is very different from psychoanalytic models where to address the process is to pre-empt experience. Therapy is aimed at training the client to 'correct the idiosyncratic negative thoughts and the underlying negative assumptions' (Beck 1979). In recognising when these processes occur and their behavioural and emotional consequences, the client has the possibility of achieving mastery over them. Guided discovery is used as a method of collaborative investigation to explore whether the client's view of a situation is amenable to be seen in a different light. The key technique here is the *Socratic method* of question and answer which assists in understanding the client's point of view and considering alternatives. Socratic questioning aims at revealing and clarifying suppressed contradictions. They address the underlying belief systems which expose incompatibility of thoughts, feelings and motives which cause conflicts and tensions (see Mace 1999). The aim of this process is to help the client learn how to question automatic thoughts and core beliefs themselves.

Little emphasis was initially placed on the therapeutic relationship other than to view it as a vehicle for the therapies stated aim of 'cognitive retraining'. CBT now views the therapeutic relationship as having historical determinants which can become significant in the here and now. Contemporary CBT recognises the value of the therapeutic relationship which previously, as with early Freud, was only thought important insofar as it hindered therapy. While used in a collaborative and explicit way (as opposed to interpreting the therapeutic process), CBT acknowledges the importance of relationship factors in helping or hindering therapy. Increasingly, psychoanalytic insights have been rediscovered by, and incorporated into the relational aspects of CBT (Safran and Segal 1990; Safran and McMain 1992). Dysfunctional cognitive interpersonal cycles can be seen to be similar to Bowlby's (1988) concept of 'internal working models' of relationships which are of central importance in therapy. The therapeutic relationship must avoid a repetition of damaging relational patterns or the exacerbation of negative core assumptions.

The concept of interpersonal *Schemata* or *Schemas* was developed in response to criticisms that cognitive therapies were not sufficiently cognisant of non-verbal communication (which may be derived from the earliest experience), the relational aspects of therapy, or the individual client's highly personal and idiosyncratic relational styles. One result of this has been the development of *schema-focused cognitive therapy* (Beck and Freeman 1990; Young 1994). Schemata are seen as cognitive structures that function to organise behaviour and experience. Together with core beliefs, they form the 'deepest level of cognition underlying both automatic thoughts and assumptions ... which are particularly important in structuring perceptions and building up rule giving behaviours' (Wills and Sanders 1997). They derive from the increasing recognition by CBT that cognitions, behaviour and emotions are influenced by early family experience, and that these schemata might not be conscious. Schemata are ways in which individuals perceive their lives, including interpersonal relationships and self-esteem. Events and experiences are interpreted through the medium of personal schemas. In effect, they function as templates in making sense of the world and 'tend to be activated when an experience occurs similar to the one earlier incorporated within the range of the template ... [they] even shape incoming data to conform to [the templates'] expectations' (Ross 1999). Schemata may be represented by *metaphor* and 'paradox' (i.e. opposites) and while it is sometimes difficult to draw a distinction between them and core beliefs, schemata are thought to consist of the developmentally earliest character structures. Consequently, they are seen to be of importance in treating borderline personality traits. Imagery techniques and dreams are ways that these schemata can be accessed.

There is comparatively little discussion of treatment length in cognitive/behavioural literature. As originally conceived, cognitive therapy offered between ten and twenty sessions if necessary, and while the length may now vary between ten and fifteen sessions, much depends on the conceptualisation of the problem. Six to eight sessions are recommended for mild depression or anxiety while sixteen to twenty sessions are recommended for more severe cases. Schema-focused work is thought to be more appropriate for longer-term, more pervasive difficulties while symptom/automatic thought-level problems may be more amenable to a shorter time frame (for a useful discussion of this, see Wills and Sanders 1997).

More recently, new cognitive therapies have appeared, partly in response to criticisms of specific aspects of cognitive therapy, but also because, despite its popularity, some people do not improve significantly with cognitive therapy. These new developments focus on issues of control and acceptance, and typically aim to alter the person's relationship to their thoughts. They have been developed in a variety of formats, including as Mindfulness-Based CBT (Segal et al. 2001), Metacognitive therapy (Wells 2008), and Acceptance and Commitment therapy (Hayes and Strosahl 2004).

Cognitive analytic therapy

Cognitive analytic therapy, as its name suggests, is an integrative model of therapy. It incorporates psychoanalytic, cognitive and object relational ideas into a brief, time-limited, structured therapy applicable to a variety of clinical settings. Developed by Anthony Ryle (1995, 1997), it makes use of the repertory grid techniques described by Kelly (1955). Kelly's personal construct theory was based on the view that the individual is 'constructed' by the way he construes and anticipates events. Change is therefore possible by placing the 'Old Self' in a 'New Role'. These constructs, linked to ascribed or perceived roles, operate as *personal templates* through which an individual's experience, and actions are processed in order for them to be made sense of and mastered. Personal constructs are relative and fluid and can be 'mapped' by what are termed repertory grids. These 'maps' were used by Ryle as a means of identifying his clients' problems and used in therapy to facilitate and chart therapeutic progress and change. Construct theory suggests that the self can be permeable and created 'as we go along', rather than dependent on one's personal history, and can either be dictated from inside or imposed from without.

Cognitive analytic therapy's model is one of a partnership which helps the client understand the nature of their behaviour patterns. The transference is actively used to facilitate this understanding through what are termed '*reciprocal relationships*'. These are roles which are repeated over time and which the client will attempt to elicit in the therapeutic relationship. In essence, they are the predictions, developed from our earliest relationships, of the responses of others to one's actions and behaviour. Therapist and client are engaged in a joint endeavour to discover and describe the client's 'harmful procedures' and, in a manner similar to that described by Alexander, the therapist offers the client a different experience by either behaving differently from the client's expectations or by drawing attention to familiar patterns of behaviour as they occur in the sessions. This enables the therapist to reflect on which reciprocal roles are being enacted/repeated in the here and now of the therapeutic relationship and is particularly important and helpful when the therapeutic relationship is under threat. This is achieved through an active partnership rather than the client's gradual recognition through insight and interpretation. The object is to 'remove the self-defeating blocks to growth' and to enable the client to 'develop a self observing and self integrating capacity' (Ryle 1995).

The treatment is generally limited to 16 sessions divided into three stages. Sessions one to three involve initial information gathering, leading to a reformulation of the client's problem. During these sessions the developing therapeutic relationship and the client's history, will lead to the identification and listing of the following:

- *the client's target problems* (TPs) These consist of descriptions of the client's problem which he wishes to address in therapy.
- *the client's target problem procedures* (TPPs). These are statements which list and describe how the client creates and maintains the actions and experiences which lead to, and reinforce, the target problems. During the course of treatment these TPPs are actively monitored through diary keeping and acknowledged as they are evidenced 'in narratives brought to the therapy and as they are enacted in the therapy relationship'.

From this process the core neurotic patterns are discovered. These can be conceptualised in terms of dilemmas, traps, and snags. *Dilemmas* consist of 'false choices and narrow options'. Although unhappy, we behave in certain ways because we fear that alternatives would be even worse. *Traps* are 'vicious circles' where, feeling bad about ourselves, we behave and think in ways which confirm our 'badness'. Traps may also include the fear of hurting others, avoidance, trying to please, etc. *Snags* (often evidenced as 'yes, buts') are self-imposed obstacles which arise out of guilt or fear. These become particularly prominent if we are apprehensive about pleasure or success.

At the end of the first session, the client is given a *psychotherapy file* to take away and read. This is a form of self-monitoring derived from cognitive therapy where clients are asked to list unwanted behaviour, variable moods and symptoms. This enables their antecedents, the thoughts and feelings experienced at the time, and their consequences, to be highlighted. The file forms the basis for an 'exploratory conversation and as a way of introducing the client to new forms of self reflection' (Ryle 1997, p. 14). The file helps to note and record how these patterns of feelings and behaviour are observable and occur over the course of therapy.

In the fourth session, a draft reformulation letter is introduced which includes the listing of the target problems and how these core neurotic problems are enacted and reinforced by the target problem procedures. *Reformulations* are central to the treatment and consist of a letter written to the client which highlights past experiences and difficulties, coping mechanisms used by the client to deal with his problems, the identification of TPs and TPPs, and examples or predictions of how these procedures are in evidence in the thera-peutic relationship. The letter attempts to include the client's *own words and metaphors*. A copy of the letter, after discussion and agreement over its contents, is then held by both client and thera-pist. The reformulation letter can also take the form of a *sequential diagrammatic reformulation* (SDR) which traces, in diagrammatic fashion, how the current procedures serve to reinforce or maintain current unhelpful patterns. This flow chart, or scaffolding, is thought particularly helpful for clients who may have difficulty with a letter.

Sessions five to sixteen focus on the reformulation letter. Change is brought about via a new experience (a co-operative non-collusive therapeutic relationship), and through the experimentation with new behaviours (role play, discussion, graded exposure to the feared situation). Homework tasks and diaries are used to facilitate these aims. Attempts by the client to engage the therapist in enacting the TPPs need to be promptly identified and all process material including the transference has to be linked with the reformulation. A 'descriptive transformation' of the client's story is attempted – this, rather than interpretation, leads to change. This process is termed the three Rs: *Reformulation, Recognition, and Revision*.

Termination, which is borne in mind from the beginning of treatment by numbering every session, becomes increasingly an issue and needs to be addressed by sessions ten to twelve. The client's feelings about the ending, including reservations about the therapist's shortcomings, what has been achieved in therapy, and anxiety about the future are incorporated into the reformulation by way of a 'goodbye letter'. The client is also asked to write a goodbye letter. This is discussed with the client and includes a realistic review of what has been achieved, based on the evidence presented by the client. A follow-up session, focusing on reviewing the joint work rather than continuing the therapeutic process, is offered some three months after the termination of treatment.

Ryle's more recent (2002) work has extended the CAT approach to the treatment of a more disturbed population. Acknowledging the fact that people with borderline personality disorders are in general thought to be contraindicated for time-limited therapy, Ryle proposes a twenty-four-session model of CAT for clients presenting with problems which have what are termed borderline features. These include: labile, unstable and volatile moods, variable self-image, self-neglect or self-harm, a history of destructive and unstable relationships, impulsivity, and identity diffusion. These tend to be traits rather than symptoms and are perhaps best described as 'borderline personality organisations' (Kernberg 1975) rather than viewed as a specific disorders (see Ryle 1997, pp. 3–10, for a helpful discussion of this problematic concept).

Given the sudden and volatile mood swings in this population a central feature of CAT is the development of the 'self state sequential diagram' (SSSD) which monitors the awareness of self and others. The self-state diagram differs from the SDR described above by showing how feelings, roles and behaviour and action, originate from different 'self states' within the personality. Self states are defined as including 'mood(s), access to, and control of, emotion, and reciprocal role patterns.' These 'self states', which are often split off and of which the client remains unaware, are manifest in relationships with others or in relation to other parts of the self. By plotting these different self states, the transitions between them, and isolating the factors which prompt or trigger sudden mood swings, these switches of 'states' can be monitored and their relationship to each other identified and discussed. This acknowledges the discreet self states in this population which, while coexisting, tend to exist as dissociated entities in the personality. The therapeutic aim is to achieve some integration between these dissociated states. It is through identifying and monitoring the SSSDs that the integration of these different self states is achieved. Twenty-four sessions are recommended for these clients with follow-ups at one-, two-, three- and six-month intervals in recognition of the extreme difficulties these clients face with termination. CAT for different clinical populations and in differing clinical contexts has recently been described (Ryle 2002; Norcross 2005).

The therapeutic traditions outlined thus far have very differing theoretical starting points but – some more than others – are beginning to address both issues of what it is that might be mutative in therapy as well as the similarities in their clinical applications. In this they are becoming more eclectic in their application, concerned with what might be appropriate for the individual client rather than fitting clients into a purist theoretical approach.

Consequently the more eclectic short-term therapies tend to be wide-ranging, drawing on various orientations in framing treatment models. Examples of eclectic short-term psychotherapy include Wolberg (1980), Anstad and Hoyt (2005) in the context of managed care, Garfield's (1998) multi-faceted approach to brief therapies and Gustafson's (1986) wide-ranging and theoretically inclusive therapy. As well as using theories from both older and more contemporary psychoanalytic thought, Gustafson's model also incorporates ideas from systemic theories and describes very brief therapeutic interventions that can have substantive effects (Gustafson 2005).

Systems theory

The systemic model considers that people are best understood in a relational context and that any individual will be shaped and developed in relation to their family and social context. Thus relationships, communication and interaction, are central to the development of identity and personal experience and are the key to understanding psychological problems (Beinart et al. 2009). Pathology is understood as resulting from interpersonal processes. For example, fundamental to systemic family therapy are the patterns that develop that connect family members in a coherent and meaningful way (described as circularity). Circularity suggests that each person's behaviour is maintained by the actions of the other, thus problems are interpersonally maintained and may be shaped by broader contexts such as dominant gender or cultural roles. Contemporary systemic therapy, used mostly within a family therapy context, uses techniques such as hypothesizing, circularity, and positive connotation. Systems theory, while used extensively by family therapists, can be incorporated into the practice of counselling individuals, and these strategies are also used by the more focal dynamic short-term individual therapists. Similarly, the short-term individual therapist is part of the wider social system (in the consulting room as well as in the wider environment) both being influenced by it and having influence upon it.

Systems theory suggests that symptoms can be seen to be maintained by and for others. Clients may maintain symptoms to protect others or to maintain their existing relationships with them. Gustafson gives an example of a daughter 'needing' to lack confidence so that her mother would feel 'a successful mother [in order] that the daughter could be friends with the father, so [that] the father could tolerate what was missing in his [relationship] with his wife' (1986, p. 263). This is termed systemic resistance. Gustafson's model is based upon finding the missing developmental piece, paying careful attention to identifying and managing resistance, (including systemic resistance) and using this to 'resolve and repair' the developmental deficit.

Solution-focused therapy

Systemic thinking helps remind the therapist that the client is part of a wider system that may help or hinder therapeutic change. An associated technique, although having different origins, is the time-limited solution-focused approach. Rather than focus on pathology, symptoms and problems, this approach looks at how clients solve problems and attempts to generalise these successful strategies to other areas of their lives (de Shazer 1982, 1985; George et al. 1990). The bottle is half full rather than half empty. This model assumes that clients are basically healthy and potentially possess the skills to overcome their problems. The underlying cause of the problem does not need to be established since change can be brought about without making this link. Goals are articulated in the context of the clients' views of what life would be like without their current problem. The therapist is active in encouraging a dialogue of 'change talk' rather than 'problem talk' (Walter and Peller 1992). As its name suggests, change talk focuses on viewing the problem positively and working on previously and currently successful patterns of problem solving. This is achieved by working through stages (Dzie-gielewski 1997). More recent work has highlighted how the client's existing competencies and strengths are utilised to successfully address the client's current problems (O'Connell 2005).

These theories have all had an impact on the practice of time-aware therapy and counselling (Feltham 1997; Dryden and Feltham 1998; Litrell 1998). Egan's (1994) influential counselling text includes a three-stage problem solving model which 'gives helpers the technology of helping'. This moves from identifying current problems including 'unused opportunities' (stage one), through to assisting the client articulate and discover a 'preferred scenario' for the future (stage two), to stage three which identifies, and supports, the client in implementing, the various strategies to help achieve stage two.

The central tenets of focal therapies are also in evidence in both transactional analysis (TA), associated with the work of Berne (1963; Berne et al. 1973) and contemporary existential therapies.

Transactional analysis (TA)

Transactional analysis, based on the discrete but related ego states of adult, parent and child, is based upon the notion of a therapeutic contract, which is clear, unambiguous and agreed to by both client and therapist. Included in the contract is consideration of the therapist's contract with the institution which employs him to practise. The notion of cure is clearly defined early in treatment and is based upon what the clients wants rather than what the therapist thinks the client needs. The contract is made when both therapist and client have clearly articulated the answer to the question; 'How will we both know when we have achieved what you are consulting me for?' The aim of the treatment is to 'cure as many clients during the first treatment session as possible' (Berne et al. 1973). Recent literature has addressed short-term therapies from a TA viewpoint (Tudor 2001). The same author has outlined an approach to brief therapy from the person-centred tradition (Tudor 2008).

Existential therapy

Similarly, existential time-limited therapy (Strasser and Strasser 1997) has as its core belief, human limitations and the centrality of time. Believing that there are a certain number of 'givens' associated with the human condition (uncertainty, unpredictability, inconsistency and the fleeting nature of existence), all existential treatments are time-aware. Issues brought to therapy converge around 'givens' and only diverge in the individual clients' feelings, attitudes and behaviour towards these givens.

The guiding theme of time-limited treatments is to help the client tease out the distinction between those 'limitations that are imposed upon them by the world and (those they) impose on themselves' (Strasser and Strasser 1997). In this model, 12 to 15 sessions, using a modular approach to the timing of the sessions, are offered with two follow-up sessions one month apart. There is less necessity for a discrete focus since existential therapy assumes many of the client's presenting problems are linked to life's central issues of being and meaning. Treatment is based on the notion that clients develop 'rigid sedimented belief systems' which have both positive and negative connotations and determine their personal values. These 'sedimented outlooks' are similar to core beliefs and can be linked to the central themes of many of the therapeutic orientations described above. Sedimented outlooks are related to four dimensions of the human condition: physical, public, private and spiritual. Treatment consists of looking at the balance between these four dimensions and questioning any 'rigid sediments' which are in evidence. The therapist acts as a guide or catalyst and prompts or challenges perceptions. Sediments, arising from life experience, can be transformable within the context of the 'givens' existing in a particular client's life.

Heinz Kohut and self psychology

Returning to contemporary psychoanalytic theories, mention needs to be made of the increasingly influential school of 'self psychology' and its relevance to time-limited treatments. Self psychology, associated with the work of Heinz Kohut (1971, 1977), set out to integrate the relational school of psychoanalysis with the drive/structural model. Kohut came to recognise that his clients depended on his active responsiveness to the subtlety of their emotional states. In drawing attention to the actual care offered to the infant, he was implicitly drawing attention to the actual care offered by the therapist to his clients. This required him to modify analytic technique and made his acceptance within the analytic community increasingly problematic. In advocating the need for the therapist to be empathically engaged with his client rather than passively neutral, it was inevitable that self psychology would become more supportive and experiential than classic analysis would allow. Also inevitable was that Kohut's later work (1984) would show less sensitivity in offending analytic sensibilities.

Kohut suggests that the 'self' develops out of the earliest interpersonal relationships and throughout life mediates between the individual and his 'object world'. What the self requires is 'constancy, resilience and cohesion' which only the relationship with another can provide. The 'others' are termed 'self objects' since in infancy they are not experienced as differentiated from the self. The concept of self object is based upon the infant's earliest experience of the provision of affirmation and recognition by his primary caretakers. Self objects can be people or, later in life, may become more abstract, such as belief systems. Responsive to the needs of the infant, these 'self objects' provide the basis for the gradual development of the self. They provide a range of psychological functions for another person similar to the way a mother or caretaker provides for her infant. Development consists of the recognition and acceptance that the functions of the self objects will eventually need to be taken over by oneself.

The experiences, which are central to the development of the self, and are provided by contact with the self objects, include:

- 'mirroring' – the infant's 'grandiose images' which the parents affirm and become related to the child's self-esteem. This includes empathy, constancy and basic nurture and is associated with maternal care. It is from mirroring that the eventual feeling that we are understood and cared for by others develops.

■ 'idealised self objects' – the infant's capacity to vicariously enjoy the idealisation of the parent which becomes the basis of the belief that there are things that are greater than ourselves which become the source of comfort and inspiration in adult life. This is associated with the role of the father.

Gradual and inevitable parental failures in both these spheres lead to what Kohut calls a process of 'transmuting internalisation'. This involves the non-traumatic recognition that 'self objects' are not perfect sources of mirroring or objects for idealisation and prompts the infant to gradually take on, or incorporate, the functions of the self objects into themselves.

Problems arise through a 'chronic failure' of parental empathy which prevents the healthy development of the child's sense of self. The development of a cohesive sense of self, based upon self-esteem and self-comfort, is thus impaired. For Kohut, this deficiency or deprivation becomes the basis for destructive or handicapping narcissism.

It follows that in therapy the client will establish a 'self object transference' based upon either 'mirroring' or 'idealising' modes and this will provide a second chance to rework an earlier faulty 'transmuting idealisation.' The therapist's 'empathic reflection' helps provide the missing developmental experiences in a safe and non-traumatic setting. This, of course, will take time as the therapist has to work through stages of empathic mirroring and idealisation before his inevitable shortcomings, or failures, can be acknowledged and addressed. These deficiencies in therapeutic care (repeating the parental shortcomings) enable the client to see the therapist in a more realistic light. This helps the client to become less dependent on therapeutic 'mirroring' and 'idealisation', and his self-esteem, or coherent sense of self, will flourish. The importance placed, in the development of the self, on 'cohesiveness, continuity and integrity' in parental care taking is reflected in the stance adopted by the therapist. It is the slow exposure to 'optimal frustrations' which is curative, thus lengthy treatments are indicated. Therapy consists of the client gradually working through childhood developmental difficulties in establishing a cohesive sense of self and the movement towards a more mature and less fractured relationship to his 'self object'. Though it is apparent that the therapeutic relationship may take a considerable amount of time to develop while the therapist adopts a passive, empathic and 'mirroring' stance, what is of interest in Kohut's work is the importance placed not on the therapeutic relationship itself, but the manner in which it is able to be established, maintained, and how it affects the client's sense of self. In this, it is crucial to listen for, and validate, the *client's frame of reference* (including language and affective states which often are communicated in symbolic forms or through subjective metaphors) as well as to interpret and focus on any resistance to the establishment of what Kohut terms a 'self-object transference'. The concept of 'mirroring' is particularly helpful when considering time-limited therapy with those clients who present with narcissistic, schizoid or borderline characteristics (Chapter 4).

The importance placed by self-psychology on ways of relating, and the connection with self-esteem, have led to increasing interest in applying these insights to shorter-term treatments (Baker 1991; Gardner 1991; Lynch 1998). While shorter-term self-psychological approaches tend to be aimed at supporting and treating current problems, in common with other time-limited approaches, these authors speak of therapy as 'getting something started rather than finished'. It is recognised that working through may take place in significant relationships outside therapy. This literature suggests that self-esteem and a coherent sense of self can be assisted by brief therapeutic relationships. Thus, the client might 'gain some benefit simply from experiencing a self object transference in relation to their counsellor without needing necessarily to work through experiences of frustration in the context of this relationship' (Lynch 1998). It may be enough to be affirmed and heard.

Integrative and eclectic therapies have been frowned upon in psychoanalytic circles which have tended to view these approaches as promiscuous deviations from pure forms of therapy. Therapeutic eclecticism is, however, based on what works, derived from empirical research. It is increasingly seen as incorporating aspects of proven therapeutic models based upon the needs of the client rather than theory-driven professionalism. Advantages of eclectic models include that they tend to be more inclusive in their selection criteria and assist therapists in focusing on which type of therapy or technique will help the individual client. However, it does assume that therapists are sufficiently flexible to be able to master and implement a variety of techniques, some of which may be at variance with their own therapeutic styles. It also assumes that one can introduce different techniques into the same therapy without changing the therapeutic process. Can one introduce techniques such as homework or diary-keeping halfway through a therapy which has not used such techniques previously without altering the therapeutic dynamic? Integration of these therapies is not made any easier by the absence of a common language; this despite the fact that, as we have seen, many of the underlying assumptions of therapy are not dissimilar.

What they share is the expectation that the therapy will be short, therapeutic hope, the need for some form of therapeutic focus, and therapist activity. It is perhaps not surprising that interest in short-term therapies has taken brevity to its logical extreme in single-session therapy and the prescription of 'no therapy'. As we have seen, many of Freud's early therapeutic successes were single-session treatments. One four-hour session with Gustav Mahler in which Freud linked the name of Mahler's wife with that of his mother was help enough but it was Donald Winnicott and his concept of the therapeutic consultation which showed how an informed brief contact can lead to major change.

The work of Donald Winnicott

Donald Winnicott, a paediatrician and psychoanalyst, is perhaps not the first person to spring to mind when thinking about brief interventions. Trained at the Institute of Psychoanalysis and supervised by Melanie Klein, it is surprising to find many of the fundamentals of time-limited treatment in Winnicott's clinical descriptions. Working as a paediatrician, Winnicott was startled to find that a great many of his patients were helped by the 'full exploitation of the first interview'. This was not what his training had led him to expect.

From this experience emerged what he termed his *therapeutic consultations*. His descriptions of 'therapeutic consultations', often consisting of only one session, appear at times to involve a form of magical intuition yet are firmly grounded in developmental theory. As a result, his consultations, predominantly with children, are aimed at removing developmental blocks and ensuring that environmental provision is 'good enough' to facilitate further progress. Hence, consultations 'loosen the knot' and assist development. For Winnicott, each individual session is a treatment in itself. As Groves (1996) points out, particularly as Winnicott got older 'he brought to each session a special type of activity that made every hour count, as if each session would be his last'. This is a helpful approach for time-limited therapists.

Familiar to many contemporary time-limited therapists, Winnicott's technique involved an active engagement with his patients including the use of both transference and counter-transference, the need for the patient to come to an interpretation themselves with the therapist as a guide, and the importance of *therapeutic surprise*. He also implied that the more serious the earlier trauma or deprivation, the less likely that standard analytic techniques would be applicable and the more the therapist needed to rely on the qualities inherent in the therapeutic relationship. This was, and still is, a challenge to traditional psychoanalytic treatments where the earlier the deprivation, the longer the therapy is likely to be.

Winnicott's therapeutic consultations with children are centred, although not exclusively so, on the 'Squiggle Game'. The therapist draws a 'squiggle' and the child is encouraged to add to it in the process of which the child communicates something of himself to the therapist. This makes the consultation 'come alive'. While not relying on an interchange of drawings, Winnicott's consultations with adults are no different from those with children in attempting to facilitate 'communications of a very personal kind' A good example of the use of a one-off consultation to facilitate change is given in 'The Case of Mrs. X' (Winnicott 1971), his consultation with the mother of a child repeatedly admitted to hospital where no physical cause was detected. Here the timing of the consultation, the active and insightful engagement with her, the use of symbols, and the skilful use of self, enabled Winnicott to make immediate contact with the patient's primary concerns. Interestingly, these bore some resemblance to what others have called core beliefs about the self arising from deprived formative experiences. Jerry (1994) attempts to develop 'therapeutic consultations' into a workable technique in brief or single-session therapy that focuses on linking past and present caretaking experiences.

Winnicott was perhaps the first to recognise and work with the *'pre-transference'*. In Winnicott's language, this was the patient's need to turn him into a 'subjective object'. Struck by the frequency with which patients recalled having dreamt of him the night before the consultation, he found that, to his amusement, he was fitting in with a preconceived notion of what the individual patient subjectively expected him to be. Being this 'subjective object' has great therapeutic possibilities but 'rarely outlasts the first or first few interviews'. It is an early example of the importance which modern time-aware therapists place on the need to recognise the clients' *anticipation and expectation, or pre-transference, of therapy*. This too is likely to be a reflection of the clients' core beliefs and fundamental anxieties.

For Winnicott, the length of a treatment is less important than making contact with his clients. Implicit in his therapeutic consultations is the belief that reaching 'deeper levels of the psyche' is not related to length of treatment; indeed, the reverse can be true. Timing and therapeutic surprise can lead to '*a sacred moment*' in a consultation which enables the client to make themselves known. These 'sacred moments' can 'be used or wasted' and appear to consist of something of the client's essence being understood by the therapist. This reinforces the client's belief in the therapeutic value of both therapist and treatment.

Therapeutic surprise is important. Winnicott believed that interpretations fail because the client experiences them as familiar modes of interaction and reacts to them in characteristic and familiar ways. When interpretations work, the client experiences them as something new, not encountered before, and so responds to them in a different way. This appears to be not dissimilar to other versions of the need for a 'different' therapeutic experience which we have described previously. Interpretation is not the main feature of the consultation. Indeed, even correct interpretations can be unhelpful as they can be technically correct but clinically damaging. Winnicott warns against making interpretations, however 'correct', solely for the benefit of the therapist. Dogmatic interpretations are also harmful since they leave the client 'with only two alternatives, an acceptance of what I have said as propaganda or a rejection of the interpretation and of me and the whole set up' (1971, p. 10). The issue of how we can avoid 'propaganda' in time-limited therapies is one we will return to in a later chapter.

Winnicott alludes to the need to transcend, if not 'unlearn', one's own training in these brief consultations. Aware of the effect that his own analytic training had on him, he states that he found 'that interpretations that seemed right ten years ago and that the patient accepted because of awe turned out in the end to be collusive defences' (1971, p. 10). All snakes might not be penis symbols, rather they might be attempts by the client to communicate something important about themselves. We shall return to this theme when we discuss the issue of training for time-limited therapies.

Winnicott believed that this approach was open to almost any level of psychopathology although recognised that some clients were too sick and damaged to be helped by brief consultations and needed containment or management. Central to the work is Winnicott's understanding of the individual's emotional development and its relationship to the client's specific environment. His idiosyncratic style, which, Groves (1996) believes should be read like poetry, 'from the heart' rather than the head, makes it appear that his technique is intuitive and difficult to either replicate or grasp. Winnicott appears to recognise this himself when he says that 'the work cannot be copied because the therapist is involved in every case as a person and therefore no two interviews could be alike since they would be carried through by two (different therapists)' (1971, p. 9). This is of little help or comfort to the fledgling therapist attempting to understand and practise therapeutic consultations. Again we shall return to the issue of intuition when we discuss training.

Single-session, and less, treatments

Single-session treatments (in essence an adaptation of Winnicott's therapeutic consultations) and other very brief interventions (e.g. Barkham's 1989 2+1 model), have tended to be a response to increasing demand for therapeutic services and ways of managing waiting lists. This is very different from the planned use of a minimal number of sessions. The work of Malan et al. (1975) at the Tavistock Clinic had already suggested that minimal contact could have positive outcomes. This piece of research followed up clients who were seen for one consultation but did not receive any ongoing treatment. The vast majority of the 45 clients in the research improved to such an extent that Malan initially thought that this was the result of 'spontaneous remission'. However, he eventually came to the conclusion (not without considerable disbelief) that it was the single consultation that had led to change; positive outcomes may be extremely widespread following a single session. Profound therapeutic effects can follow from a single interview – 'the ripple effect'. Malan finally came to the conclusion that what they were seeing was not spontaneous remission (or other non-therapeutic effects such as 'flights into health' and 'transference cures') but the outcomes of one-session psychotherapy.

This has led to increasing interest in single-session treatments. Talmon (1993), under the therapeutic maxim of 'Think complex, do simple', questioned the widely held belief that there is a conflict between brevity and effectiveness. Using techniques such as reframing, linking, making symbolic connections and narrative, Talmon suggested that much can be achieved in a single session by encouraging clients to use what they found helpful in their sessions to utilise change. Brunning (1998) gives an account of the successful treatment of a young agoraphobic woman using these techniques. Bloom's (1992) single-session model is two hours long and explicitly attempts to assist the client become aware of something that was previously unconscious and to begin a process of change after the end of the session. Stadter (2004) suggests three conditions must be present for single-session therapy to be effective. First, a positive client–therapist relationship which includes a *positive contextual transference*, the client's belief that they, rather than external forces or others, can be an active agent of change, and the client's readiness to change. The single-session clinician has to ask themselves the question: What can I do now? An equally challenging question for the short-term therapist would be: 'What would I do if I would never see this client again?' Both questions exert require considerable discipline on the therapist. Single-session treatments, where specific problems are articulated, potential solutions explored, and new approaches developed, have an increasingly positive evidence base (Cameron 2007).

There is growing recognition that there are times when the proscription of no therapy is the (non) treatment of choice (Frances and Clarkin 1981). While this may appear the logical extension of ever briefer therapies (and an unconscious Freudian 'death wish' for the therapeutic profession!), it does allow for the fact that the clinician's duty is to do 'no further harm'. There may be times when therapy becomes, if not directly harmful, then at least unhelpful. As Frances and Clarkson suggest 'the psychotherapies, like drugs, can produce addiction, side effects, complications and overdoses if prescribed in an unselective fashion' (in Groves 1996, p. 450). They suggest various categories of clients for whom treatment may be harmful which include the psychotic and severely disturbed but also those for whom 'treatment has become a way of life rather than a means to an end'.

The 'no treatment' suggestion may also function as a paradoxical injunction to clients who lack motivation or are passively referred by third parties. By speaking to, and appearing to agree with, the part of the client who is resisting therapy, the part of the client that may be wishing to establish a therapeutic alliance is provoked into responding:

A 30-year-old woman who had recently arrived in the country to pursue a course of further study, sought out therapy. She described herself in a passive and matter of fact fashion describing a diffuse and non-specific sense of ennui, and was clearly taken aback when the counsellor asked her why she had come for therapy at this stage in her life and enquired as to what she might want from the experience. She had talked at length about herself but without any sense that there was an acute problem that she wished to address. Also absent was any suggestion that there were long-standing issues which needed some attention. The counsellor was faced with the choice of either finding a way of making the counselling 'helpful' for her (in the face of her bemusement as to what it may focus on) or putting responsibility on her to define how counselling could help. He chose the latter course. It turned out that this young woman was the daughter of two psychoanalysts and had been in therapy since she was very small. She had assumed, in line with her parental beliefs, that therapy was indeed 'a way of life'. Having signed on for her academic courses, paid for her accommodation and joined a number of college societies, she thought she would book in for counselling as it was both an unquestioned assumption on her part and an expectation of what students did. She had no particularly enjoyable or rewarding experiences of previous counselling and just thought it 'was something one did'. The suggestion that she might not need therapy as a lifestyle requirement was met with surprise and relief. She left the consultation rather stunned, believing that her 'old compliant self' had been liberated and saying, with more liveliness than had been in evidence throughout the previous 40 minutes, that the thought of managing without any therapeutic 'help' was extremely exiting. Metaphorically of course this consultation was all about her separation from her parents. The therapist's response would hopefully allow this process to continue beyond the consultation and generalise to other areas of this young woman's life; the 'ripple effect'.

This is not dissimilar to the 'research chemist' described by Malan (in Groves 1996, pp. 493–4) who, disturbed by the thought of seeing a therapist, was so relieved that his consultation had resulted in the therapist saying he did not need treatment that his symptoms immediately disappeared. Clients can be very relieved that they might not need therapy and gain considerable benefit from the suggestion that they may be able to take more responsibility for their own lives than they believe themselves capable of doing.

Having come to the point of suggesting that some of our clients might not need therapy we can now move on to a discussion of how to help those that do.

Summary

In this chapter we have developed the notion that therapeutic interventions are an interactive process where both participants influence each other. In dynamic terms, this can be seen to represent the object relations school of therapy and is influenced by post-modern notions of intersubjectivity. We have also looked at various non-dynamic therapies and seen that they incorporate many psychodynamic ideas and applications. Equally, in true intersubjective fashion, we have seen how the more purely dynamic therapies have sought to harness insights from the more structured, less process-driven therapies, in developing short-term interventions which are briefer, structured in requiring a focus, and require more therapeutic activity on behalf of the therapist. Contemporary dynamic focal therapies often make use of metaphor and symbols. These assist clinically in the move away from excessive reliance on interpretation to the use of linking, the importance of the 'here and now' processes of clinical sessions, and using the therapeutic process collaboratively to understand and assist the client's problems. In addition to the intrapsychic and object relations schools, we now need to add insights from attachment and narrative theory to develop a contemporary model of short-term focused interventions. But first we will look at the similarities in the therapeutic traditions described thus far to assist us in articulating a model of short-term psychodynamic therapy.

3

Idiom, the Therapeutic Triangle and Transference

If the patient is to fight his way through the normal conflict with the resistances which we have uncovered for him in the analysis, he is in need of a powerful stimulus which will influence the decision in the sense which we desire leading to recovery ... At this point what turns the scale in his struggle is not his intellectual insight ... but simply and solely his relationship to the doctor. (Freud 1917)

The result of our review of time-limited and briefer therapies in previous chapters has been to focus attention on some common themes. Issues which have emerged to be of central importance include:

- the importance of the therapeutic *frame*;
- the attention paid to the therapeutic *process*, including the 'here and now' relationship, as distinct from the 'there and then' content of sessions;
- the importance of *affect*, i.e. feeling as opposed to solely intellectual understanding, in dynamic short-term therapy;
- the need to link the presenting problem with both the client's history and the here and now therapeutic process; what Malan has termed the *triangle of insight*.

What has also become apparent are some basic similarities among all the theories discussed in the previous chapters. Although very different in their theoretical models and in their clinical applications, all the theories appear to show some fundamental similarities. All appear to moving towards recognition that it is the quality of, and attention paid to, the therapeutic relationship, which are of central importance. In addition, they share a belief in the immediate and active engagement, and a demand, on both therapist and client, for mutual collaboration. However, they also suggest that there is something in the client's 'way of being in the world' and its immediate clinical manifestations, which is crucial in time-limited therapies. If we, for instance, look at the following concepts we can see that they are in actual fact addressing very similar themes:

- Adler's 'faulty beliefs' and 'unstable opinions';
- Ellis's 'core irrational beliefs';
- Felix Deutsch's concept of 'associated anamnesis'. Deutsch (1949) drew attention to recurring themes in the client's discourse of which the client may not be fully aware. These may be key words, affects or behaviours.
- Malan's 'repetitive patterns';
- Weiss and Sampson's (1986) 'pathogenic beliefs' similar to cognitive therapy's maladaptive automatic thoughts;
- Horrowitz's 'schematic representations and personal schemas';
- Strupp's 'cyclical maladaptive patterns';
- Strupp and Binder's concepts of personal 'maps';
- Milton Erikson's (1980) 'organised themes';
- Budman and Gurman's 'faulty learning' leading to personal 'templates for future behaviour and relationships';
- Mann's 'chronically endured pain;';
- Cognitive analytic therapy's 'reciprocal relationships' and 'reciprocal role procedures';
- Beck's 'false cognitions' and 'automatic thoughts';
- Cognitive behaviour therapy's concepts of 'core beliefs' and individual 'schemas';
- the 'internal objects' of psychoanalysis which can be seen to be similar, despite differing theoretical assumptions, to 'core beliefs';
- the 'sedimental values' in existential therapy;
- Kohut's 'self objects' and the importance placed on the client's 'frame of reference'.

In addition, attention has been paid to specific moments in therapy which are seen to be of significance:

- Davanloo's 'subtlety loaded words';
- Balint's 'important moments';
- Winnicott's 'sacred moments';
- Stern's 'now moments'.

Freud in the Ego and the Id (1923) had referred to internal perceptions 'which arise in the most diverse and deepest strata of the mental apparatus' which can be viewed as a way of describing a process through which a sense of self, or a personal idiom, is created.

Idiom: towards an integrative model for time-limited therapies

As can be seen, these are all terms which refer to a specific aspect of the client's 'being' in the therapeutic relationship. They all draw attention to the language, behaviour, posture, appearance, and belief systems of the individual client. These are ways of being in the world and ways of relating (including the anticipation of encounters with others) often in evidence by a recurring word, behaviour or affect in individual sessions. These give clues to the individual's *recurring motifs* which become central to the therapy. These recurring motifs often centre on feelings and experiences (anger, sadness, betrayal, hope, fear, etc.) and relate to what the individual expects from others and how the individual views himself. They form mental representations of the place of self and others in the world and include specific expectations in the way the world is perceived and experienced. These can be derived from faulty learning (behaviour therapy) or result from experiences that lead to a discrete way of 'object relating' (psychoanalytic and dynamic therapies). Whichever theoretical model is preferred, all are based on the notion that what the individual internalises from his own specific developmental history is a *relational template* which shapes the individual's experience of both himself and others. This is the basis of how the individual relates to others and how he expects others to relate to him. Although these beliefs can arise from real experiences (and symptoms are often failed attempts to master traumatic experiences), they can also result from fantasies, hopes, fears and straightforward misunderstandings.

Clinically recurring motifs can be conveyed by oft repeated single words (leading to those 'sacred moments'), personal themes and the transference, as well as the client's perception of, and response to, the therapist's verbal and non-verbal communications. They may also represent discrete ways in which the client relates to the therapy itself. Single words, the description of specific experiences or attitudes towards the therapist can be important. The particular moment in the session when these appear (in terms of their context and timing), and the feelings and behaviour – frequently expressing disappointment, hurt, rage fear, rejection, etc. – associated with them, often convey a 'secret' motif that can become the organising theme for the subsequent therapy.

These personal templates are central to time-limited therapies since they speak directly to the client's way of being in the world and his way of approaching and mastering conflicts. The Oxford English Dictionary defines 'idiom' as:

- a form of expression peculiar to a language [and] person;
- the language of a people [and] the specific character of this;
- a group of words established by usage and having a meaning not *deducible from those of the individual words*, a 'characteristic mode of expression' which might be private if not secret.

I would suggest that *idiom* is a convenient shorthand way of describing these common themes which have emerged from the literature. We can use the term 'idiom' as a way of describing these similar, but differently named, concepts which depict the individual's way of being in the world.

Idiom, used in this sense, is similar to the description of a distinctive personal style outlined by Bollas (1992). Bollas considers us to have a range of personal idioms, not all of which we are aware of, that consist of a repertoire of 'ways of being' which are waiting to be called up in our encounters with others:

> without giving it much thought at all we consecrate the world with our own subjectivity, investing people, places, things, and events with a kind of idiomatic significance. (1992, p. 3)

The self is made up of a plurality of idioms waiting to be called up and discovered. Our idiom is our mystery. We may seek out others to activate dormant (what Bollas calls 'unthought' but sensed) idioms. In this way, we seek out others to express parts of ourselves. While some objects may have more significant idiomatic meaning for us than others, we seek out and select objects to express different parts of ourselves. The self, or personality, is made up of many idiomatic representations. A person's idiom, 'partly inherited, partly acquired', actively 'shapes their relational world according to the idiom of their internal world'. Idioms only come about through interaction with others and these interactions (or what Bollas terms the 'collisional dialectic') leave a trace on the person. This would imply that we actively seek out those 'objects' that can give expression to discrete notions of our idiom. For Bollas, 'a day is a space for the potential articulation of my idiom' (1992, p. 24). This suggests some degree of choice, albeit unconscious, in the selection of an activity. When deciding whether to read a book, see a friend or see a therapist, we are 'choosing' to bring alive an aspect of our idiom. In this sense, the therapist has to be alive to the manifold idioms potentially on offer while at the same time being aware of his own idiomatic response to his client. It is the neutrality, framework, structure, and boundary of the consulting room and therapeutic relationship which enable idioms to appear thus to become therapeutically meaningful. Hopkins (2006) quotes a rather magical consultation that the film designer Tony Walton had with Winnicott who was able to intuitively tune into Walton's idiomatic sensitivities (2006, pp. 121–2). Whereas Bollas sees idioms as being revealed over time, my contention is that they are immediately apparent. They cannot be hidden: a person's idiom is the one thing they cannot not express.

Tina

Tina shows us the way that idiom can relate to clinical practice:

Tina, a 25-year-old woman, consulted a counsellor, just over a year after the sudden death of her mother. In a frustrated and irascible way she explained that she was becoming listless, irritable and low, feeling reluctant and unable to get up in the mornings. She was aware that she was withdrawing from friendships and social relationships. Without any prompting from the counsellor Tina somewhat wearily (although indicating that she was complying with an anticipated request from the counsellor) spoke about her background and the events leading up to her mother's death. Her elderly father, originally from continental Europe, had a history of manic depressive illness necessitating numerous hospitalisations, most recently on the anniversary of her mother's death. One of the mother's roles in the family was to support the temperamentally labile father. Tina, the eldest of three daughters, was now taking on this maternal role with little enthusiasm. She told the counsellor that while she supported him as best she could, she found his often tearful distress somewhat tiresome. She experienced it as a paternal demand that the daughters should grieve in the same fashion. Tina felt unable and unwilling to respond in the same way; she did not want to cry with, or could not cry for, him.

Tina's mother had been ill for some time but the family did not think that her frequent bouts of poor health were life-threatening. Tina's maternal grandmother had died some three years previously after which Tina's mother had developed a range of psychosomatic symptoms which, Tina stressed to her counsellor, she understood to be her mother's way of dealing with the loss. At this point the counsellor was beginning to experience unease, sensing a certain provocative hostility in the room and puzzled – as well as anxious – about how he was going to be able to make a helpful contribution to the session since Tina did not appear to welcome or allow any verbal participation in the session from him. He was sensing Tina's dismissive attitude to him but felt a need, out of professional self-respect if nothing else, to comment on the maternal link in patterns of grief. Tina brushed this aside saying she had already thought of that, which left the counsellor feeling silly for having 'stated the obvious', and summarily dismissed.

Prior to her mother's illness, Tina had been working abroad where she learnt of her mother's hospital admission but thought it unlikely to be serious so had arranged to see her mother on her return in two weeks time. The following day, she was informed by fax that her mother had died. Tina felt numb and by her own account 'went through the motions'. She had at that time actively dealt with 'what needed dealing with' and, having mourned her mother, was puzzled as to why she was currently experiencing these symptoms. The counsellor who by now was recovering from the earlier dismissal and feeling more comfortable with (and more warmly towards) Tina was beginning to build up a picture of a very competent young woman who, although at times 'listless, irritable and low', 'gets things done'. He was, however, still aware of a certain anxiety which, when reflected upon, appeared to centre on his lack of verbal contribution and a wish to become more involved in the session. He was nursing a sense of unease that his silence, and his feeling of being barged out and excluded from the encounter, were instrumental in leading him to feel a certain desperation to become 'involved'. This, combined with a feeling that Tina needed somehow to be appeased and mirrored through support and reassurance, led him to say something about the stages of grief and that people dealt with them in their own idiosyncratic ways. Tina, giving the counsellor a withering and dismissive glance, said she knew all about that – she knew the theory and did not believe in stages anyway – and continued to talk at her counsellor while he retreated to lick his wounds and consider further lines of approach. He was left wondering about his 'stages of grief' comment, and again felt clumsy and inane.

Tina went on to talk about her mother and their relationship. They were the 'best of friends', rather than mother and daughter, and this friendship had to be mourned. She would miss the almost sibling-like affection. Without her mother, she was experiencing herself as boring, something that the counsellor was beginning to feel in relation to Tina – he could only bore her with his 'insights'. Tina felt that she had nothing to talk about with her friends other than her mother. She was so disinterested in other areas of her *life that she was 'allowing' her boyfriend to pursue interests in other women. She just did not care. Tina began to talk about having nightmares at which point the counsellor began to perk up a bit, thinking that he might have something to offer here – if he did not have anything to contribute when dreams were being discussed, he was surely redundant! One fleeting daydream which Tina reported was a thought of taking an overdose or throwing herself in the river as a wish to end the pain. At this point the counsellor felt brave enough to comment that these thoughts may symbolise how much she might miss her mother and Tina's wish to be reunited with her. Tina's withering expression suggested that she had thought of this some months ago; it was literally water off a duck's back.*

What was happening here? How are we to understand this thera-peutic encounter? One way is to identify and name Tina's predomi-nant idiom. It is by reflecting on the session's process rather than content that we are able to recognise Tina's *idiom*. Tina's idiom was her self-sufficient competence ('gets things done'). She had dealt successfully with all life's challenges by being busy and successful. Until the death of her mother she saw herself as someone who did not need anybody and this idiom was brought into the session with her counsellor (witness the counsellor's counter-transference of wishing to become more involved but being left to feel inept and excluded). The difficulty, however, as with all idioms, is that under stress or pressure, they may become dysfunctional and part of the problem. Characteristic ways of being are rarely flexible enough to cope with all eventualities.

Tina's expectation on herself was to cure herself of these feelings of sadness and grief without anyone else's assistance. Her counsellor had nothing to say – Tina had covered every angle and thought of everything. She was clearly as uncomfortable in coming to see the counsellor as the counsellor was in her presence; what both Tina and her counsellor felt in these opening minutes pointed to where the real problem lay.

We can see that during the session that certain themes emerged and continuously recurred:

■ Efforts at empathy and support were rejected. Tina was dismissive of all the counsellor's verbal interventions.
■ Tina was relentlessly counter-suggestible. Her father's suggestion that signs of grief were part of the mourning process was met with dismissal by Tina who was not going to mourn the same way as him; a warning to the counsellor that any prescriptive (or

even normative) approach by him was likely to be dealt with in the same fashion.

■ Tina's attitude to her low mood and irritableness (observable and experienced by the counsellor during the session) was one of frustration and self-reproach – she ought to be able to conquer these feelings herself.

■ Tina's attitude to sadness, or more specifically tears (as representing her more vulnerable side), was harsh – she was not going to cry like, or for, her father. The statement that she was not going to cry for him was an important transferential comment – she was not going to either do what she assumed the counsellor wanted (show her vulnerability in her tears) or 'cry' in front of a man. When Tina said she was not going to cry in front of her father to either please him or grieve in the same way, the fact that her counsellor was male could not but indicate that the same process and dynamic were alive in the session.

■ The fact that Tina spoke of her mother as more of a sibling indicated that there were possible conflicts for her around the issue of being mothered and mothering. This was confirmed by both her discomfort and reluctance to 'mother' her father as her mother had done, and by her response to the counsellor's attempts to 'mother' her, e.g. Tina's reply to the 'stages of grief comment'. This could be a pointer to why Tina's grief reaction was both delayed and prolonged; Tina harboured considerable unexpressed ambivalence towards her mother's maternal role. This had been exacerbated by her death. This ambivalence would also be apparent in her attitude to counselling and the counsellor.

■ Tina needed to actively control the therapeutic encounter and any suggestion that she became more passive (or even allow a reciprocal dialogue) with others was dealt with harshly.

■ Here was a woman whose personal template led her in her first meeting with the counsellor to replicate her characteristic way of approaching problems (and people). She was attempting to cure herself of the consequences of being bereaved just as she had single mindedly solved previous problems in her life.

These recurring motifs formed Tina's idiom which became central to the therapy. Apparent in the opening session, Tina's idiom needed to be linked with the therapeutic triangle of history (relationships with parents), current symptom (delayed and resisted grief) and the process relationship with the counsellor.

For this to be done, it was important to view the therapeutic process of the session in the context of the therapeutic triangle. The counsellor decided that the first most important element to address was Tina's attitude to counselling, the counsellor, and, by implication, parts of her self. When Tina said, not unsurprisingly, that she did not think regular counselling would be either helpful or indicated, the counsellor, using his experience of being shut out in the session, suggested that this was possibly contributing to the current problem. Tina had worked it all out herself and knew what was going on but this did not lead her to feeling any better. She knew everything but could not change how she felt with that knowledge. It was the expectation that she placed on herself that was the problem. Her own self-knowledge could not help her but the expectation she placed on herself (her idiom) was that it should. Could it be that it was this – the way her current symptom challenged her personal idiom – that needed discussing? Perhaps this was what counselling could offer? Tina would treat any form of counselling in much the same way as other demands on the self. We can see here how this idiomatic metaphor represented both her current problem and relationships with significant people in the past.

During the course of the next eight time-limited sessions, other elements of the therapeutic triangle were in evidence and addressed. These included the following questions:

- How was Tina's sense of idiom of herself (as someone who needed to solve problems without letting anyone else in) established and maintained?
- How did it manifest itself in the therapeutic relationship?
- Was her response to her own vulnerability gender-related in terms of her father, counsellor and men in general?
- Was this idiom derived from her earliest experiences?

Central importance was attached to the need to address the personal idiom as evidenced in the therapeutic process as soon as possible. This was particularly important in relation to negative feelings which were communicated both verbally and through counter-transference discomfort. In this sense, the counter-transference is understood and used to work with the idiomatic transference. Tina shows us how her affects and recurring motifs in the opening session, which represented her idiom, were interlinked with the therapeutic triangle.

The present complaint: This would include Tina's irritableness and self reproach that she should be able to 'manage' her feelings of loss; the counsellors fear that he would have nothing to say and Tina's feeling that she had nothing else to talk about other than the loss of her mother. This needed to be linked with Tina's *personal history*. How did family relationships (including both her father's wish that she should grieve in a certain way and 'idioms' of mothering and being mothered) link with the *transference*? This was in relation to what counselling represented in Tina's idiom and internal world as much as to the counsellor as person.

Seen in this light, the therapy could (and indeed did through the use of symbol and metaphor) address all three dimensions of the triangle concurrently via the mechanism of Tina's personal idiom.

Despite being an internal construct or template, an idiom implies that there is always another with whom we are interacting. Idioms are formed and maintained through our relationships with others. They are recurring patterns of interpersonal behaviour which determine how we construct and perceive past, present and future experience. Fantasy plays its part but it is important to acknowledge and appreciate the impact of real-life experience in the construction of an idiom. It is important, however, to value the important adaptational aspects of personal idioms although, as we have seen in the case of Tina, they can, at times, be maladaptive.

Time-limited therapies pay specific attention to these idiomatic representations as they appear and develop. It is the relationship between this idiomatic representation and the therapeutic triangle that becomes the central organising focus in time-limited therapies.

The therapeutic triangle

A central organising focus is crucial to time-limited therapies. Ideally this needs to incorporate various significant aspects of the client's difficulties. These have been conceptualised as triangles (see Malan, discussed in Chapter 2) (Figure 3.1).

The important aspect of the triangle of persons (Figure 3.1) is to link therapeutic material with all three corners of the triangle. This usually includes the therapist, significant people in the client's current life who impact on the presenting problem, and significant people in the past including parents, siblings and caretakers. An additional aspect of this is the importance, as we have seen with Tina, of including how the client's relationship with themselves is connected with their relationship to others, including the therapist (Stadter 2004).

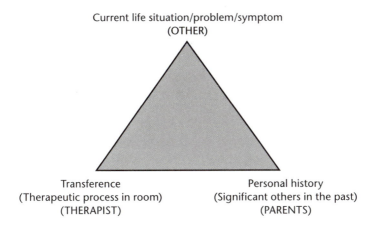

Current life situation/problem/symptom
(OTHER)

Transference
(Therapeutic process in room)
(THERAPIST)

Personal history
(Significant others in the past)
(PARENTS)

FIGURE **3.1** Triangle of persons/insight

The triangle of defence, or conflict (Figure 3.2), illustrates the attempts made to master and manage anxiety. An example comes to mind when I recently needed to undertake a complex rail journey. Having decided the night before that I would use the journey to complete a work task, I found myself intrigued by a novel which I was reading and had the thought (impulse, hidden feeling) that I could continue this on my train journey the following morning. This caused some anxiety as I would not be completing my work task. The following day I purchased a newspaper to read on the train to defer the decision whether to work or continue with the novel (this act can be viewed as a defence against the anxiety of the previous night) only to find when I got on the train that I had forgotten my spectacles. The 'forgetting' of the glasses can be seen to be comparable with how the unconscious creates symptoms. This is despite the attempts of the triangle of defence to prevent their formation.

While this is a fundamental psychoanalytic way of viewing the creation of symptoms, all therapy is an attempt to break the causal links between the three sides of this triangle. Cognitive behavioural therapists would see the triangle more in terms of the interaction between thoughts, emotions and behaviour. Clinically, Figure 3.2 is linked to Figure 3.1 since the anxiety and defence are likely to be in evidence in relation to the three points of the triangle of persons.

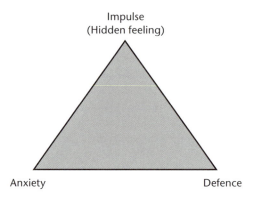

FIGURE 3.2 Triangle of defence

The therapeutic triangle (Figure 3.3) provides the framework for learning the client's specific personal idiom which in turn provides the raw material for making a formulation and treatment plan in time-limited therapy. Anita provides us with an opportunity to attempt to link the material of the first session with the therapeutic triangle.

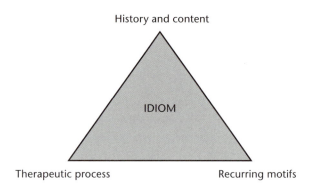

FIGURE 3.3 Therapeutic triangle

Anita

Anita, a mature student in her mid-thirties, referred herself for counselling after the long summer vacation, anxious and fearful for the coming academic year which was to be her final one. She was finding it impossible to concentrate and becoming increasingly agitated and depressed. She had spent most of the summer plucking up courage to come since she was 'not the kind of person to require counselling'. Last term, she had been a Welfare Officer to other students and had become aware of drug use on the campus which she had reported to the University authorities. They appeared not to take much interest so, after being assaulted by one of the drug users, she had informed the police which had left a great deal of ill feeling towards her on the part of both fellow students and the campus authorities.

Anita was the oldest of three. She had twin brothers seven years younger than herself. She matter of factly described having poor relationships with her censorious parents – although closer enquiry revealed that she meant predominantly her mother – and left home at age 14, abruptly severing contact with her family, to live with her best female friend's family. She lived with them for some time before spending three years travelling. On her return, she took a succession of menial jobs during which time she reported that she had been 'quite wild'; by that she meant drugs, alcohol and promiscuity. Eventually, acknowledging her unsuccessful schooldays, she decided to go to college, live independently and 'have fun'. On getting a place at university, Anita's mother became more involved, much to Anita's annoyance – 'she just wants to live off my success'. On her arrival at university, Anita fell out with her best friend and her best friend's family on their discovery that she had had a relationship with their youngest son when still in her teens. While they disapproved of this liaison, they still wished to maintain contact although Anita wanted nothing more to do with them. She then threw herself into her academic work. Soon after her arrival at university she met a fellow student, became engaged and married him four months later. Passing reference was made to a baby who was born towards the end of her second year.

Anita talked at length, looking provocatively directly at the counsellor. She came over as a very 'matter of fact' woman, quite adult in her manner, with little evidence of any emotional contact – it felt as if her emotions were under quite firm control. While the counsellor felt able to make a good initial contact with Anita, he was aware of a quality of seductiveness on her part which made him cautious and concerned about maintaining boundaries. Reflecting on this subsequently in supervision, the counsellor felt Anita may have experienced this as his passivity and withdrawal. He was also struck by his own feelings which were dominated by a preoccupation with Anita's infant child.

Anita was worried that she would not be able to 'compartmentalise' her work and home life and was perplexed at how suddenly she had become a mature student, married and with a family.

Using the therapeutic triangle as a framework for understanding this opening session we would be seeking to take into account and link the following factors in making a tentative hypothesis.

■ *History and content:* we have a narrative account of Anita's progress to becoming a mature student. The precipitating event leading Anita to make a counselling appointment was the long summer holidays and the forthcoming 'final' year. It may well be that this precipitating event can be seen to have an emotional significance in common with Anita's past family history; she left her family before her first major educational examinations.

In addition, and idiomatically important, are:

■ Anita's assertion that she 'is not the sort of person to require counselling'. This is made all the more interesting given the knowledge that she had been a Welfare Officer herself and 'counselled' others.
■ Anita appears to have made intense attachments which are then abruptly jettisoned – a warning here to the counsellor?
■ Drugs: Anita's recent experience of reporting drug users; does this have any relevance to her past drug use? By reporting it, did Anita believe that responsible adults ought to have taken note of her own previous drug misuse? Were the authorities by 'not taking any notice' reacting in the same way as previous 'responsible adults' in Anita's life? Was this also a warning to the counsellor that Anita needed to be taken notice of? Adults needed to take the initiative in being authoritatively containing – had that been lacking in Anita's childhood and was she looking for that from the counsellor?
■ *Therapeutic process:* Anita did not present as in any way maternal. She appeared cold and somewhat indifferent to her child, yet described an almost passionate distrust and dislike of her mother who was depicted as appearing 'to want to live off my success'. Was this almost parasitical description a more general comment about Anita's experience of relating to others?

The nature of Anita's attachments appeared to consist of impulsive, if somewhat desperate, engagement, followed by an equally swift disengagement. A certain reckless impulsivity was also in evidence in Anita's drug taking and promiscuity and may explain the counsellor's wariness and caution in the face of what at times appeared a provocative seductiveness.

The counsellor's identification with Anita's child is not without interest given Anita's 'adult' presentation. There was very little childlike in Anita's manner although her wish that the adults (e.g. the university authorities) would take some responsibility could indicate that Anita herself wanted to be relieved of this 'adult' burden. After her own volatile past, had she gone to the other end of the spectrum and become precociously adult?

Recurring motifs: Linking with the above, was there a wish for her male counsellor to take adult responsibility in a manner absent from her own paternal care? The repeated challenging looks and absence of a potent paternal figure in her childhood could well have represented a wish for just such a figure to save her from an intrusive and damaging mother.

Not to be ignored was the fact that Anita herself had recently become a mother and appeared indifferent to her child. Was this an 'idiom of mothering' that she had experienced from her own mother, in which case, would this have transferential implications? How competent were the people in positions of responsibility towards others? Were they able to look after others?

Like Tina, Anita appeared to have a complicated relationship to her own vulnerability, but, unlike Tina, dealt with it by impulsive action. A recurring theme, and one which began and ended the session, was Anita's wish to be able to return to 'compartmentalising' her life. This is the help which Anita was requesting from counselling. This, what could be termed 'splitting', could be seen as a functional 'idiom' which was now in danger of breaking down.

Other themes which were apparent, and could be seen to be in evidence, were Anita's need to escape her mother, the cultivation of an air of unsuccessful self-sufficiency, and some ambivalence about the pain of endings as evidenced by Anita's difficulty in saying goodbye to those closest to her. In this context it is not without interest that she presented for counselling just at the time when she was beginning to have to go through the process of leaving university and sitting her 'Final' examinations.

From this it is not too difficult to construct Anita's idiom which then influences the way the problem is formulated and the therapy's frame and plan. Using content, history, process and motif, a therapeutic narrative can be established. What happens in these encounters is that the therapist *attends to the story as it unfolds but pays primary attention to the repetitive motifs through which the client's idiom is rendered intelligible.*

In making a formulation, attention is paid to the precipitating event, or reason, for seeking therapy, and discovering its emotional significance in terms of previous life events or experiences. Tentative hypotheses are made which are based upon the pattern of previous relationships and the developing relationship – or difficulty in establishing one – with the therapist. The therapist then needs to translate his body of knowledge into the client's idiom or private language.

Transference and the therapeutic relationship

One of the most contentious issues in the debate between time-limited and open-ended therapies is the issue of transference and the associated matter of the therapeutic or working alliance. Transference, as classically defined, concerns the totality of the client's attitudes, beliefs and feelings towards the therapist. These are based on previous experiences of relating and can be seen to be incorporated into the client's template or idiom of relating to specific situations or people. As such, transference is more in the realm of fantasy or a construct of the client's mind rather than necessarily based on objective reality. It is interesting to note that in both the history of psychoanalysis and that of the more behavioural therapies, transference was initially viewed as a problem. For the early Freud it was something which got in the way of curing the client (clients could not be relied upon to accept the objective reality of their therapist and his interpretations) while for behaviour therapy the therapeutic relationship was seen merely as a vehicle for the delivery of treatment. In psychoanalysis all that changed when Freud (and Breuer) recognised that the 'irrational' responses of their clients – often creating the therapist into something they were not – needed further investigation. Since then, and particularly in the object relation school of therapy, transference has become the central 'tool' of psychodynamic treatments. Similarly, with the advent of schema-focused cognitive behavioural therapy, greater attention has been paid to the need to recognise and use the therapeutic relationship. Transference, which was a problem, is now a major part of the solution. However, the historical legacy, as Langs (1976) has pointed out, has cast an unhelpful shadow over contemporary open-ended psychoanalytic therapies. Clients, according to Langs, are still viewed, 'as the enemy and as resisting ... [an attitude which still] ... dominate[s] the analyst's unconscious image while the patient as ally and as curative is still far less appreciated' (in Groves 1996, p. 363). This is not the view of time-limited therapists who seek the client's active collaboration and agreement at every stage of treatment.

Traditionally, psychoanalytically oriented therapists have tended to view transference as something that is 'subtle and that only through listening and waiting patiently in an atmosphere of stringent therapist neutrality and abstinence will it emerge in a convincing way' (Messer and Warren 1995). Time-limited therapists view the concept of transference as a multifaceted one. A distinction needs to be made between the concept of transference as ubiquitous (that it is everywhere and a normal part of life and social interaction) and the transference neurosis (the transfer, both conscious and unconscious, of fantasies, emotions and attitudes from the past onto the therapist) which is a specific illusion of the therapeutic setting. Therapists, despite their frequent protestations, can be quite active (even through their passivity and silence) in encouraging the latter form of transference. Time-aware therapists do not encourage a transference neurosis and do not view the establishment of a neurotic transference as a prerequisite for helping their clients. For change to occur it is not necessary to recreate the client's conflicts in the leisurely development of the transference neurosis. Rather,

[Transference] is viewed more modestly as [clients] experience of the therapist in ways akin to their view of significant figures, especially from the past ... clients cannot help but relate to the therapist in accordance with their set patterns, templates or schemas, and it is the therapist's job to discern the role relationships into which they are cast, bring them to light, and relate them to other enactments in the present or past. A regressive transference neurosis ... promotes dependency which may not be resolved in a brief therapy ... Transference is understood not as a distortion or projection by the [client] onto the blank screen of the neutral analyst, but rather as the inevitable expression of the patients' construction of interpersonal reality, shaped and determined by his or her personal experience. (Messer and Warren 1995, pp. 50, 143)

This also applies to the working alliance or therapeutic relationship. Time-limited therapists do not accept that the development of a therapeutic alliance necessarily requires time. They do, however, view basic trust in the therapeutic process as a positive feature for treatment. This basic trust applies to the therapist as well as to their clients. As will be seen when assessment is discussed, this is reflected in the importance placed on previous meaningful relationships in the client's life. This is also shown by the requirement for therapeutic activity on the part of the therapist since this can facilitate the establishment of a collaborative and positive working alliance. In order to do this, the therapist is always both participant and observer.

This view of transference points to the importance of taking up any transference manifestations, however defined, immediately. These manifestations may well be characteristic ways of relating to people in the client's current life. They demonstrate how they have been used with other people in the past and how dysfunctional or inappropriate they may currently be. The time-limited therapist must not wait for the transference to appear later in therapy as a full-blown resistance but must be alert to the transference idioms which appear in the first and subsequent sessions. These transferential idioms are often in evidence as early manifestations towards the setting, process or frame, which need to be addressed since they deal not only with any early anxieties which the client has, but also to prevent any incipient transference neurosis. Transference in this sense represents aspects of the client's idiom which seeks understanding. It is not always possible or desirable to 'use' or 'work' in the transference; the transferential idiom needs to be understood, acknowledged and linked to the central therapeutic focus or triangle.

Becky

Becky was a very compliant and self-effacing client in her first session. Incapacitated by crippling social anxiety, she haltingly revealed her story of an overbearing and critical mother with whom she needed to constantly agree while feeling a pervasive sense of getting things wrong. Her mother would not tolerate any arguing. Becky felt 'she never knew her own mind'. Her passive, rather distant father always seemed unavailable to Becky, who grew up into an anxious, pleasant and compliant young woman. The therapist thought he had made good contact with her in the first session, linking her somewhat cowed manner with her childhood experiences and current interpersonal relationships. In the follow-up session, Becky reported no change in her presenting problem and said she had returned to her GP 'to see whether medication could also help'. We can see here how the client's idiom was present from the first session and how the transference to the setting and process, as well as to the (female) clinician was enacted immediately. Becky's return to her GP could be seen as a way of expressing, in action, the negative transference to the therapy although this could only be done surreptitiously and indirectly mirroring her annoyance with her overbearing mother for which she had no outlet as a child. Returning to her male GP can also be seen as seeking paternal advice and involvement (as well as a disguised wish for him to stand up to her controlling mother) which she had missed as a child. For the treatment to survive, this had to be dealt with immediately although the therapist had to approach this through metaphors and symbols rather than interpret Becky's behaviour in reconstructive terms. The therapist commented that perhaps Becky had felt disappointed with her first session, although it might be difficult to say that for fear of offending the therapist. It was very important for Becky to feel that those responsible for her care were working in tandem so that she felt safe and able to make informed decisions rather than 'never being able to make up her own mind' which might involve having to be less compliant to those around her and sometimes 'get things wrong'. In this sense, this negative action toward the therapy was linked with Becky's difficulty with her own sense of active agency (not being able to be critical of the therapy) but also positively connoted in that it showed that she was able to act on something she had felt. Working on this in the second session enabled Becky to continue for a further eight sessions. Eventually the 'ripple effect' enabled Becky to get cross with some her friends for being 'too bossy' and to express her annoyance when she felt her therapist was behaving in a similar fashion. What this shows is the oblique way in which transference was used, and how negative acting out was understood as a positive attempt by Becky to address her problems.

The client's feelings towards the totality of the therapeutic process are crucial.

In time-limited therapy it is frequently more helpful to work with the many 'transference' possibilities which are apparent rather than foster a regressive personal transference to the therapist. *Transference to the setting* in which the therapy occurs may be extremely important. This can include transference to the therapeutic context such as an educational institution, a hospital, a GP's surgery, etc. It can also include factors as diverse as transference to one's own development, to what education or medical 'sickness' represents in one's personal idiom, to joining and leaving an institution, the institution itself and what the therapist might represent in the setting in which he practises. This can become the basis for therapeutic encounters – not who the therapist is, or what the client neurotically invests in him or turns him into – but what the setting, and the therapist in that setting, symbolises in the client's idiom. Transference to setting becomes important. This can include: feelings about receiving help, limited help, not being encouraged to regress and issues about the ending. These are frequently in evidence from the first session and become predominant themes for therapy. This more multifaceted view of transference implies that the therapist needs to adopt a more oblique third party role which some may find problematic. It follows that if transference is ubiquitous, then one can even have a transference to time-limited therapy (and a counter-transference of course too).

These transferences, to the therapeutic process and context, can be evidenced by:

- the student who comes to counselling expecting the same frame-work as a lecture, and the same response which he had recently received from a dismissive lecturer;
- the client who is referred to a general practice counsellor feeling 'fobbed off' by their doctor and wishes to continue to medicalise their distress;
- clients who are either elated or disappointed by the number of sessions offered;
- clients who view the place of counselling within the institution in a denigratory fashion, perhaps as a repository of vulnerability and shame;
- clients who experience their need for counselling as a failure on their part.

Many of these 'transferences' can be seen to be anticipatory – in that sense, they function as a *pre-transference*. The client's initial hopes, fears, expectations and overall presentation both in, and prior to, the first session, can reveal much about the client's idiom and 'transference' to receiving help. What are the client's hopes, fears and expectations from the first appointment? What does he expect to happen? What role does he think the therapist will play? What part will the client play in the process? Is he relieved or disappointed with the first encounter? What are the client's first words or gestures? How the initial appointment is made, kept, as well as the interaction with any other (e.g. secretarial or administrative) staff can be very revealing and help in understanding the individual's template to coming for therapy. These, however, must only be initial tentative impressions, amenable to modification over time, rather than judgements frozen in stone. All these 'transferences' are part of the client's subjective idiom and can form the basis of the therapy.

These 'anticipatory transferences' also have the potential to contribute to 'therapeutic surprise' (see below). Clients will often be surprised that such minute attention is paid to their relationship with the therapy and therapist and gain considerable relief that the safety of the therapeutic frame can shed light and assist in helping with current (and previous) interpersonal conflict.

Counter-transference

Comparable considerations also apply to the concept of counter-transference. Having undergone a similar transformation as transference in the development of psychoanalysis (from being an obstacle to a primary therapeutic tool), its use in time-limited therapies has been further modified. Counter-transference is classically understood as the therapist's feelings and attitudes towards his client which may result from unresolved issues in the therapist, a means of communication of affective states between client and therapist and as a subtle and non-verbal way in which to client seeks to control the therapist. Jacobs (1988) has variously described these counter-transferential manifestations as 'classical' (the therapist's 'transference' to the client), 'neurotic' (the therapist's own unresolved personal issues), 'role' (the therapist's response to the role the client has put him in), and 'complementary' (where the client communicates unconsciously to the therapist his own feelings and experiences). In time-limited therapy counter-transference is a vehicle for the empathic learning about the client's idiom. Inevitably the therapist will be exposed and drawn in to the client's' template or idiom and it is this process (and its link with the therapeutic triangle) which becomes central to the therapy. When and how the therapist becomes so 'unavoidably co-opted' (Levenson 1995) in experiencing what is like to be with the client forms the basis of assessing whether the client's idiom is in any way related to the presenting problem and whether it has historical antecedents. Counter-transference then can shed light on whether the therapeutic relationship represents the client's 'most pervasive and chief problematic style of relating' (Levenson 1995). It frequently assists in adding to the dynamic focus since the therapist's feelings and actions towards the client will be a microcosm (and parallel) of how the client functions with others, and their reactions to him, in the real world. The therapist uses his response to being invited into the client's idiom (and his experience of being part of it) to facilitate the therapy and help further understanding of how the idiom may or may not help the resolution of the problem.

Understood and used in this fashion both transference and counter-transference aid the use of the 'here and now' therapeutic relationship. While the problems may originate in the past, they are maintained in the present and it is the use of the current therapeutic relationship which provides the most efficacious method of facilitating change in time-limited therapies. The past is accessed via the present, not vice versa. The therapeutic relationship provides both client and therapist with a glimpse, and the possible re-enactment, of what gets the client into difficulties in the outside world. It is the interaction between client and therapist and its possible historical antecedents which form the basic building blocks for therapy.

June

June shows how pre-transference, transference, counter-transference, and the 'here and now' aspects of the therapeutic process can lead to the discovery of a personal idiom. This then can be incorporated into the triangle of past, present and therapeutic process.

June had made two previous appointments to see a counsellor, neither of which were kept. When making these appointments the administrative staff mentioned that June had seemed anxious and tentative on the telephone. On the second occasion she phoned shortly after the session was due to end saying that she had forgotten but wished to make a further appointment. She arrived a quarter of an hour late for this appointment in the company of a friend who had accompanied (June's phrase was 'brought') her.

June explained that it had 'been suggested' that she sought counselling after the break-up of a four-year relationship. It subsequently transpired that her friend who had 'brought' her was the boyfriend from whom she had so recently separated. He was concerned at the depth of June's depression and, feeling neither he nor June's other friends could cope with her, had insisted she come to see the counsellor. June's first words were 'I am not sure I should be here; I don't think you can help.' Here we have aspects of the negative and fearful pre-transference which needed to be addressed before anything else (including getting a history or description of the problem) could be attempted. The acknowledgment of her pre-transference reluctance to come enabled June to explore her fear that counselling (and the counsellor) would in effect 'blame' her for not being able to 'sustain' the relationship and view her as a failure in this as in other areas of her life. It transpired that June was the eldest of four daughters whose parents were continuously

on the point of separating and had indeed had a number of temporary sepa-
rations after violent arguments. Both parents told June that they had to stay
together for the sake of their daughters. Consequently, June as the eldest
always felt responsible for attempting to keep her parents together although
suspecting that in reality relationships were, like the parental one, difficult
to 'sustain'. June had also felt responsible for the behaviour and feelings of
her younger siblings.

She spent most of the first session in tears, evidently in great distress,
but continuously apologising to the counsellor for being so 'weak and
emotional'. An oft repeated word was 'sorry', frequently followed by the
phrase 'you must think I am silly' accompanied by a tearful and nervous
giggle. June said she felt the counsellor would inevitably see her as 'hope-
less', and a 'failure' at relationships, not unlike June's perception of her
parents. It transpired that these were the reasons which her boyfriend had
given for the break-up of the relationship. She believed that the counsellor
would only want to get 'rid of' her. This was a not unreasonable assumption
given June's perception that her ex-partner had brought her for counselling
for similar reasons which was subsequently borne out by the fact that he was
to have no further contact with June once he knew that she was coming for
counselling.

The counsellor felt co-opted by June's idiom not least by the fact that
her late arrival had ensured that, since he needed to stick to the time
boundary, there was limited time available to contain June's distress
and work on enabling June to return for a further session. Her
boyfriend, by staying with her until she saw the counsellor (not
unlike her parents staying together for the sake of the children) was
also adding a further dynamic. All of which led to the counsellor
needing to ensure that June did not feel 'dumped' after the opening
session which would have confirmed June's fear that she was unable
to 'sustain' relationships. The counsellor had to attempt to accomplish this while simultaneously processing a feeling of irritation
with June for her passivity and victimhood.

We can see that June's idiom of feeling weak, emotional, and her
'inability to sustain' relationships, while feeling responsible for
others and needing to keep them happy and together, was in
evidence by the tortuous route she adopted in approaching counselling. The counsellor had to process his counter-transference in
order to understand and use June's transference to him, the setting
and her own vulnerability. The reasons why she came for counselling at that specific time, the way she presented herself to the counsellor, the counsellor's feelings in the session with her, her current

relationships with friends, and the small amount of historical information which initially came to light, all contributed to a tentative hypothesis regarding June's core conflict. It was by linking these in statements which incorporated her pre-transference anxieties, current emotional crisis, real-life concerns, and the process of what happened in the 'here and now' of the shortened counselling session, that the counsellor was able to help June return for a further exploratory appointment – without the necessity of being 'brought' by someone else – and to begin the process of a ten-session counselling contract which took as its focus many of the triangular issues which were already in evidence in the first meeting.

In addition to the notion of a personal idiom, and the use of a slightly more oblique way of viewing both transference and counter-transference, short-term therapy is increasingly using insights gained from attachment and narrative theories

Narrative and attachment theory in time-limited therapy

At first glance, it may appear that attachment theory, which places emphasis on the nature of the bond that is established between the infant and his caretaker, poses specific difficulties for the time-limited therapist. Surely, attachment, trust and safety take time to establish? On closer examination, however, the concept of attachment is one that has clinical implications for focal therapies and can be usefully incorporated into a time-limited model. Attachment theory is less an alternative model of therapy than a template underlying the practice of all therapies. Bowlby, the originator of the notion of primary attachment, expressed considerable optimism about the potential contribution of attachment theory to brief psychoanalytic psychotherapy.

The work of John Bowlby

Bowlby (1953, 1988) drawing on his studies of the newborn infant's dependence and helplessness, drew attention to the nature of the developing bond between mother and infant and suggested that future development and mental health were in some measure dependent on the constant and safe predictability of this early bonding process. His neo-Darwinist belief that humans will inevitably attempt to bond for survival's sake is very different from the original analytic position which placed hunger or sex as the basis of the need to attach and 'seek out gratifying objects'. Thus, attachment theory states that the mother 'does not become important because she gratifies ... she is important from the start' (Greenberg and Mitchell 1983).

Attachment theory proposes that the making and breaking of affectional bonds are central to the human condition; primary and innate, rather than a secondary response to frustration or absence. This places separation and loss, and the work of grief and mourning, at the centre of our experience. Consequently it is inevitable that this issue in its varied forms will form the basis of most clinical therapy.

Bowlby saw development primarily in terms of the effects of external environmental influence. Genetic endowment, instinctual drives and fantasy are less important than the interactions with others which lead to models of attachment behaviour. For Bowlby, the environment was essentially the mother although towards the end of his life he accepted that this could include the father and other caretakers.

It was these views which led Bowlby to be only ambivalently tolerated by the psychoanalytic community, a position which is gradually changing with the renewed interest in both Bowlby's original work (Bowlby 1953) and contemporary developments in attachment theory (Holmes 1993, 1997, 2001; Kraemer and Roberts 1996). Bowlby had originally hoped and expected that attachment theory would illuminate and strengthen object relations theory – not unreasonable given the relational core of both approaches – but attachment, and the importance it placed on environment rather than fantasy, were viewed as a threat to, and betrayal of, psychoanalytic theory and practice. (For an interesting discussion of Bowlby's wary relationship with the analytic community, see Holmes 1993, pp. 3–9.)

Bowlby suggested that the origins of insecurity occur early in life. His main achievements were to highlight:

- the effects of maternal deprivation;
- the importance of the bond between children and parents;
- the need for a secure base;
- the importance of feeling attached throughout life;
- loss and its relation to stages of grieving.

Clinical implications of attachment theory include the ideas of the therapist as a secure base, the internalisation of a secure base, and feeling understood as an aspect of secure attachment. A consequence of this is the notion that profound affective experiences are linked to attachment:

Many of the most intense emotions arise during the formation, the maintenance, the disruption and the renewal of attachment relationships ... because such emotions are usually a reflection of the state of a person's affectional bonds ... emotion is found to be in a large part the psychology and psychopathology of affectional bonds. (Bowlby 1980)

This is no less true of the clinical couple as of the maternal one. The short-term therapist's task, from an attachment theory point of view, is to promote a safe, trusting relationship as well as to facilitate emotional exploration. To the mirroring of emotional states of self-psychology is added the safety to deal with distress rather than being overwhelmed by it.

Modes of attachment are internalised by the child through 'internal working models', templates of early relational experiences, which lead to either a secure or anxious attachment.

Bowlby contrasted the notion of 'secure attachment', a result of safe, predictable and continuous (maternal) care, with 'insecure attachment'. Ainsworth et al. (1978) suggested that insecurely attached children fall into two distinct patterns:

- *Anxious/avoidant* who appear detached from their parents showing little protest when separated and 'hovering nervously near them when reunited'.
- *Anxious/ambivalent or resistant* who cling desperately to their parents and are unable to be pacified when reunited.

A third group has more recently been added:

- *Disorganised/disoriented* who show an inconsistent response to separation ranging from 'frozen watchfulness' to behavioural and emotional breakdown.

These patterns of childhood reactions to separation have been linked with various parenting styles (one could call them 'idioms of parenting') and are likely to be repeated in any therapeutic relationship. They also 'carry through into ... adult life and affect the way we make sense of, and ascribe meaning to, our world' (Holmes 1993). In other words, they assist in the formation of our personal idiom. Therapeutically significant is the link between attachment styles and what Holmes has termed 'autobiographical competence'. Secure attachment tends to foster autobiographical competence which is 'the ability to talk coherently about oneself and one's life including painful experiences'. Insecure attachments preclude the achievement of autobiographical competence. The insecurely attached and avoidant tend to be 'monosyllabically dismissive when talking about their pasts ('can't remember' or 'fine'). Insecurely attached ambivalents are frequently 'bogged down or enmeshed in past pain, often weeping inconsolably when asked to recall their early childhood'. Alternatively, they may cultivate an air of self-sufficiency when dealing with loss to mask their ambivalence.

Initial attachment styles, or idioms, can give some indication of how clients are likely to respond to therapy and what form of containment they may need.

Paul, Philip and Tina

Paul had been abused as a child and his current life was dominated by often violent mood swings, feeling others had let him down or were hostile to him. His relationships were always unsuccessful despite his expressed wish for more satisfactory contact with others. In his opening meeting with the therapist, for which he arrived late, he presenting with sullen suspicion and a reluctance to engage in therapy. He was anxious about any form of attachment fearing that it would inevitably be either abusive or lead to betrayal. Frozen and suspicious, he could be seen as 'disorganisedly' *insecurely attached. Attachment theory implies that Paul needed a more supportive, less emotionally intense or interpretative response.*

Philip was immediately preoccupied with the therapist's room and personal appearance. Excessively polite and submissive, expressing concern as to the health and well being of the therapist, minimising his own distress while speaking with excessive warmth about all his friends and family, Philip could be seen as ambivalently *attached. It rapidly became apparent that as an only child of fractious and argumentative parents, his role had been to pacify them and 'keep them happy' at the cost of his own needs or wishes. He would need a firm, reliable and safe setting in which to begin to experiment with notions of difference in relationships*

We have seen how Tina initially exhibited 'avoidant' *insecure attachment by minimising her own needs for attachment, partly to avoid rejection. The difficulty she experienced in overcoming the loss of her mother a year after her death, speaks to the avoidantly attached need to remain in some, often distant, contact with the person who has rejected them. Close contact with another was associated with pain and possible rejection. Her response to the therapist's comments indicated that she experienced them as intrusive attacks on her. She needed a more 'conversational' and flexible therapeutic relationship.*

These patterns of attachment may shed light on how the individual approaches intimate relationships in adult life. For an interesting further discussion of the clinical relevance of attachment modes, narrative style, generational transmission and parenting, see Main (1995).

Emotional stability is dependent on the availability of attachment figures. The expectation of available attachment figures is built up over time and is dependent on positive experiences with parents and caretakers. While originally referring to the physical presence of a caretaker, Bowlby, and subsequent attachment theoreticians, have also acknowledged the importance of emotional absences. It has become apparent that it is not the loss per se which is necessarily of crucial importance (grief can be successfully mourned) but the nature of the previous attachment and the circumstances following the loss. These are more likely to predispose the person to subsequent depression or psychological problems (Rutter 1985). As we saw with Tina, it is the person's emotional and behavioural response to loss and separation which is of central importance.

Theory of mind, mentalisation and self-reflective function

More recently (Fonagy 2001), attempts have been made to link child attachment patterns with adult states of mind with respect to attachment. Securely attached children would value attachment relationships, while insecurely avoidant childhood attachment patterns would link with dismissing adults who would be prone to 'deny, devalue, idealise or denigrate' past and current attachments; insecurely ambivalent children would become preoccupied adults who 'are overwhelmed and confused' by present and past relationships, while insecurely disorganisedly attached children, who have often suffered trauma, would be vulnerable to becoming 'disorganised/unresolved' adults. There is also some evidence that parental modes of attachment predict subsequent mother–infant attachment modes and can define adult states of mind with respect to attachment. These developments are potentially very encouraging since they raise the possibility of some degree of predictive capability in linking attachment styles with both the likely differing client transferential presentations, and attachment style with length of treatment. To some extent this is in evidence in the descriptions of Paul, Philip and Tina above.

Linked with attachment theory is the concept of mentalisation which can be defined as the capacity to understand that both one's own behaviour and that of others are motivated by thoughts and feelings, i.e. internal states of mind (Fonagy 1998). Mentalisation is the ability to see ourselves as others see us and the recognition that human activity is filtered through the mind (ours and others). Therefore, all our 'perceptions, desires and theories', are, as Holmes (2008) states 'necessarily provisional'. Short-term therapy can 'enhance mentalisation skills and identify situations where mentalisation skills are impaired' (Holmes 2008) by focusing on the minute therapeutic interactions in individual sessions between client and therapist. This process of examining and thinking about feelings between ourselves and others and their manifestations, intent and meanings, is central to short-term therapy. Associated with this is the understanding that one's perceptions of others are representations of a form of reality (with a substantive subjective component) rather than the way it actually is. Others are different from us with differing needs, wishes, relational templates which will predicate their perception of, and behaviours to, us. Understanding this can be both difficult and painful.

This is closely linked to the idea of a Theory of Mind (Fonagy et al. 1991) – the ability to decode others' emotions and thoughts – and the associated capacity of reflective self-function where the child develops a sense of his own mind and that of the other. It is suggested that traumatised children – or borderline adults – lack a theory of mind in that they have difficulty in 'accurately defining their own inner world', and viewing others as having feelings, desires or intentions independently of themselves (Holmes 2001) which may be different from their own. This is a clinical as well as a developmental achievement since it involves the child's (and the adult's) ability to 'ascribe thoughts, feelings and intentions to others' (Sharpe 2008) which is central to our capacity to anticipate the behaviours of others and to respond empathically using our own self-reflective capacities.

Reflective capacity, the ability to process our internal and external worlds in the context of those of others, is helpful in that it makes our internal and external worlds more meaningful. In attachment terms, this is linked to the capacity to talk cogently and coherently about one's difficulties. Inevitably this is linked to early experience of the caregiver's capacity to transform sensations and experiences via the process of mentalisation into internal working models of self and other relationships. This depends on the opportunities that the child has had early in life to 'observe and explore the mind of his primary caregiver'. This involves the recognition that the caregiver has her own needs, interests and aims and to take these into account in considering one's own wishes and behaviours. Inevitably secure attachment provides a base for this process, missing in insecure attachments, to be facilitated: 'the avoidant child shuns the mental state of the other, while the resistant child focuses on its own state of distress to the exclusion (of the other)' (Fonagy 2001).

Borderline pathology thus arises out of this faulty ability to conceptualise and integrate the recognition of self and other difference. The achievement of this reflective process can be facilitated by 'one relationship with an understanding other through which the impact of trauma can be transformed' (Fosha 2000). It is suggested that 'the other' need not need to be a 'dominant attachment figure' but merely the provider of a safe relational frame for emotional exploration and experience. This is what the short-term therapist seeks to provide.

Bowlby's work links with modern relational theories since it posits an infant and caretaker who are aware of each other from the start, what Trevarthen (1980) has called 'primary intersubjectivity'. The concept of 'attunement' (Stern 1985) describes how the basis of secure attachment is formed through the 'emotional alignment' of infant and caretaker. Stern gives an example of this process as:

> a 9 month old girl becomes very excited about a toy and reaches for it. As she grabs for it she lets out an exuberant 'aaaah!' and looks at her mother. Her mother looks back and scrunches up her shoulders and performs a terrific shimmy with her upper body, like a go-go dancer. The shimmy lasts about as long as her daughter's 'aaaah!', but is equally excited, joyful and intense. (1985, p. 140)

Short-term therapies are becoming increasingly interested in this concept (Fosha 2000; Malan 2006) particularly in respect of how strong feelings are modulated in clinical sessions.

It is, however, the quality of this emotional interaction rather than its quantity which is important for future development. This is a significant way in which attachment theory informs time-limited therapies which stress the immediate engagement, on an emotional level, with the client and place the active use of, and 'attunement' in, the therapeutic relationship at the centre of therapy.

Attachment theory has placed separation and loss at the forefront of human experience and thus clinical practice. Since these are the inevitable consequences of being human, they will need to be continually negotiated throughout our lives. Time-limited thera-pies address this issue directly, not least since the issue of time is apparent in every session. Time-limited therapies are informed by attachment theory in this respect – both ascribe significance to loss and separation (which may be actual or in fantasy) but clinically crucial is *how the loss is emotionally perceived, responded to and resolved by the individual.*

Towards the end of his life, Bowlby was advocating a therapeutic approach which suggested that therapy should focus on current interpersonal relationships and how these are based on previous formative relationships. Implicit in this is the notion that these forms of attachment, or non-attachment, will be in evidence in the 'here and now' consulting room. It is highly likely that an idiom of attach-ment will be evident in all aspects of the therapeutic triangle.

This relates to patterns of parental management and handling which are internalised as internal working models, templates or personal idioms. The idiom of attachment is what Bowlby would call transference. Attachment becomes internalised as a template or working model for all close relationships. Since all therapeutic relationships are essentially ones of attachment and separation (this applies particularly to briefer therapies), attachment theory offers a way of thinking about past, current and future relationships within the context of a finite therapeutic process. In this way, attachment theory, including patterns of relating to separation and loss, can assist time-limited therapies not least in the importance paid in briefer therapies to the therapeutic frame and how it is responded to and used. Attachment theory also sheds light on the struggle to convey both verbal communication and affective states in a setting where time is limited. The therapist must offer a secure and safe base while focusing on real-life experiences 'at the expense of deep interpretations based on primitive fantasy' (Holmes 1997).

In stressing the need for a secure base, Attachment theory 'requires ... reliability, responsiveness and the capacity to process negative affect, especially in relation to separation and loss' (Holmes 1997, p. 122). The key to successful attachment is active and recip-rocal interaction. It is *less a question of the amount of time a caretaker (or therapist) spends with the child (client) than the nature and quality of how the time is spent.* These are also the core conditions for time-limited therapies which place emphasis on viewing therapy more like a 'conversation' and where the therapeutic alliance is one of 'compan-ionable interaction' (Heard and Lake 1986) much like the 'playful-ness' made possible by a parentally secure base.

Bowlby recognised that attachment can never be entirely reliable; it must sometimes be shared and will inevitably be lost, sometimes prematurely. The capacity to separate from attachment figures and to form new ones is viewed as a developmental challenge and achievement throughout life; the frame of time-limited therapies speaks directly to this.

Time-limited therapies also place emphasis on 'autobiographical competence'; telling one's story facilitates attachment. A dilemma for time-aware therapists is how to allow for substantive attachment and trust to develop without the client becoming too dependent; the notion of 'idioms of attachment' is helpful here. Bowlby's own preferred therapeutic stance assists the development of a non-adhesive or dependent attachment:

> While some traditional therapists might be described as adopting the stance ' I know, I'll tell you', the stance I advocate is one of 'You know, you tell me' ... the human psyche, like human bones, is strongly inclined towards self-healing. (Bowlby 1988)

It might not take long (or much) to facilitate a process which sets in train the client's ability to 'heal themselves' provided the initial 'attachment' is secure and that the therapist is 'attuned' to the client's idiom and to what the client, as opposed to the therapist, wants.

Our idiom of attachment becomes internalised as a 'self-narrative'. The way we make ourselves known to others is through our narrative styles which consist of our personal, and often secret or untold, version of our life stories. Autobiographical competence leads to narrative coherence. Holmes (1993) implies that there is a strong connection between the kind of childhood attachment patterns and the narratives that people tell about themselves years later; 'securely attached children tell coherent stories about their lives, however difficult they may have been, while insecure children have much greater difficulty in narrative competence, either dismissing their past or remaining bogged down in it' (1993, p. 9).

Since attachment experiences are linked to autobiographical competence and narrative coherence we now need to look at how storytelling can be used in time-limited therapy.

Narrative in time-limited therapy

On one level, narrative in therapy is relatively straightforward. Offering someone the opportunity to tell their story – a story that may never have been told before – is helpful and enables them to feel heard and understood by another. Narratives help to validate our experience and give us a voice. Narratives function as self-revelatory stories which 'help us discover who we are' (Sugarman 1996) and enable our lives to have some form of thematic continuity and direction. Narratives are closely linked to personal development; they give a voice to who we are, where we come from and what we want to become. They link the internal world of the 'me' with the external world of the 'us'. Narrative 'turns experience into a story which is temporal, is coherent and has meaning … it gives a person a sense of ownership of their past and their life' (Holmes 1993). As we have seen, it is advantageous to be able to tell one's story coherently.

Narrative is important in time-limited therapy. Having a loosely linear story enables both therapist and client to maintain a focus and link therapeutic material to the emerging narrative. Putting our stories into words, and contextualising their cultural and familial aspects, help a framework to emerge which is based more on normative, as opposed to pathological, explanations. This non-pathological approach is significant in time-limited therapy since it enables the client to contextualise his experience rather than blame himself or take a victim or sick role. Being able to tell one's story objectifies experience so that the person is at one remove from it – it becomes a symbol of our personal idiom rather than raw and unprocessed feeling. By converting a series of seemingly unrelated experiences, often painful, into a coherent narrative, we are able to use past experience as a vehicle for symbolisation. This can then be reflected upon rather than either acted out or painfully experienced as a series of unrelated misfortunes. Autobiographical competence and narrative coherence enable the emotional processing of painful past events

Narratives are composed and determined by personal development, life events and time. It is the subtle interaction between personal development, societal norms, life events/experience and one's idiomatic way of managing these phenomena that constitutes our personal narrative. Central to the idea of narrative coherence is the balance between continuity and change. This enables us to feel 'a sense of being the same person [we] have always been – despite the gradual incremental changes associated with ageing – and despite major life disruptions' (Sugarman 1996, p. 291). We struggle to change while remaining the same.

Coherence and making sense of our experience tend to help us have some control over what otherwise may be experienced as random and disassociated events and feelings. Random descriptions make little sense. Since our lives are complex, more than one story can be told; in narrative therapy, client and therapist 'choose' which experiences and events are of significance in the emerging 'plot'. In short-term therapy this is likely to form the core focus. This is helped by the fact that we make sense of our experience when it can be ordered according to recurring themes. 'Emplotment' (Ricoeur 1984), like the development of a plot in a novel, helps us to organise our personal narrative. Narratives can be conveyed in metaphors, images, and recurring themes as well as through the expression of our personal idioms including those of attachment.

All narratives are personal and idiosyncratic. However, just as in literature, there may only be a limited or finite number of plots in our lives. Elbstree (1982) identified five generic 'plots' which form the basis of all stories. How these plots intersect with the developmental stages of the life cycle influence the construction of our personal narrative. For instance the acts of, and the feelings associated with, love or betrayal may link with the various developmental stages which can make a significant contribution to our plots. Shafer (1976) suggests that the narrative paradigm, which includes the subjective account of perceptions and feelings in the context of the external environment, may well be as therapeutic as the arousal of transference feelings in successful therapeutic outcomes. It is the therapist's job to attempt to make sense out of things that don't quite fit or make sense although the client may not have previously questioned them. What Holmes has called 'thematic analysis' attempts to find a dominant theme in a client's discourse which may be revealed 'through a significant tone' or word (or affective state) which permeates everything that is said: 'sadness, injustice, victimhood, recklessness, abandonment or fear, blaming others or oneself or vice versa'. The theme is closely linked to the client's idiom which Holmes views as akin to, and unique as, a fingerprint since it reveals the specific pattern in intimate relationships which characterises the individual's interactions with others.

Narratives are inevitably subjective accounts of our experiences. They may bear little relation to factual events. Therapy is concerned with narrative as opposed to historical truth (Spence 1982). Therapists are interested in their clients' subjective accounts not only because they rarely have access to objective/factual information, but because it is the client's experience of events that shapes their narrative and idiom and it is this which is important in therapy. This links with our discussion of attachment – *it is the subjective emotional content of an event rather than its factual occurrence (or the therapist's own assumptions about how that event should be proc-essed) which is therapeutically important.* It is the way, manner and form that the narrative or story unfolds or is told which are of central significance.

The importance of a story in time-limited therapies

The use of narrative is particularly helpful in time-limited therapies since it incorporates aspects of the triangles of therapy and persons, discussed earlier. As clients discuss their present experiences, reconstruct past events, the present, including the therapeutic relationship, can be linked with the past. The narrative is not merely the client's story or history, it also throws light on the development and current status of the therapeutic relationship. This is frequently told at one remove in the context of specific metaphors. Therapy then becomes an exercise in 'story repair and reconstruction' which 'encourages the powerless to tell their stories [and confers] a clear and constructive identity on the teller' (Sugarman 1996, p. 304). Clients come to therapy with their own stories which the therapist helps to elaborate, reconstruct or focus.

Short-term therapy can be seen as a short story which 'typically focuses on a single theme, a few characters, and [a] slice of life … long-term therapy is more akin to a fully developed novel, incorpo-rating plots and sub plots, a panoply of characters, and a great variety of situations in which human drama unfolds' (Messer and Warren 1995, p. 211).

Susan

Susan, a pretty and articulate young woman, consulted a therapist in considerable distress, puzzled and worried about panic attacks which seemed to have no meaning or cause – 'they just do not make sense'. They left her 'frightened, confused and scary.' While the attacks had shown some sign of improvement since her doctor had prescribed tranquillisers, Susan was still anxious as she could not identify why they occurred. 'I am normally such a relaxed and easy going person.' She had recently left home to attend univer-sity and, having chosen to study Law, saw herself as a 'logical, rational' type of person for whom panic attacks just did not make any sense. Susan's mother thought the anxiety might relate to coming to university.

Anxiety attacks, when the rational cause cannot be identified, are likely to be problematic for people whose personal idiom is one of logic or, as in Susan's case, the person views themselves as themselves as calm and relaxed. A time-limited narrative approach to Susan's difficulties proved helpful.

Susan spoke about never 'having had any problems before.' Discussion revealed that aged seven Susan needed to go into hospital suddenly for a major operation. The suddenness of the admission 'surprised and confused' her. Having to spend a few days in hospital in unfamiliar surroundings, lacking the familial supports, was 'scary' and 'frightening'. A link was made between this experience and coming to start her University career – she had after all used similar words to describe both going into hospital and her current anxiety attacks. This appeared to make sense to Susan; important given her personal idiom of logic and rationality.

Susan did not initially want to come to university, preferring to have a gap year to think through what she really wanted. Her mother had linked the symptom with going to university and discussion revealed that Susan's mother had not been able go to university herself, needing to attend to her problematic father. Her mother had always regretted this and this sense of lost opportunities had dominated Susan's childhood. Susan felt generationally compelled to leave home to study before she was really ready.

Susan was studying Law 'as I always thought I was temperamentally suited to it'. Allowing Susan to talk and construct her own narrative revealed that her maternal grandfather had spent some time in prison and throughout Susan's childhood it had been impressed on her both how unjust and shameful this was. Studying Law would correct these wrongs.

A narrative approach allowed Susan to explore her personal idiom – the kind of person her childhood self had assumed she was – and to begin to consider whether this was actually a realistic picture of herself; perhaps she was more complex, less rational, than her past had led her to imagine?

Susan was able to use the construction of a personal narrative to help her master her panic attacks. However, sometimes life is not as linear and ordered as it seems. On those occasions the narrative needs to be deconstructed.

Ibrahim

Ibrahim was a large ungainly man whose parents were African but who presented himself to his therapist in a very traditional anglicized fashion both in manner and appearance. Ibrahim had been 'sent' for therapy by his Doctor who could not find any physical cause for Ibrahim's aliment. Ibrahim took a long time to explain that he was preoccupied by a facial skin complaint which, while barely visible to the therapist, caused Ibrahim much distress and led him to avoid close physical contact with people. He had been attempting to cure himself by attending to his diet but this only had the effect of making him feel 'inauthentic'. People also did not appreciate how tortured he was by his symptom since others could not see it. His GP had prescribed various medications but none was effective. Ibrahim did not know what to make of his GP's suggestion that he seek counselling: 'For what?'

Ibrahim had a 'wonderful childhood'. Born in the Sudan, he had arrived in Britain when he was 3 years old, his father a medical student having preceded him leaving the Sudan immediately after his birth. His mother never really settled in Britain and returned to the Sudan together with a younger brother when Ibrahim was 7. Father remarried when Ibrahim was 10 and he had a mixed race younger sister. Ibrahim had spent the whole of his childhood and young adulthood in the north of Scotland and in an East Anglian village which was 'great'. However, he was always worried about his physical appearance and sought various medical treatments, none of which were helpful – in itself not without interest given his father's profession. This was revealed in a matter of fact manner with no hesitation, pause for thought or reflection; a coherent, circumscribed, understandable narrative. The only problem was that it lacked any emotional conviction. Narratives need to have some emotional resonance which links with the person's life experience.

Ibrahim's skin was revealing something he would rather conceal. In the same way, his narrative, by being so straightforward and seemingly coherent, was hiding something more complex and personal which could not be thought or talked about but could only be experienced as a physical ailment. Here was a narrative which needed to be deconstructed. For Ibrahim, any form of self-exposure was problematic whether it was his skin or his 'authentic' story. His childhood, and particularly his experiences in British schools, had been excessively problematic but this was defended against by his convincing, at least to himself, narrative. The emotional content of this had to be displaced elsewhere: onto his sensitive skin. We can see clearly here the operation of the triangle of conflict; how feelings are repressed and form symptoms.

Ibrahim's ambivalent relationship with his father, which could not be voiced, was enacted by his dealings with his various medical advisors, none of whom were experienced as helpful. Ibrahim was seeking recognition as 'authentic' but the only way his narrative allowed this to come about was via the treatment of his various physical ailments.

Ibrahim was a very complex and troubled young man but the important point from our perspective is that Ibrahim demonstrates how psychological problems can be evidenced by too coherent a narrative. Narrative theory holds that the self only exists in the telling of our stories. The purpose of telling a story is to reaffirm the self and make a coherent narrative. There are, however, times, and this is particularly true of psychosomatic problems which tend to reflect the split between the emotional and the physical, when the narrative needs to be broken down so that a different story can emerge.

The importance of surprise in time-limited therapy

Of significance in the construction (or deconstruction) of a therapeutic narrative is surprise. It was Winnicott (1971) who first drew attention to the importance of therapeutic surprise. In describing the use of the 'squiggle game' with 9-year-old Iiro, Winnicott drew attention to a point in the game when Iiro 'had surprised himself' by what he had drawn. The capacity to surprise oneself and be taken unawares by one's own thoughts and feelings can function as potent and significant moments in therapy.

Therapeutic surprise and revelation are important aspects of therapy. Like the best novels, narratives which maintain our curiosity tend to be those which surprise us; discovering alternative scripts with our clients about their lives can be exciting, surprising and helpful. Therapeutic surprise '[is] a very special type of pleasure, ... it opens up, liberating an area like a key fitting a lock' (Bollas 1992). Narratives pull together bits of our stories in the knowledge that other stories are always possible; it is the elucidation and discovery of other possible scripts or stories which inform time-limited therapy.

Narrative surprise has the most profound effect when it is coupled with what Enid Balint has called an 'Erlebnis' in therapy. Roughly translated, this means a new experience in the 'here and now' relationship between client and therapist. This assists new ways of being and relating, as well as challenging our existing narratives. Focal therapy needs to be an affective experience as well as a verbal or behavioural interchange. A new understanding is coupled with a new experience. An experience is more important than an explanation since what is therapeutic is the experiential emotional tie between the client and his therapist rather than didactic learning through interpretations. A new relational experience with a therapist need not primarily be a 'corrective emotional experience' (according to Alexander) to repair a 'deficit' but can help the client have a different sense of themselves. Surprise can involve clients having a different experience (hopefully more meaningful and benign) with the therapist than they had with significant people in the past or present. It can also hold out the possibility of the discovery of alternative scripts of their lives. Therapeutic surprise enables the therapist to offer 'not suspicion about the patient's motives and the exposure of a truer meaning known only to the [therapist], but a variety of complementary (and sometimes paradoxical) meanings that open up to new experiential options' (Mitchell 1997).

Therapeutic surprise links with the theory of change in time-limited therapies. While open-ended therapies tend to assume that change only comes about as a result of the working through of as many problematic areas of the personality or fantasy systems as possible, time-limited therapies tend to believe that by sticking to the core focal problem a 'ripple' effect will be set in motion. If you change your attitude and feeling in respect of one central issue, it is likely to change and affect other areas or parts of your life. This enables clients, by being able to gain some mastery of a central aspect of their emotional lives, to extend and generalise this experience and knowledge to other areas of their lives. A client who works on a core focus of self-reproach and lack of confidence in their therapy may well generalise their experience of therapy to other settings after the therapy is finished. This is aided by the fact that the core focus is generally a metaphor for various different areas of a client's life.

Lee

Lee exemplifies some of these issues. Surprise, experiential learning and the ripple effect of focal therapy are all in evidence:

Lee, a 32-year-old man from the Far East who had arrived in Britain to study for a professional qualification, consulted a counsellor to express his disappointment with his host country. Lee had arrived with high hopes of discovering a stimulating academic environment and a welcoming community but had found neither. The academic standard of his course was not 'up to much' and he found British people 'inscrutable'; by that Lee meant diffident, closed and unwelcoming. Perhaps, Lee asked, the counsellor could teach him some 'social c(l)ues'? The counsellor, unsure he was able to recognise any social cues, let alone teach them, offered Lee ten sessions to discuss Lee's adaptation in Britain and his need for social cues. He arrived regularly if frequently late for sessions. A number of issues presented themselves including Lee's need to escape his country of origin (he had studied abroad for the last six years). It rapidly became apparent that Lee's idiom was one of harbouring high and unattainable expectations of himself and others. The therapist sensed this by experiencing a sense of therapeutic failure in every session. Not surprisingly, Lee thought others saw him as arrogant, although Lee himself was not bothered by this; they were merely jealous of his ability as a scientist to work things, including relationships, out from 'logical first principles'. During the sessions the counsellor, increasingly aware that the core problem lay in the area of Lee's general social manner rather than one of cultural dissonance, was becoming concerned that the day of judgement would soon arrive when Lee would ask the counsellor to come up with some 'social cues'. The counsellor himself felt clumsy and in need of some therapeutic clues. Lee had talked about how enraged, bitter and disappointed he was becoming with his academic institution (a metaphoric reference to the therapeutic relationship) for not giving him what he wanted. This was a contradictory demand for, on the one hand, more guidance, and, on the other, more recognition of what a special person he was.

In his sixth session, Lee arrived uncharacteristically a few minutes early, and instead of reporting to the receptionist and waiting in the waiting room, Lee went straight up to the counsellor's consulting room, entering without knocking to find the counsellor on the telephone. The counsellor, surprised and aware of his irritation with Lee, asked him to wait in the waiting room until the agreed time. Lee looked shocked and affronted by this request. The space enabled the counsellor to think about how best to incorporate this action, and the feelings it had elicited, into the impending session. When Lee arrived, the counsellor spoke about Lee's strange entrance; the 'custom' in the counselling service, as Lee knew from previous visits, was to check in with the receptionist and wait in the waiting area. Perhaps by ignoring this he was expressing both his dissatisfaction with his counsellor and the 'customary' ways of doing things in the service? When the counsellor explained the rationale for the operation of the service, Lee said it was 'nonsense' – i.e. not logical. People knew he was due, the counsellor did not have an engaged sign on his door, and he found it humiliating and degrading to be asked to use the waiting room. This turned out to be the turning point in the therapy. The emotional response to be asked to wait was linked to a discussion of the personal meaning of social cues for Lee. The wish to be taught social cues (which Lee's defensive grandiosity would not allow him to learn) linked with a number of core difficulties in his life. The remaining sessions focused on related issues including what place logic vs. custom and rituals had in Lee's life. For Lee, customs, including how people related to each other, were governed and regulated by logic and could be worked out in a scientific way. It followed of course that Lee was frequently disappointed and annoyed that others did not recognise the superiority of his logic and abide by it. He was then faced with having to adapt to customs and rituals imposed on him from the outside which was what had made him furious when he was asked to return to the waiting room. The demand that he do so had no basis in logic and led him to feel he was complying and losing any sense of an active subjective self. To conform to ritual and custom was to lose the self. Alternatively Lee could choose not to adapt to custom or social cues and risk the kind of social, personal anxiety and dissatisfaction that he had originally talked to his counsellor about. Importantly, this was enacted as an in vivo experience with the counsellor. The counsellor's feeling that he was going to 'fail' Lee and be 'not good enough' was a reflection of Lee's own fear of failure hidden behind his grandiosity. Lee, at some level, was wishing that his logic would be found wanting, if only because it had condemned him to a peripatetic and migratory existence in his desire to find the illusory custom/ritual or relationship which was governed by logic. The counsellor suggested to Lee that adaptation to external rites of passage or customs was a choice he was constantly facing. In making that choice, he was losing something of himself. One way of looking at customs or rites of passage is that they are there to help us conform or tame something dangerous in ourselves. This story surprised Lee not least since it had considerable emotional resonance as a result of Lee having had an 'Erlebnis' of it in the session. The 'ripple' effect of this experience was manifested in the concluding sessions, where Lee's choice of when and how to present himself to the counsellor and the service was significant. It was also in evidence in Lee's experimentation with 'non-logical' interactions with others outside the sessions.

Lee's 'Erlebnis' in the session began a process of looking at himself, others and his own circumstances somewhat differently. We have seen that, in what we could call therapeutic micro-moments, change can happen and a process set in motion that continues over time. Winnicott's 'sacred moments', Davanloo's 'subtly loaded words', Balint's 'important moments' – also termed 'aha' experiences – can be linked to Stern's (2004) 'present' or 'now' moment, which, together with therapeutic surprise, can set psychological change in motion.

Externalising the therapeutic alliance in time-limited therapy

Transference in psychoanalysis has always had an 'as if 'quality. It is not 'as if' the therapist is the client's actual parent, although a transference neurosis might stimulate a regression which leads the client to feel 'as though' the therapist is their parent as opposed to a parental figure. As we shall see in Chapter 5, therapeutic activity on the part of the therapist in time-limited therapy acts to prevent the development of a regressive transference. The use of the therapeutic alliance in time-limited therapy demands a therapeutic stance which maintains not merely an 'as if' position ('you are behaving and feeling towards me as if I were your parent') but also requires the therapist to adopt an oblique third party role. The exploration of a personal narrative aids this process. A joint exploration is embarked on where both therapist and client view the developing narrative 'as if' it were a collaborative story engaged upon by two separate people. To be able to do this also provokes a different form of attachment (an attachment to the narrative) and requires the client to maintain an observing ego. By this I mean the client will be encouraged both to experience what the therapeutic alliance is like and to reflect on its emotional impact in terms of past and present, i.e. outside the therapy, in past and present relationships. In this way the therapeutic relationship becomes objectified. This is similar to the concept of the 'externalising conversation' in family therapy (White and Epston 1990) where the therapist 'maps' the effects that the problem has on a client's life, helps them notice the influence the problem has on differing areas of their lives, and then assists the client in 'organising and fighting against' it. Here the problem is given a name ('Sneaky Poo' in the case of an encopretic child) and the family discuss how to get the better of 'old sneaky poo'.

This functions, as in time-limited therapy, to put both the symptom/problem, as well as the therapeutic relationship, at one remove and enlist the 'observing ego' to fight against it. 'How are we going to outsmart Sneaky Poo?' This can equally well apply to concepts – dependence, for instance – which is named and then discussed rather than, as tends to be the case in longer or open-ended therapies, slowly experienced and worked through. Externalising the problem is associated with the narrative approach and helps to do the following:

■ give the problem human characteristics and a will of its own;
■ locate the problem/worry either as part of the self or place it outside the self so that it becomes less persecutory;
■ plan a strategy to defeat it.

This is in many ways similar to Gestalt techniques where parts of the self are placed in an empty chair and spoken to, and helps place the therapeutic relationship in a similar frame. It is something to be named, reflected on, and linked with other, outside the consulting room, experiences. The fact that both therapist and client maintain an 'observing ego' helps contextualise the therapeutic alliance. The importance of this is borne out by the finding that what helps positive outcomes in focal therapy are the links that are made between the 'here and now'- transference – and the 'there and then' – parent or significant caretaker (Malan 1976). The transference is externalised and enlisted in the understanding of core relational patterns in both the past and the present.

This 'externalising conversation' has the function of assisting the move from 'people having problems' to the idea of 'problems having people' (Eron and Lund 1996). This enables the person to be 'separated from the problem and helps … [the client] marshal their resources against problems' (1996, pp. 32, 33). Externalising conversations also assist in the construction of alternative stories – and alternative solutions. This speaks to the delicate balancing act in time-limited therapies where the therapist seeks not to become too important (which may in itself be problematic for some therapists). Positioning the therapeutic alliance as an externalised third party experience and linking it with significant past and current relationships ensures that the dangers of an intense dependence are kept to a minimum. An example of this is the treatment of a depressed and adhesively dependent young woman whose idiomatic wish/fear of becoming dependent on the therapy was named enabling both she and her therapist to 'work together' to prevent this happening (Coren 1996).

The externalising conversation also has the function of placing the therapeutic dyad in the area of Winnicottian transitional space where the therapy itself becomes a transitional phenomenon. Just as short-term therapy mediates directly between the inside and outside worlds and maintains a focus which straddles both, so symptoms, affective states, and problematic character traits can be placed in the space between the therapeutic couple, making them amenable for dispassionate consideration without them needing to be experienced as too persecutory.

Tim

Tim, a rather schizoid young man with few friends or interests, complained of feeling empty and alone but blamed others for his predicament and, after a few sessions of counselling, was beginning to include the counsellor among those that had let him down or were unhelpful. He had made a number of unsuccessful and short-lived approaches to women who had rebuffed him and he blamed them for their dismissive and cruel response to his advances. Rather than viewing this as evidence of either a pernicious and rejecting world or Tim's social and relational deficits, the counsellor encouraged Tim to give his feeling of emptiness and loneliness a name (he chose Noddy which had a childhood resonance) which then functioned as a space into which all Tim's feelings about both himself and others could be placed – in that sense, not experienced as persecutory objects – as well as an area where speculation as to how Noddy could be confronted to improve Tim's life were discussed.

This process can also be aided by the language of 'part objects' – by addressing 'part of the client' the clinician acknowledges the complex nature of the client's self, avoids a possible persecutory spiral (where client and therapist struggle to break a cycle of mutual incomprehension and both experience the other as attacking) and enables the client to reflect on parts of herself. Other 'parts' then become accessible to address the part which is experienced as problematic.

Narrative and the therapeutic process

We have seen how the concept of narrative can refer to two specific areas of the therapeutic process. Primarily, it describes the telling, retelling and reconstruction of the client's life story and associated emotional life. However, narratives also have what Brunner (1986) calls a 'paradigmatic' function; that is they describe the ongoing 'here and now' therapeutic process. They provide a commentary on the progress or otherwise of the therapeutic relationship. They are stories that are told in therapy but also, and it is this which gives them their emotive power, experientially enacted in the relationship between client and therapist. They provide a commentary on the day-to-day aspects of the therapy while simultaneously communicating something about the client's core idioms.

More often than not, the commentary needs to be decoded since it is communicated through metaphors of the client's life and experience. Metaphors are frequently used to convey aspects of the transference, the treatment alliance and the client's core idioms. They can encapsulate aspects of the self that speak to the core conflict, or focus, and represent key aspects of the self and its relation to others as well as issues of personal development and therapeutic change. Metaphors which are often brought to therapy can be about the client's working or leisure life, sport, literature, popular culture, pastimes and hobbies, the weather, etc. All have some personal or interpersonal resonance. Metaphorical narratives assist in the search for a common language and they provide a vehicle for decoding or reframing the symptoms message.

Dorothy

Dorothy had approached counselling with problems in her marriage but increasingly used sessions to express her anger at aspects of daily life. Not a person who was able to reflect on experience or make links between different experiences or feeling states, her thinking was very concrete. She complained that her husband was 'unreliable and directionless' who often ' did the opposite' to what she wanted. Dorothy came regularly to sessions using them to report on the weekly rigours of her life. On one occasion Dorothy reported that she had just come from the supermarket where she was unfortunate enough to pick up a shopping trolley which was ' unreliable', did not follow her directions and kept going the wrong way. The counsellor, aware that Dorothy had used the same words to describe her husband, encouraged Dorothy to talk about her supermarket experience thinking that by discussing Dorothy's choice of a dysfunctional trolley, she was also talking symbolically about her husband and possibly other objects in her life that were, or had been, unreliable or counter – suggestible, including the counsellor. By using the metaphor of the supermarket trolley, the counsellor was able to begin to help Dorothy think about how strange it was that she was choosing unreliable objects in her life and how these were in evidence from her past, her marriage and also occasionally in her relationship with her counsellor. How had this arisen and what could Dorothy do about it? Dorothy remained a rather concrete thinking and unreflective person but she was able to begin to think about how she could actively avoid dysfunctional trolleys in the supermarket and deal with an unresponsive husband.

Here, the issue of 'the shopping trolley' became a way of charting change as it developed over the course of a brief therapeutic contact. A similar therapeutic metaphor was in evidence with the young man who talked incessantly in sessions about whether he should buy a mobile phone. This conflict came to represent profound issues about independence, isolation and loneliness as well as separation from what were perceived as over-involved parents. Core developmental issues can often be addressed by focusing on metaphors particularly with clients who are more concrete in their thinking (see next chapter).

Summary

Time-limited therapy is 'an introduction to a process through which [clients] expand their conscious awareness of the nature of their problem, their role in creating it, and the potential to do something about it' (Messer and Warren 1995, p.27). Time-limited therapies place more emphasis on the 'here and now' (including the therapeutic process) of problems as opposed to their 'there and then' origin. The question is less 'What does this mean?' than 'What is going on here?' or 'What are we doing to each other?' History is used to shed light on the present rather than the reverse. We have seen that focal therapies which are based on psychoanalytic theories have incorporated concepts and techniques from other orientations and traditions. To the symbolism and relational approach of psychoanalysis has been added the need to challenge attitudes and cognitions from cognitive therapy and the technique of reframing, linking and ways of dealing with resistance from more systemic therapies. Attachment, narrative and metaphor all contribute to the short-term therapist's framework. However, the central point of all time-limited therapies is increasingly the use of the therapeutic relationship; it is here that all approaches are beginning to coalesce. One of the advantages of a degree of eclecticism is that it allows for a broader and more diverse population to be included and benefit from time-limited therapy. From this, it is evident that no single approach is appropriate for all clients and it is important to match the therapy to the client rather than vice versa. Detailed assessment is the crucial element in choice of therapy and this will be discussed in the following chapter.

4

ASSESSMENT FOR TIME-LIMITED THERAPY

This chapter discusses the concept of assessment as it applies to focal therapies and discusses the various clinical populations for whom it might be appropriate, bearing in mind that differing clinical presentations may require different responses. The issue is not as straightforward as it might appear since it tends to depend on the model used and the preference of the individual clinician. Traditionally, there have been two schools of thought with regard to suitability for short-term therapies – a more restrictive one and one that is more inclusive but, as we shall see, these have become somewhat blurred in recent times.

The concept of assessment

It has always been a source of bemusement to me that a client's opinion of his therapist is called transference while the therapist's opinion of the client is called assessment. This is a legacy of the history and development of the concept of assessment in psychoanalytic thought. As we have seen, classical drive theory was essentially a one-person psychology; the therapist, as 'scientist-observer', stands apart from the therapeutic material and dispassionately assesses the client's problems. Freud originally suggested that assessment consisted of gauging the patient's intelligence, financial situation and moral character. Although this is more palatable than it sounds when viewed from a temporal and cultural perspective, it placed the concept of assessment in a moralistic, if not judgmental, frame, which psychoanalysis has found difficult to transcend. Greenson (1981) spoke of the 'requirements' which psychoanalysis made on the patient which included:

- *motivation* (this included the 'will to be analysed' and the suggestion that the level of 'neurotic misery' should be such that the 'person is able to become a patient');
- *capabilities* (which included 'elasticity of character'; the ability to regress and progress and relinquish control; to be able move in and out of reality testing;
- *personality traits* (symptoms and pathology).

Already we see here a factor which has been problematic for time-limited focal therapists coming from a psychoanalytic background; the suggestion that the purpose of assessment is to exclude, rather than include, people from a 'pure' form of treatment. The preoccupation with pathology, motivation and 'character' has over the years ensured that more people were excluded from psychoanalytic treatments than were included. This was not the intention of Freud and his original followers.

Greenson's requirements for the therapist were even more daunting. The therapist needed to do the following:

- understand the unconscious;
- show a 'high intelligence and cultural level';
- demonstrate skill, theoretical knowledge, character and motivation;
- possess empathy;
- be able to communicate to the patient (i.e. a one-way process).

Much of the early discourse on assessment raised the question: is the client capable of 'producing material' or 'working'? This has had the effect that the ethos of 'work' (as opposed to play, for example) has come to dominate the discourse in psychodynamic circles. Therapy can only succeed if it is seen as 'work'. The early dynamic literature on the subject of assessment reflected the observer-observed quality of psychoanalysis at that time; analysis was not seen as an interactional process. The move to an object relations, and with it to a dyadic, framework for dynamic psychotherapy, recognised that there are two people (at least) in any therapeutic relationship and has placed assessment in a more interactional framework but traces of the early evaluative and judgemental flavours remain. It is part of the generational legacy of psychodynamic practitioners.

Recognition of the interactional nature of the therapeutic dyad has placed the concept of assessment in a more fluid and reciprocal framework (see Mace 1995; Mander 2005, for a useful overview of the concept as it applies to various different therapies and settings). Assessment can be broken down into three main areas:

1. *Purpose.* What do we hope to achieve? What is it for?
2. *Aim.* Where do client and therapist want to be when the process is complete?
3. *Content.* How do client and therapist go about the task? This is determined in no small measure by the answers given to purpose and aim.

The purpose of the assessment process differs according to the context in which it occurs. Both therapist and client may have different hopes, expectations and fears arising from the process. It may function to reassure therapists that they have some indication of (or control over) the nature of the therapeutic task while clients may experience the process as either reassuring or worry that they are being evaluated and judged.

Therapeutic tasks in the assessment process

Bramley (1996) describes three interlinked stages and therapeutic tasks in the assessment process:

1. *The establishment of a therapeutic alliance* – This includes the bonding, or attunement, of client and therapist and a joint commitment to work together as well as finding a common language, or idiom. These factors are more important than the concept of psychological mindedness which has had the effect of excluding many clients who may have benefited from a short-term dynamic approach.
2. *Making a dynamic formulation* – This would include: (a) which therapeutic approach might realistically achieve common goals?; (b) the recognition of any past therapy and its usefulness; (c) taking a psycho social history including any previous psychiatric involvement; (d) what internal and external resources are available to the client during the course of what may be an anxiety-provoking (or emotionally 'churning up') therapy; and (e) attending to the client's anxieties about the therapist or treatment.
3. *Making the contract* – Namely, a practical and psychological commitment to work together.

A helpful way of incorporating the different forms of therapeutic material into the formulation is by distinguishing between the text (what is said), the subtext (what is not said) and the context (the setting in which therapy occurs).

Tantam (1995) considers the aims of assessment as including the following:

- *Establishing rapport* with the client which forms the basis of any productive therapeutic work;
- *Obtaining information.* This aids:
  - the making of a *formulation* which includes what form of treatments may best be suited to the client and his difficulties;
  - assessing the client's *strengths and weaknesses;* can treatment be damaging?;
  - determining *why now?* Why has the client sought help at this particular moment in this specific context from this particular person?;
  - the consideration of the *external and internal variables* in determining how the difficulty has arisen.
- *Giving information.* Basic information about the proposed treatment.
- *Enabling the client to feel understood and giving hope.* This would include a coherent narrative. Focal therapy would aim to conceptualise this in the context of the therapeutic triangle.
- *Giving the client a 'taste' of the treatment.* This could involve a 'trial interpretation' (in focal therapy, a linking, triangular comment) as well as the therapist 'modelling' the form the treatment may take.
- *Arranging for any further assessments.* This includes further physical or psychological investigations.
- Ensuring that the *client/therapist mix* is not going to be harmful
- The making of the *practical arrangements.*

Tantam concludes that a combination of the following should be included in any assessment process:

- current complaint or predicament;
- any current 'habit disorders' (eating disorders, substance abuse);
- history of key previous relationships including previous therapeutic relationships;
- mental or physical illnesses;
- preconceptions of the therapy;
- expectations of the therapist.

It is not without interest that considerable importance is placed on what we have termed the pre-transference; the hopes, expectations and fears that the client has about the therapy and therapist. This suggests that the information-gathering aspect of the assessment process may be less of a priority than many therapists imagine and that equal, if not more, attention needs to be paid to the 'here and now' anxieties of the assessment process. This certainly applies to the contemporary emotionally expressive therapies (ISTDT, PIT). This is particularly true in focal therapy where learning more about the client's idiom is paramount.

A number of additional questions are raised when thinking about the purpose and aim of the assessment and the therapist's contribution to the process:

- Is assessment distinct from treatment or do the two run concurrently?
- Does the therapist place specific emphasis on history taking and therefore see assessment as an opportunity to ask questions, take the initiative or control the process? Or does he see it as an opportunity primarily to reflect on the process, in which case, questions are of less importance than enabling the client to reveal themselves in whichever way they choose?
- Is the assessment process one of observer–observed, an interacting dyad, or even a triad as in the case of third party referrals or where there is an institutional dimension?
- Is assessment the same as diagnosis in medicine?
- What part, if any, does intuition play?
- Is the emphasis placed on pathology (ego deficits) or development (the client's strengths)?
- Does assessment take into account the nature of the therapeutic task? (i.e. will the client respond more to a reflective as opposed to a more directional approach and is the client likely to benefit from an interpretative as opposed to a non-interpretative framework? Is the client more comfortable with a compartmentalised approach to his problems or does he gain from linking various different areas of functioning?)
- Is assessment a static or dynamic process? Does it only apply now, or in a week's, a month's, a year's time? Should it be continually part of the process which is built into the therapy?
- If its function is to reassure – who does it reassure, the client or the therapist?

- Is what we call 'assessment' a way of prematurely controlling material which, however satisfying for the therapist, may over time impede spontaneity and understanding?
- If we as therapists are engaged in something called assessment, does that mean that therapeutic progress is being made?

Therapists too can have transferences to concepts, including assessment, that are difficult to relinquish. A balance needs to be struck between the therapist's need, and professional duty, to have some idea of what form of approach and treatment might benefit whom, what individual clients are likely to need or find helpful, and the danger that 'assessment' can be a means by which the therapist defends, or avoids, a real engagement with the client. There is a danger that over-reliance on theories of 'assessment' can give the therapist the illusion of safety, control and predictability and blind them to the values of being open to the therapeutic process as it unfolds in surprising and unexpected ways. Assessment, as a static and diagnostic concept, can merely function to convince the therapist that they know what they are doing. It is then likely to be set in stone and not be amenable to change, review or modification over time in the light of clinical material arising during the course of therapy. However, it remains true that a thorough, evidence-led and comprehensive assessment is required in considering suitability for time-limited therapies to ensure that it is the treatment of choice for the individual client.

Open-ended dynamic therapies have highlighted the following areas when considering whether psychodynamic psychotherapy is likely to be indicated:

- motivation;
- capacity to form some kind of treatment alliance;
- capacity for reflection;
- psychological mindedness;
- capacity to distance oneself from the immediate emotional experience (that is the ability to reflect on experience rather than deny it or act out);
- capacity to link symptom or current problem to current relationships or history (a trial interpretation is frequently used to test this out);
- the ability to distinguish between internal and external reality;
- is the client open to, and does he enjoy, introspection?;
- some capacity to recognise internal unconscious life.

What, then, are the differences between the assessment processes for open-ended and focal, briefer therapies?

Assessment for short-term focal therapy

Assessment and selection are controversial concepts in the field of focal therapies. Freud, who analysed himself and whose own treatments had been brief, had originally suggested that treatment could be shortened for the healthier client. As a result, many early brief therapists developed stringent selection criteria which suggested that those clients most likely to benefit from briefer treatments were relatively healthy, highly motivated individuals who were able to form successful relationships. In other words, indistinguishable from people likely to benefit from any form of therapy. Malan's (1979) selection criteria (mild illness, recent onset, high motivation, satisfactory personal relationships, good contact and response to trial interpretations) are still helpful but the nature and context of shorter-term therapies have changed considerably and with it issues of client (and therapist) suitability for a range of short-term therapies. These tend to be tailored to specific client-presenting problems and characteristics rather than intrinsic to a specific therapeutic orientation.

While there is a wide variation in selection criteria depending on therapeutic orientation, in general, time-limited focal therapy has increasingly looked towards a model which highlights treatment length rather than explicitly focusing on inclusions/exclusions. This is in keeping with a belief that different clinical presentations require different responses and the increasing optimism that presentations which previously were felt to be contraindicated for short-term therapy may now, with sufficient flexibility, be amenable to a shorter-term approach

Box 4.1 lists client characteristics, with those above the line being either less suited to a briefer approach or likely to take longer to treat than those below the line.

Box 4.1 Short-term therapy – length and suitability for treatment

Circumscribed problem
Psychological mindedness
Capacity to form relationships
Flexibility to defences
Oedipal focus

Capacity to form treatment alliance
Capacity to reflect
Recognition that problems have an emotional component
Introspection/curiosity about oneself
Tolerate some frustration and anxiety

Pre-Oedipal problems
Exclusively borderline problems
Termination problems – deep-seated difficulties re loss
Exclusive reliance on projection
Reliance on acting out in dealing with emotional problems

It can be seen that Box 4.1 reflects the distinction between Oedipal and pre-Oedipal areas of functioning. What it reflects is the rule of thumb that Oedipal problems are likely to be appropriately dealt with in shorter therapies while pre-Oedipal issues may be more complex and take more time. Initially, short-term clinicians thought that those suitable for briefer therapies tended to be clients who presented with Oedipal problems while those presenting with what are seen as pre-Oedipal difficulties were excluded. Contemporary short-term therapists are less likely to make that distinction, believing that the latter may merely take longer, and require a different therapeutic response, than the former.

Generally, it still remains the case that the earlier developmentally the roots of the difficulty or problem are, the longer it will take to resolve. This holds true in short-term therapy where a borderline client will need more sessions than a client labelled or diagnosed as neurotic.

However, what can be seen from the above discussion is that the criteria for open-ended or longer-term dynamic psychotherapy are in essence the same, or very similar, to those considered prerequisites for good outcomes in focal, shorter therapy. It seems that all dynamic therapies are looking for the same clients. Needless to say these 'ideal type' clients are rarely to be found in consulting rooms. However, it still remains the case that it is difficult to accurately predict who will do well or badly in briefer therapies not least since, as we will see, short-term interventions tend to differ depending on the nature of the client's problem.

Contemporary theories of assessment and selection for focal therapy are more linked to the populations who present themselves for therapeutic help than on static criteria of pathology or health, which have previously functioned to exclude more people than they include. We are looking to suit the treatment to the client rather than the other way round. However, the literature on focal and short-term therapies tends to suggest that if any of the following criteria are in evidence, extreme caution should be exercised when considering briefer treatments:

- psychotic illness including severe depression;
- severe personality disorder;
- extreme self-destructive behaviour including severe drug or alcohol abuse;
- the difficulty of establishing a focus;
- those clients unlikely to be contained by a time-limited or focal approach;
- clients who do not seek or want brief therapy (this has major implications for the contexts in which short-term work is practised).

When assessing for short-term therapies, a developmental paradigm is likely to be more helpful than one which relies excessively on psychopathology – one is not attempting to 'cure character' but 'solve problems', although the ripple effect of change suggests that the two are not mutually exclusive. This is similar to what Wiener and Sher (1998) have termed the 'life audit' function of short-term therapy.

From the previous chapter, we can see how the concepts of both narrative coherence and autobiographical competence may have a part to play in the assessment process. If clear and coherent stories are told by the securely attached and muddled, incoherent ones are evidence of the insecurely attached, then 'autobiographical coherence' ('the ability to make meanings out of unstoried life, ... especially out of loss and disappointment', Holmes 1993, p. 146) is likely to be a good indicator of the length of any prospective therapy. Models of attachment may be linked with the length of treatment. The inability to tell a story may suggest that it may take more time for the individual to construct one. In a similar vein, therapeutic goals could be linked to a client's attachment history. Able storytellers may require less time as do those people who are able to move comfortably in and out of relationships at transitional points in their lives. This reinforces the importance placed on the quality, as opposed to the quantity, of the client's previous relationships in the assessment process. Of *particular significance are any previous therapeutic relationships*. These are likely to colour the client's pre-transference and need to be acknowledged and addressed immediately.

Initial considerations in the assessment process

Time-limited therapy, because of its selective focus and time constraints, needs, during the assessment process, to address two central issues (Aveline 1995). First, the establishment of an early, positive, therapeutic alliance. This is achieved, in part, through therapist activity. Focal therapies place great importance in client selection on an active positive engagement. Second, the prompt acknowledgement and addressing of any negative feelings evident in first few meetings.

Attention having been paid to the contra-indications for focal therapy, a *formulation* of the client's difficulties needs to be arrived at and coupled with a statement as to how therapy might address them. This is based on the triangles of persons and therapy as they affect the following areas:

- content, including presenting problem;
- autobiographical competence;
- history, especially of inter-personal relationships;
- idiom, narrative, personal template;
- affective expression;
- the context in which therapy takes place.

When they first meet a client, short-term therapists have two main sources of dynamic information: the manifest and latent content of the narrative that unfolds, and the interactive process between themselves and their clients. This material can then be incorporated into the three triangles mentioned in Chapter 3. Given that the short-term therapists' aim in making an assessment and arriving at a formulation is to link the clients' presenting problems with the 'core idiom and conflict', these will assist in arriving at an understanding of the client's way of being in the world intrapsychically (triangle of conflict), their history, present problem, relationship with therapist (triangle of persons) and their characteristic idiomatic way of relating (idiomatic triangle).

In general, it is helpful to begin an assessment with a discussion of the client's current pain, including their feelings about coming for help. This can be a guide as to the client's idiom in relation to intimacy and closeness. This also serves to elucidate the links between the past, present and how the client's idiom might be manifest in the room. What is also helpful at this stage is to ensure that specific examples of the client's problem are given to ensure that vagueness is kept to a minimum and the evolving focus can be refined. First sessions need to focus on what the client has brought to the treatment in the context of their previous experience and their relational history. The short-term therapist's psychodynamic formulation, when arrived at, should be able to highlight the clients 'core issues and dominant motivation in a way that makes sense of the [client's] symptoms, precipitating incident, functioning, way of being in the therapy, subjective experience, and past conflicts' (Fosha 2000).

The formulation is then able to take the form of a working hypothesis which client and therapist use and is amenable to change or redefinition over time. Both client and therapist 'play' with inferential material stemming from the personal history and the affective quality of sessions in order to test out the validity of the dynamic formulation. In this sense, assessment in focal therapy is a dynamic process which lasts throughout the therapy and is interwoven with treatment.

The nature of object relations and defences in the assessment process

Two factors which assist in the assessment process are the nature of the client's quality of object relations and their use of defences. Given that a central feature of the model of short-term therapy outlined here is how the therapeutic relationship is used, it follows that specific attention should be paid to the client's current and previous relational history. Box 4.2 (Quality of Object Relations Scale, Azim et al. 1991) outlines a relational model based upon the distinction between Oedipal and pre-Oedipal levels of inter-relating.

Box 4.2 Distinction between Oedipal (three person/neurotic) and pre-Oedipal (two person/borderline) dynamic

1. **Primitive Organisational Level**
   Repeated patterns of intense, unstable and destructive relationships. Others either idealised or denigrated. Alternating between clinging and aloof behaviour. Preoccupation with destroying or being destroyed by the other.

2. **Searching Organisational Level**
   Repeated infatuations with heightened fear of loss, rejection and abandonment. Feelings of anxiety and emptiness in the absence of the other. Self esteem dependent on their availability.

3. **Controlling Organisational Level**
   Attempts to control or possess others in relationships. React to others' attempts at control with either defiance or compliance. Anger and rage when unable to control the other.

4. **Triangular Organisational Level**
   Repetitive involvement in rivalless triangular relationships.

5. **Mature Organisational Level**
   Tolerance of bad as well as appreciation of good in others. Capacity to express tenderness and concern for others while able to be assertive. Ability to mourn.

As can be seen, these categories link with the previous chapter's discussion of attachment theory. They are a useful way for the short-term therapist to conceptualise their client's quality of relationships, and, although perhaps not to be used as discrete categories (we can move from one category to another in different contexts) can function as a guide to the nature and length of the treatment required with fewer sessions needed for clients in (5) and more for those in (1).

Equally, the nature of the client's characteristic defence mechanisms can give some indication of the likely length of treatment based on a developmental model. Table 4.3 distinguishes between two sets of defence mechanisms.

TABLE **4.3** Defence mechanisms and developmental stages

Primitive (Pre-Oedipal)	Mature (Oedipal)
Splitting	Repression
Idealisation	Reaction formation
Devaluation	Undoing
Introjection	Displacement
Projection	Emotional isolation
Projective identification	Intellectualisation
Denial	Rationalisation
Regression	Sublimation

Exclusive reliance on the more primitive defences – developmentally earlier – would suggest treatment needs to be longer, and perhaps more focused and structured. However we need to be aware that these are not discrete positions and that a combination of defences are used by most of us most of the time.

More recently, attention has focused on therapeutic modality rather than client pathology as indicators for focal therapy. The key question is the form of therapy most likely to be helpful for this particular client rather than necessarily its length. In the final analysis, it is likely that the question is less a matter of whether long- or short-term therapy is indicated, rather than what form of therapy (e.g. interpretative or non-interpretative, structured or reflective) is likely to be helpful. In this, the client's idiom or personal/relational style – whether concrete or reflective – is likely to be an important consideration. As Malan has pointed out, healthier clients get selected for interpretative work, sicker ones don't. By the same token, the more disturbed the client, the more partial the focus needs to be in time-limited therapy. For less healthy clients, work in the transference needs to be more indirect – often working exclusively in the 'at one remove' metaphor – and more reliance needs to be placed on 'ego building' supportive techniques. Assessment or selection by treatment modality would gauge how supportive, exploratory or interpretive the therapy, or therapist, needs to be with any individual client rather than solely looking at aspects of the client's pathology in deciding whether focal treatment is indicated or not. Clients will require differing responses depending on whether their idioms are reflective or concrete.

Some short-term therapists suggest a period of 'trial therapy' to ascertain whether the client can benefit from a more circumscribed focal approach. During this period both parties can monitor whether the therapy is likely to be helpful. Given that short-term therapies range from the emotionally expressive to the more supportive (often related to the context in which they are delivered), clinicians have to gauge the client's degree of emotional/ego strength for more expressive work while also taking into account the client's capacity to use metaphor and symbolisation as therapeutic tools. The assessment process can take place over a number of sessions before the decision to work together is made and an inclusive therapeutic focus identified. It is less a matter of the client being able to 'work' in the therapist's idiom or orientation than assessing what the client's personal idiom may be and being guided by that as to the choice of therapy.

Focal therapies suggest that it is important that the assessment process includes informing the client of the structure, purpose and methods which the therapy will employ.

William

William arrived for his first session with a counsellor having been referred by his GP 'to see whether having a chat could help'. He was a worried and anxious young man, of a concrete and practical bent, who had spent some years on anti-depressant medication and whose pre-transference to counselling was one of bewilderment. It subsequently transpired that he thought he would be seen for a few minutes and given literature to read, not unlike his experience of consulting his doctor. The counsellor, assuming that an idiom of the counselling process was shared, suggested they meet weekly and 'see where we get to …' William was bewildered by the next session where the counsellor said little and William, not knowing what was expected of him, even less. The counsellor thought William defensive and hostile which, had these sessions continued, would have turned into a self-fulfilling prophesy. In supervision, the counsellor was encouraged to explain to William the basic structure and process of how counselling proceeds. William was relieved to be told that they would meet at a specific time weekly for 50 minutes, that if he arrived late, the time could not be made up. The task was to think about William's anxiety and depression (which the counsellor thought had to do with aspects of William's background and current life) and that this would be attempted by William talking about what he considered at the time to be important issues as well as anything which came into his mind. The counsellor would help William think about them by commenting on William's thoughts and by adding some of his own. William was visibly relieved by these guidelines and made substantive progress over the 12 sessions offered.

This elucidation of the focal psychotherapeutic setting and framework shows that the therapist takes the frame, and the client's anxieties about it, seriously, but also clarifies for the client what is expected of him (and the therapist) in therapy. Many clients, particularly those referred by third parties, have little concept or idea of therapy and benefit from the clarification offered by the therapist. This also applies to people from different cultures whose views of therapy and psychological counselling maybe radically different from those of the therapist or counselling agency. Clarification, where appropriate, also helps the client decide whether the form of therapy on offer is what they want. Since the assessment process requires the active participation of two people, clients need to have access to basic information which assists them in assessing the prospective therapy and therapist. 'Trial therapies' have a similar function in empowering the client. This is a very different approach from that used in longer-term therapy where the explanation of the frame and possible content of therapy by the therapist is viewed as pre-empting the therapeutic process.

It is becoming increasingly apparent that it is difficult to lay down hard and fast criteria that favour one form of therapy over another, let alone between open-ended and focal time-limited therapies. The therapist needs to bring imagination, curiosity and an openness to the use of metaphor and symbols to the assessment process. This is what enables therapeutic conversations to take place independent of strict assessment criteria. It is worth noting in passing that this raises the issue of how such things are to be taught. However, in considering assessment, the simple rule of thumb remains true: *the earlier the developmental arrest or problem, the longer the treatment is likely to be* and, in shorter therapies, the more a circumscribed focus is indicated.

What needs to be guarded against is any unthinking encouragement, on the therapist's part, which may lead the client to become deeply attached to the therapist or therapy and then for this attachment to be suddenly terminated. Therapeutic activity and the maintenance of an agreed, and regularly attended to, focus, help to minimise the risk of this occurring. However, it does bring up the issue of whether therapeutic attachments can be regulated. It may well be that different therapeutic styles lead to differing modes of attachment.

Looking at contemporary time-limited therapy which advocates a high level of activity on the part of the therapist; a confidence in technique and outcome which is conveyed to the client; where resistances are challenged directly, and therapeutic material is encouraged, we can see that this is very similar to the early Freud. However, as psychoanalysis became preoccupied in earlier and more primitive developmental phases and conflicts, therapies became longer and ostensibly more rigorous in order to treat these conditions. The current challenge for focal and time-limited therapies – and one could say for all therapies – is to examine whether they have anything to offer those clients who present with borderline characteristics or who are, more simply, difficult. It is here that a careful assessment is especially important.

Focal therapies and the 'difficult' client

As we have seen, the early short-term therapists thought that focal therapies had little to offer those clients who presented with what are termed pre-Oedipal problems. By definition, these included people with the most complex, often long-standing, problems, who were also less likely to be able to enter into or sustain a therapeutic alliance. These clients were thought to be contra-indicated for briefer therapies, often on the basis that they lacked 'motivation'. Motivation, however, has always been a problematic concept in psychotherapy:

> Until the late 1970s I ... considered motivation an important criterion; but since then my position has changed totally based on my research. I consider motivation a criterion created by therapists who cannot treat highly resistant, complex patients ... Until 1980 I considered a fragile character a contraindication ... but our research data ... shows that they are the best candidates and that we can bring about major structural character changes. (Davanloo 1994)

Clients who are perceived as 'difficult' (although the term presupposes that others are 'easy' which is debatable since all clients are likely to pose therapeutic challenges at some point during therapy) may be those who are deemed unsuitable for a specific therapy or therapist. However, there is evidence that certain clients present specific difficulties to whatever therapeutic approach is attempted. This is particularly true in relation to short-term focal therapies.

Whatever assessment criteria are used, the reality is that, particularly in public sector settings, many clients are included in short-term therapies who might on reflection not be the most suitable candidates for short-term therapy. Economic concerns should not lead to the belief that time-limited therapy is necessarily the treatment of choice for every client. This is a concern that we will discuss in more detail in Chapter 7.

However, it remains the case that clients showing a predominance of borderline states of mind or behaviour pose specific difficulties for any therapist under any conditions. The nature of the problems presented in many therapeutic settings is increasingly leading to the need to consider of how shorter focal therapies can address the multifaceted difficulties which are brought by the borderline personality client. This is in some ways an opportunity for the profession since many of the advances in psychotherapy have been made when learning from clients initially considered not suitable for a specific therapy; as Messer and Warren (1995, p. 249) point out, 'Today's difficult patient is tomorrow's new conceptual and clinical vista.'

The concept of borderline

'Borderline' is a difficult concept to define and some would say that it is a category devised by the therapeutic profession to describe people that it would rather not treat. In that sense it has acquired somewhat moralistic overtones. However, descriptively it can be a helpful term which identifies certain character traits, behaviour, actions, affects and states of mind which are likely to have a central bearing on any prospective therapy. The phrase describes difficulties which lie on the frontier between neurotic and psychotic states of mind; in that sense everyone has the capacity, under pressure, to swing in and out of borderline states of mind. However, the concept does suggest that there are certain characterological traits which, when concurrently in evidence, contribute to a way of functioning, or being, that (because of their complex, disconcerting and challenging presentation) require specific therapeutic attention. These include:

- labile and unstable mood swings, which are particularly sensitive to slights, real or imagined;
- fragile boundaries between the self and others;
- a wish for closeness (fusion or merger) coexisting with a fear of engulfment. This can frequently lead to fierce oscillations between the hope for, and dread of, intimacy.
- low tolerance of frustration and angry outbursts;
- faulty reality testing;
- unstable interpersonal relationships which are dominated by oscillations between idealisation and denigration;
- relationships which tend to be dominated by demanding, distrustful, envious and rivalrous feelings and behaviour;
- self-harming behaviour, including drug and alcohol abuse;
- pervasive feelings of emptiness, meaninglessness and boredom;
- identity diffusion and confusion. These manifest as basic conflicts around ego integration and object constancy where the normal differentiation between self and other has not occurred or been attained.

These characteristics potentially present major challenges to the establishment of a working therapeutic alliance. Since borderline character traits involve, on the one hand, a dread of closeness and engulfment, while concurrently yearning for intimacy and attempting to seek it, this dynamic will be constantly enacted in the therapeutic relationship:

These people experience the harrowing dilemma of extreme dependence coupled with an intense fear of closeness. They believe that closeness to the other person will be mutually destructive. The true danger arises not so much from their aggression as from the more tragic fact that their love is destructive. They feel that to give love is to impoverish oneself and to love the other person is to drain him. (Model 1968)

Fonagy (1991) has described this form of presentation as one of 'stable instability', which succinctly sums up the constant, if variable, difficulties these clients experience. Many of these people will have had unstable and neglectful childhoods which may have included emotional, physical or sexual abuse. It follows that these clients may be problematic to engage in any reflective therapy and, once engaged, pose considerable challenges to orthodox therapeutic approaches:

The therapist is ... used as a receptacle for the patient's feelings, and may be filled with anger, confusion, fear and disgust in a way that, for the inexperienced, is unexpected and difficult to tolerate. The patient treats therapy in a very concrete way, and may become highly dependent on the therapist, seeking comfort in fusion with a rescuing object who is, at other times, felt to be sadistic and rejecting. These latter aspects emerge especially at times of breaks, or when the therapist lets the patient down, as inevitably he will. (Holmes 1993)

However, clinicians need to remember that it is their empathic understanding of the client's inner world that is important and facilitates therapeutic change, and this is as true of the borderline personality as it is of any other client group. In this sense it is important not to be distracted by symptoms or pathology but to attend to what the underlying personality factors represent for each specific client. Specific attention needs to be paid to the clinician's counter-transference – these clients can evoke strongly negative counter-transferences which will need to be processed and contained. Equally, clinicians may have to accept that outcome goals need to be more limited and circumscribed than with other client groups.

Assessment and the borderline personality

Caution needs to be exercised when considering such clients for focal, time-limited therapy. These clients often evidence traumatic losses which make treatment approaches that place a high premium on termination problematic. Similarly, narcissistic clients who exhibit fragile self-esteem may find short-term therapy problematic seeing it as evidence of the therapist's rejection of their importance or neediness. Borderline clients tend to present with diffuse and global problems which make the clarification of a clear focus more difficult. Excessive reliance on idealisation, splitting and denigration ensures that their perception of the therapist changes in rapid and unpredictable ways. The capacity for symbol formation or the use of metaphor may be impaired, making the use of language, including interpretation and clarification, more problematic. Profound anxieties over dependence and separation ensure that these clients split off and minimise experiences of abandonment, intrusion or neglect or act them out outside the therapeutic frame. Rigid character defences, often in evidence in psychosomatic complaints, make a time-limited approach more complex and challenging. Modifications in therapeutic technique may be necessary for this group of clients. The conundrum is how short-term dynamic therapists can modify their therapeutic approach while still achieving something of psychodynamic value with these clients. This applies particularly to clients with whom it is difficult to make emotional contact as a result of their defensive structures described above.

Messer and Warren (1995) suggest the following criteria be borne in mind when offering focal or short-term therapy to a borderline client:

- Capacity for engagement with the therapist in some meaningful way.
- Capacity to disengage at termination. With those clients who have not satisfactorily disengaged from their 'primary objects', or have suffered traumatic losses from primary relationships, the therapist must avoid recapitulating the loss at termination.
- The need for some degree of focality in the client's difficulties. For some clients (e.g. adolescents) the lack of a focus may become the developmentally appropriate focus, while for others, if combined with excessive borderline functioning, this lack may make short-term work difficult.
- The client's capacity to tolerate the emotional requirements of therapy. This will vary between clinical models and therapists but all short-term therapies would make some demands on the client's ego strengths and take into consideration the availability of environmental and personal supports.

While it is true to say that people with severe borderline personality disorders tend not to be treated by time-limited models, there is an increasing literature suggesting that, with some precautions, a modified form of focal therapy may benefit some borderline clients (Magnavita 1997). As with selection criteria in general, a premium is placed on the client's interpersonal relationships and history when considering focal therapy for this client group.

In Chapter 2, we discussed how cognitive analytic therapy (Ryle 1998) has specifically set out a time-limited treatment for border-line or difficult to treat clients which offers up to 24 sessions focusing on the client's awareness of self and other states of mind. Rather than length of treatment, central importance is given to the consistent, reliable therapeutic response from both setting and therapist. The therapist needs to track and remain attuned to the client's emotional state and be alert to the constant invitation to repeat current or previous traumatic experiences of intimacy which the client has come to expect, and may, albeit unconsciously, seek to re-enact.

It may be helpful to break down borderline personality disorders into dependent, schizoid and narcissistic categories to highlight the nature of therapeutic responses required.

Borderline/dependent personality

Sonia

Sonia arrived despondently at the counsellor's consulting room but soon became tearfully agitated when describing her fear that her husband might leave her for another woman. Despite her becoming increasingly submissive and attentive to him, he appeared to be less interested in her. She was unable to think about how to proceed and was having severe difficulty making day-to-day decisions in her life. She adopted a submissive and victim-like demeanour with the counsellor, constantly asking him what she should do, complained of a range of physical symptoms, and was reluctant to leave at the end of sessions. The counsellor felt overwhelmed by the depth of Sonia's distress and his initial response was to refer her for long-term therapy. Sonia's feeling of being overwhelmed by her predicament and her feelings of powerless in relation to it were being projected onto the counsellor who was able to use supervision to process these issues and subsequently begin to work on a focus with Sonia which would incorporate her physical complaints, wish for others to take responsibility for her and the nature of her previous and current attachment relationships.

Stadter (2004) outlines common treatment considerations with these clients. These include the mistaken early belief – a result of the client's grateful submissiveness – that the treatment will go smoothly, the 'urge' to make the client independent, the temptation – arising out of the dependence – to be directive and take over, the client's fear that independence will lead to abandonment, the counter-transference difficulty of recognising the client's destructive relationship and the temptation to help them give it up, and the difficulty the client may have with termination leading to the therapist being tempted to offer more; this is generally a mistake since it reinforces the dependent client's passivity and helplessness. In some senses, short-term treatment can be the treatment of choice for these clients since open-ended longer-term therapy can 'encourage the fantasy – in both therapist and client – that more growth, satisfaction and time are always available'.

Borderline/schizoid personality

Laurence

Laurence appeared to many as aloof and detached. He had few friends or acquaintances and only had regular contact with members of his family of origin at holidays and festivals. His major activity, apart from going to work where he was employed in a job with regular and predictable routines not involving others, was playing computer games and surfing the internet. He reluctantly came for counselling; it had been suggested by his employer who was concerned about Laurence's isolation and avoidance of others in the workplace. The counsellor offered a limited number of sessions which focused on how Laurence could convince his employer that counselling was not necessary – a metaphor for modulating relationships with others. Laurence appeared relieved that the counselling relationship was planned to be brief.

With schizoid clients, it is important to respect their personal space while simultaneously attempting to make contact with them. Setting a limited number of sessions 'can help the client with fears of intimacy or of being engulfed' (Stadter 2004). Frequently intermittent therapy may be of help to these clients (see Chapter 5). The therapist's counter-transference may be dominated by feelings of frustration at the lack of affect and contact demonstrated by these clients. Close attention needs to be paid to the balance between interpersonal involvement and non-involvement since these clients are often able to function well in the domain of the intellect. Stadter also suggests being open to adjusting sessions to the need of the individual client (a 50- minute session may not be appropriate for clients struggling with intimacy and intensity), that structured interest groups might be indicated (as it was for Laurence on computer bulletin boards) and periodic follow-ups.

Borderline/narcissistic

Matthew

Matthew sought out his counsellor since the counsellor had come highly recommended as very bright and able and, Matthew felt, would be one of the few people who might understand him. He felt he was one of the most able in his workplace and that others did not give him sufficient recognition for his achievements. He felt others were exploiting his achievements and was planning their humiliation when, as inevitably would happen, he would be in a position of authority over them. He was prone to bouts of self-contempt and had experienced a neglectful childhood at the hands of a vain and preoccupied mother and absent father. He was functioning rather better in the world than either Sonia or Laurence (described above) and had developed a moderately successful false self-personality which made him popular with others although he was contemptuous of their approbation. It was unclear why he had sought help but used sessions to attempt to convince the counsellor of his high opinion of himself and his denigration of others. Matthew, whose self-esteem, despite external appearances, was very brittle, needed a therapeutic response which 'mirrored' him and posed no threat to his sense of identity. He needed more sessions than Sonia or Laurence since he needed to feel a sense of the counsellor's value of him and respect for his complex false self-organisation before he was able to tolerate any questioning of this grandiose defence.

Narcissistic clients who present with complex symptomatology commonly evoke difficult counter-transferential responses from their therapists, ranging from feelings of inadequacy, exploitation, and a pressure to prove oneself as a result of the client's latent idealisation of them, to anger at the client's lack of empathy and ruthless use of them. It is important to view these as projections from the client rather than respond to them viscerally. Maintaining empathy is central since the narcissistic client will be very sensitive to being judged or seen as vulnerable. Since the narcissistic client is very ambivalent about receiving help, premature termination is always a possibility (and can be spoken to by a transparent dynamic focus). Once sufficient trust has been established through the 'mirroring stage', the therapist can begin to question the client's grandiosity (and feelings of inadequacy which lies behind it) and begin to question how the client's lack of empathy for others might be addressed by gently asking the client how others might feel about him or his actions. Narcissistic clients sometimes see themselves as 'special' and may ask for special treatments (times, fees, etc.) or question the short-term frame experiencing it as a narcissistic humiliation. Transference, too, needs to be sensitively addressed. Since the client has a grandiose and idealised version of themselves (however brittle), they may not respond well to the therapist interpreting the idealising transference, which the therapist, experiencing the idealisation as discomforting, might want to address (Stadter, 2004).

Leibovich (1996) presents a comprehensive rationale and framework for time-limited therapy with borderline clients. Client and therapist choose a single recurring personality trait as a focus (low frustration level, overvaluing or devaluing relationships, narcissistic slights) while the client's tendency to become diffuse is discouraged. The fact that therapy is short is emphasised from the beginning which places central emphasis on separation and ensures that it is linked in some way to the central focus. Since borderline clients are sensitive to real or imagined rejections, 'planned abandonment makes it less devastating'. The time frame gives clients a sense of purpose, frequently lacking in borderline functioning, while the actual fact of having persisted with a therapeutic task and relationship can be experienced as a considerable achievement.

Leibovich suggests that since the therapeutic task and focus are clearly articulated they can be more easily understood by more concrete borderline clients than longer-term, open-ended, therapy which places a premium on growth and personality change; diffuse concepts which may have little resonance with these clients. Through his active, empathic but structured stance, the therapist conveys a message that therapy is a task which can be ordered and problems solved; behaviour is not entirely affected by the past so it is possible to create an anticipation that shifts can occur in a limited time. Therapeutic activity ensures that the therapist speaks to the danger that silence and passivity can be experienced as threatening and intolerable to the borderline client. It also assists the client's 'self-definition, differentness and separateness by demarcating and accentuating the boundary between two individuals'. The therapist maintains a presence as a real person drawing attention to attempts by the client to merge or fuse as well as disengage, and linking them with relationships outside the therapy. Short-term work, by limiting and making explicit the therapeutic relationship, enables the client to feel less threatened by fears of fusion and engulfment.

Therapeutic passivity leading to symbiosis is avoided while the borderline client's need for his immediate and concrete needs to be met are continually reality tested in sessions by stressing the client's determination to directly face and address his problems with all possible haste. Achievements, however minor in the areas of self-assertion, competence and individuation, are reinforced which address the client's impaired sense of autonomy or active agency. Minute examination of the emotional impact of the sessions are linked to the client's fear of being overwhelmed and completely at the mercy of their own labile moods. Since the therapeutic relationship is viewed as an experience of reality rather than transference, and the emphasis is on current conflicts and the 'here and now' experience, the borderline client's frequently defective capacity to reality test is helped by correcting any distortions or misperceptions as they arise; in the 'more nebulous framework of some long term therapies ... the patient's grip on their own reality ... [is impaired] ... engendering panic, insecurity, confusion and disorganisation' (Leibovich 1996, p. 444). The structure and predictability of sessions provide a containing environment which speaks to the borderline client's poor impulse control.

Focal activity, and the encouragement of the client's active participation in the therapeutic alliance, assist the client's realistic expectations of what therapy can achieve. Small, gradual achievements in the area of the focus assist the development of self-esteem which 'neutralises the rage so typical of the borderline and avoids the primitive transference so frequently the cause of therapeutic impasses'. While a short-term therapy which is structured, stable, consistent, empathic and focus-oriented may be helpful for some borderline clients, it needs to be pointed out that Leibovich suggests a framework of between 36 and 52 sessions. This is at the higher end of short-term treatment sessions. However, it does indicate that a 'focal way of thinking' can assist in treating a diverse and complex group of clients. Tony shows how a borderline personality structure with a history of unstable relationships, impulsivity, rage, a fragmented sense of self and suicidal ideation, can be addressed within a short-term framework.

Tony

Tony, a 40-year-old middle manager in a computer software company, was referred for counselling after the break-up, with no explanation, of a brief (three-week) relationship with Sue, a younger woman. This had precipitated loss of concentration and interest, anti-depressant medication, bouts of heavy drinking and an intention of stalking his former friend to 'show her how much I am suffering ... I do not deserve to be treated like this.' He felt tempted to harm himself to punish her. On the one occasion that he insisted on meeting with Sue, in the company of a third party, she had subsequently become alarmed and contacted the police saying Tony was harassing her. Tony reacted to this action with barely controlled rage. Tony had come up against a brick wall: 'What should I do?'

Tony had grown up in an expatriate family and returned to Britain with his mother on the parental separation when he was aged 7. After living alone with his morose and uncommunicative mother he was sent to boarding school at 11 where he had an 'uneventful' time. He had a number of relatively short-lived relationships which ended as he thought none of his partners was quite good enough for him. This was what made the current situation unbearable; the knowledge that Sue was 'perfect' for him. They got on very well, both were 'unemotional' and ambitious, and she had a high status occupation which made Tony feel they were equals.

A plausible narrative could be sketched which linked his current devastation with the loss of his father, his tense and eventually abandoned relationship with his mother, the need to distance himself from the emotional impact of his family's upheavals, and his own ambitions for himself. However, Tony did not want to know any of this, beginning every session with a detailed (and monotonously repetitive) account of his week's ruminations, and the injustice of Sue's actions. He was so angry that he wanted to punish her and attempted this by avoiding going into work, or when there, sitting still, disconsolately refusing to begin his scheduled tasks – 'That will show her just what she is doing to me.'

During the initial three assessment meetings Tony became increasingly annoyed with Sue, bewildered and frustrated at his own inability to manage himself in response to her departure, and continuing to threaten to harm himself as a way of communicating his distress to her, and by implication, the therapist. The therapist was by this time feeling irritated and annoyed with Tony. He was aware of a feeling of dislike towards him which manifested itself in the hope that Tony would not come to appointments. In supervision the therapist recognised this counter-transference rejection as something Tony was unconsciously seeking to bring about. It was also clearly linked with the acute 'here and now' difficulty which Tony was experiencing. In response to this, the therapist suggested to Tony the following focus for sessions: Given just what a turbulent effect Sue's action was having on Tony's life, therapy would monitor the day-to-day emotional repercussions of such a profound rejection which was made worse by the fact that no reason was given for Sue's actions. Given that Tony had some experience of not being given reasons for events that affected him – his parents' separation, for instance – we needed to ensure that therapeutic reasons were given for everything that occurred in sessions. Tony could assist in this task by thinking about how he had managed to deal with previous separations and even noting how he was managing the time between the weekly sessions. Tony agreed that this might help – it would also give meaning and structure to his week – but wanted to be reassured that he would not have 'to come forever'. What were his associations to the thought of coming forever? Tony replied, 'It would kill me' which subsequently provided a useful ancillary focus: What was it about contact with others that could be so (self-)destructive?

Tony also provides an interesting example of the use of metaphor discussed in Chapter 3. During the course of treatment Tony talked about being 'dropped' by the football team that he played for; this was extremely unfair as he had trained all season only to be displaced by someone who was friendlier with the Captain. Football, and the emotions it could provoke in Tony's life, were to become a central theme of sessions which could be clearly linked with the feelings evoked by Sue's departure. The fear of being 'dropped' was pervasive, but, said Tony hopefully (without any obvious malice and referring to his own future development rather than a yearning for retribution) in his last session, 'We need to remind ourselves it is a game of two halves!'

In working with borderline clients, a more supportive (as opposed to emotionally expressive) approach may be called for. Less attention is given to interpretation, confrontation or insight and more importance is placed on containment, improving self-esteem, and a decrease in anxiety through the experience of being with a benign therapist whose boundaries and framework are clear and safe. The focus may need to be circumscribed to the client's immediate here and now situation and it is only this aspect of the therapeutic triangle that is available to be directly addressed. This does not mean that negligible therapeutic benefit can result, merely that there is greater reliance, and respect for, the 'ripple' effect in the therapy. Significant others may need to be enlisted in the treatment, or a 'care network' set up to maintain a safe therapeutic structure and contain acting out.

As we have seen, when working with these clients, greater attention may need to be paid to the therapist's counter-transference. The time limitation and the clinical demandingness of these clients may elicit more negative counter-transference feelings. It is these negative, sometimes hostile, interactions with borderline clients that the therapist needs to process since they tend to be central to the client's relational problems. If unrecognised, they are in danger of being acted out in the therapy by the therapist in destructive and untherapeutic ways and lead to the persecutory spirals referred to in the last chapter.

The therapist needs to be able to acknowledge and deal with any excessive therapeutic zeal ('I can cure this impossible person') as well as avoid 'therapeutic nihilism' along the lines of 'it doesn't matter what one does, the patient is too disturbed to be helped' (Messer and Warren 1995, p. 274). These can be counter-transference responses which parallel the client's oscillation between grandiosity and self-denigration. Messer and Warren note that the therapist's own self-esteem and need to feel effective and competent are likely to be challenged when working in a focal fashion with borderline clients since, unlike open-ended therapies where this can be postponed to an indefinite future, the sorrow of recognising the limitations of the therapy is more immediate. Both therapist and client are made painfully aware of the limitations of therapy and what cannot be achieved from the outset of treatment. Therapist and client need to recognise the value of 'partial solutions, compromises, [and] ambiguous outcomes' however difficult this may be for them. Therapist guilt, always in danger of arising in short-term therapies but pervasive with borderline clients, at not having done or helped enough – and the associated belief that if only more time was available the outcome would be better – can also be a reflection of the therapist's defence against an imperfect, if realistic, outcome.

Summary

Arguably the most important assessment criterion is the client's ability to form a collaborative therapeutic relationship and it is precisely this that our most challenging clients find most difficult. With regard to assessment criteria, it is perhaps most important to constantly question such 'truths' that we consider 'self-evident' (Stadter, 2004) since every therapeutic encounter has the capacity to surprise. Every client should perhaps be considered for short-term therapy; clinicians need to ask themselves, how can I help this person in the shortest possible time? Rather than having exclusive criteria, notwithstanding the issues highlighted in this chapter, we should cultivate a short-term state of mind in every consultation unless there are substantive reasons not to – it should, in the parlance of our time, be our default option.

5

DIFFERENCES IN THERAPEUTIC TECHNIQUE BETWEEN OPEN-ENDED AND TIME-LIMITED THERAPIES

The therapeutic alliance

Short-term therapies are distinguished by their relative brevity, the careful attention which is paid to assessment and selection, the need to establish a discreet therapeutic alliance, therapeutic activity and clinical focus. Having discussed assessment and selection in the previous chapter, we start with the nature of the therapeutic alliance as it is established in short-term therapies. Central to the success of short-term therapies is the ability to establish, maintain and repair any ruptures to the therapeutic alliance. We have seen how the establishment of trust and safety are central to the establishment of a therapeutic relationship and leads to a therapeutic stance which is conversational, co-operative, active and engaging. The more a client feels safe with the therapist, the quicker a facilitative attachment relationship can be established and, by definition, the quicker, therapeutic work can proceed. The core conditions for the establishment of a short-term therapeutic alliance are not dissimilar to the establishment of an open-ended therapeutic alliance (non-judgmental empathic attunement, respect, competence, etc.) but this needs to be done concurrently with the therapist creating the foundations for the establishment of a therapeutic focus and modelling to the client the nature of the therapeutic contact.

This need for the therapeutic relationship to be established reasonably quickly includes the necessity for both verbal and affective contact to be made between therapist and client. The need to establish this quickly carries that danger that the therapist can become impatient and try to hurry the process along. The client has to feel understood and the therapist needs to convey hope that progress can be made. Short-term therapies are a particularly intense form of encounter that require close attention to every aspect of the therapeutic relationship, so the establishment of the alliance becomes a precursor for any subsequent therapeutic work. The therapist also needs to pay heed to the acknowledgement of the notion that the relationship itself will be an object of study and the feelings it engenders respected and used in the service of the client. As a microcosm of the therapy, the initial session(s) (and each individual session) need to take into account the stages of therapy which may follow – that of the initial honeymoon, followed by ambivalence and separation. Equally, it is important that in establishing and developing a rapid therapeutic alliance, the 'central issue ought to include material, topics, verbal expressions and central themes from within the inner world of the patient, in his language and according to the quality of his … (subjective) experience' (Shefler 2001). The therapist needs to enter the client's idiom. It is always helpful for the therapist to use the same words, expressions and metaphors which have been used by the client.

The initial aim of the therapeutic alliance is to assist in the mutual discovery of a circumscribed therapeutic focus and an agreement to work together towards addressing it. Unless the client can be engaged and agreement established to work on a meaningful issue from the first session, therapy is likely to be longer than it need be. The establishment of a relationship, agreeing a focus, making substantial emotional contact (Stern's 'now moments', Winnicott's 'sacred moments', and Balint's 'Erlebnis' can be very important in expediting therapy when they happen in the first session) as well as encouraging the client to develop a self-reflective capacity by thinking about the focus and the experience of the encounter with the therapist, can assist in enabling the client to become their own therapist during the course of treatment which is, in some sense, the aim of short-term interventions.

The therapeutic focus

The concept of a therapeutic focus has a long history in the dynamic therapies. French (1952) introduced the concepts of the focal and the nuclear conflicts. Focal conflicts are 'preconscious, close to the surface' and 'explain most clinical material in a given session'. They are derivative of earlier, developmental nuclear conflicts, which 'underlie behaviour and lead to focal conflicts'. Thus 'nuclear' conflicts would incorporate early history and traumatic experiences, previous difficulties and their precipitating events, family constellations and the repetitive patterns associated with all three.

The establishment of, and working within, a core focus are among the most problematic issues which those coming from a psychodynamic background and training face when beginning open-ended therapy. This is a result of the need to pay *selective attention* and *benign neglect* in focal therapy. Both are ways of avoiding becoming overwhelmed by the sheer volume and breadth of clinical material. Both challenge orthodox analytic practice where the therapist enters every session 'without memory or desire' and all material is 'relevant'. In true post-modernist fashion, no material is implicitly more important than any other. This is not the case in time-limited therapy where material in the realm of the core focus is considered significant, while clinical material falling outside the immediate realm of the focus needs to be set aside or considered solely in terms of whether it has any bearing on, or relevance to, the central focus.

The focus serves to protect both therapist and client from becoming overwhelmed by clinical material which neither party can make sense of; it is a case of being able to *see the trees through the wood*. Since it is mutually agreed near the beginning of therapy and constantly borne in mind and refined thereafter, the dangers of the therapist imposing a therapeutic focus on a bemused and unsuspecting client are reduced. It is important to note that the focus is not the result of an insight or interpretation by the therapist. The focus is mutually arrived at and agreed by both client and therapist, and, ideally, is 'something that the [client] has always known, sometimes clearly, but most often as a vague, never ending, disturbing haze of consciousness' (Shefler 2001). As such, the focus is not imposed on the client or excessively rigid and can change over time. It is inevitably initially tentative and incomplete; it does not explain everything: 'it is a map, not the territory itself' (Schacht 1984). The focus enables a sense of narrative coherence to be maintained; it provides the central theme which weaves together sessions which may appear unrelated, and helps organise therapeutic experience. The risk of 'therapeutic drift', as evidenced in many open-ended therapies, is also avoided.

Contemporary dynamic therapists tend to take a relational, emotional or dynamic issue as their central focus. Foci can be related to content (based on an issue or difficulty) or process (e.g. the importance of being able to develop a self-reflective mindfulness in relation to other people and self states). The latter is particularly helpful in relation to borderline states of mind. It maybe that part of the focus will be the client's transference to time in relation to the therapy. This can be both positive and negative. For example, the client may be relieved that he does not have to attend for a long time or that he can be helped in a short time or, more negatively, angry that he cannot have as long as he wants or feels he needs. Often these will be revealed only by paying minute attention to the therapeutic process (speech, mannerisms, metaphors, use of body) and the affective communication as experienced in the counter-transference.

The central, 'umbrella', focus is generally in the area of the client's *recurrent interpersonal patterns*, and how they are created, developed and maintained in the client's current life. More specific 'sub-foci' are given by Groves (1996). They may reflect the following:

- a developmental stage (such as separation);
- a state (such as grief);
- a conflict (such as writer's block);
- a symptom (such as anxiety);
- a drive (such as sex);
- a life pursuit (such as a job);
- a role (such as being a parent);
- an identity (such as being gay).

As Groves (1996) says, the list is relatively endless but will also depend on the specific theory of emotional development held by the therapist. The focus is in part determined by the therapist's theoretical approach which could place differing emphasis on establishing a focus which is either primarily symptomatic, based on a specific issue, or broadly characterlogical, based on a personality trait. An interpersonal focus lends itself to more emotionally expressive therapy while a purely symptomatic focus is likely to lead to the therapy being more supportive. Developmental considerations play a part in considering a core focus – the same event may have a different meaning at different ages and developmental life stages.

What unites dynamic therapists is that the factor underlying the major focus is in the area of the client's significant relationships including the therapeutic alliance. How the discrete sub-foci link with the core relational conflict will inform the therapy. The therapeutic triangle provides the structure for the focus to be addressed. Many sub-foci, since they are not mutually exclusive, can be in evidence concurrently.

Generally short-term therapy reformulates the discrete presenting symptom or complaint in relational terms while returning to it when the therapy, or session, is in danger of becoming diffuse. Friedman and Fanger (1991) advise beginning with the metaphoric function of the symptom, which becomes a foci, then planning a course of therapy with the client which, couched 'in positive language' isolates issues that 'are dear to [the client], ... are [therapeutically] possible', and are congruent with the client's idiom and culture.

The formulation of a focus in itself poses problems for the analytic short-term therapist:

> Formulating a focus ... demands a high degree of sensitive observation, a good knowledge of psychoanalytic theory, *freedom from compulsive ways of thinking about psychopathology* and above all, *resisting the attraction of well worn psychoanalytical phrases.* (Enid Balint, in Balint 1973, my italics)

Dynamic therapists may find these difficult to relinquish.

It is important for the central focus to remain relatively fluid. The therapist needs to strike a balance between too rigid an attachment to the focus, in which case, therapy will become formulaic and mechanistic, and allowing the therapy to drift – or to follow too many discursive meanderings – so that little of substance will be fully addressed. The focus becomes a 'navigational beacon' (Stadter 2004). A useful discipline for the therapist is for him to ask himself when a sense of drift in the session appears 'how does this relate to the focus?' This can lead to the reaffirmation of the focus incorporating new material or to the realignment of the focus as a result of new material. Stadter believes that less experienced therapists set the focus too quickly before the therapeutic alliance has been consolidated, while experienced long-term therapists tend to need a 'lot of evidence' before setting a focus, leaving little time for it to be addressed. The danger exists that formulating a specific focus too early runs the risk of getting it wrong and, in neglecting other material, ensuring that the therapy proceeds up the wrong path. However, clients, as active participants in the therapeutic process, tend to point this out when it happens. Leaving it too late runs the risk that the therapy may be almost over before the therapist knows how to proceed and intervene. A useful guide to the timing of the focus is when the therapist has some inkling and knowledge of the client's idiom and relational functioning. This can generally be identified relatively early in therapy. Enid Balint calls this the 'aha' experience where the focus 'arrives in a flash' while Malan views the focus as something that crystallises between therapist and client relatively early on in therapy. 'In a certain sense,' states Groves, 'once the two people sit down together and begin their relationship ... the focus chooses itself growing naturally out of the subjective space between the two' (1996, p. 99). In general, the focus arises out of the meeting of the client's presenting complaint and narrative, the affective contact with therapist and the therapist's philosophy of cure and treatment. The client's idiom meets that of the therapist.

One way of conceptualising, and thinking about foci is to see them as an area where the therapeutic process and relationship meet the client's developmental/historical stage. This is represented in Figure 5.1 where the vertical axis represents development and the horizontal axis represents the therapeutic process. The focus can be established by plotting where the two axes intersect.

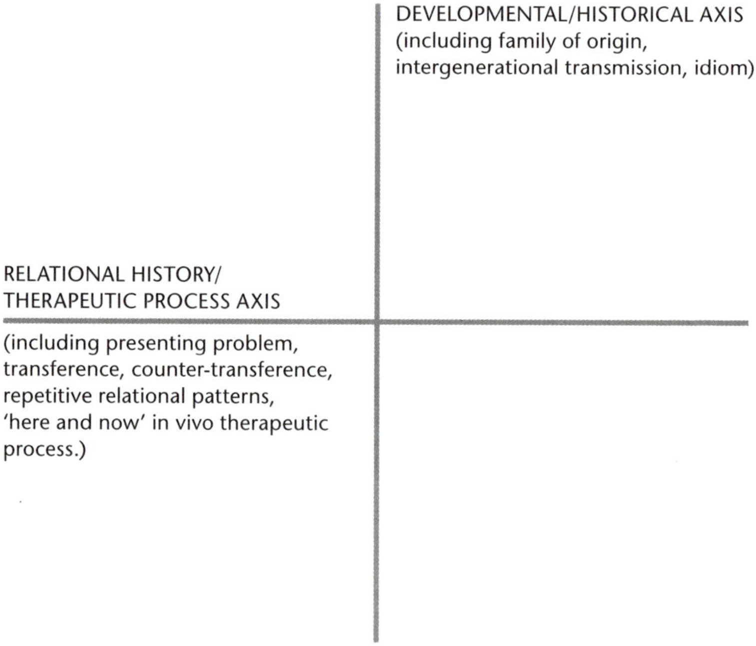

DEVELOPMENTAL/HISTORICAL AXIS
(including family of origin, intergenerational transmission, idiom)

RELATIONAL HISTORY/
THERAPEUTIC PROCESS AXIS

(including presenting problem, transference, counter-transference, repetitive relational patterns, 'here and now' in vivo therapeutic process.)

FIGURE 5.1 Establishing a therapeutic focus

Of the manifold foci that can be set, it is also possible to view foci from differing levels of the client's presentation and development. Stadter (2004) distinguishes between *symptomatic* and *dynamic* foci.

It will be noted that this is not dissimilar to French's *focal* and *nuclear* conflicts. The former address the symptom and how handicapping it might be in the client's life as well as the distress it has elicited, while dynamic foci centre on the client's underlying intra and interpersonal structure and how it affects their relationships with themselves and others. Optimally both foci are addressed simultaneously; by addressing the dynamic focus, one is inevitably also speaking to the symptomatic one. In some form, it is advantageous to be able to work with a dynamic focus although where this is not possible working on the symptomatic focus may well be sufficient. An important distinction here is that working with the dynamic focus is likely to be emotionally expressive while working solely with a symptomatic focus is likely to be more constricted and supportive, although appropriate for certain clients and contexts. These ideas have been elaborated by Smith (2006). The importance of the focus in this context is that it must be limited enough for progress to be made on it within a short-term time frame and that it engages the client's interest and curiosity. The latter cannot be underestimated. While the long-term therapist approaches every session 'without memory or desire', the short-term therapist needs to be aware of the issues which the therapeutic couple is working on at any given time. The short-term therapist must also be free from preconceptions when setting a focus. Setting a focus is a genuine process of mutual discovery between therapist and client and the task itself can be extremely therapeutic. One can also think of having a 'trial focus' where a focus is tentatively presented and the client is encouraged to accept or reject it. Here it is important to see whether the client's curiosity is engaged – again, the issue of therapeutic surprise might be helpful in facilitating this.

A further way of conceptualising the focus has been elaborated by Smith (2005) building on the four approaches to brief therapy elaborated by Messer and Warren (1995). The *drive/structural model*, related to the use of the triangle of person and the triangle of conflict, enables a focus to be generated by the use of the two triangles while the *relational model* would use the interpersonal process, narrative, idiom and the cyclical maladaptive relational pattern to construct a focus. *Integrative models* would give primacy to empathic mirroring and the client's experiential state and self esteem to construct the focus. Finally, more *eclectic models* (Gustafson) would combine psychodynamic and systemic frameworks to attend not only to the intrapsychic and interpersonal domains of experience, but also to the social context in which they occur. These are not mutually exclusive and it is possible to construct a focus which relates to all four domains. Metaphors, symbols and the client's personal idiom prove particularly helpful in this context. Personal Idioms/ Metaphors (relating, say, to Intimacy, Control, Dependency, Trust, Anger, Sexuality, Boundaries, Rejection, Separation) can be linked to all four domains and form the basis of a generic focus.

Alan

Alan was a young man who consulted a counsellor because he felt 'off the rails'. In his second year at college, he felt he was not coping and was unsure whether he wished to stay or leave the institution. He felt rather hopeless and did not expect anything of use would come out of his consultation – he had consulted counsellors before without any real sense that they had helped him and was unsure whether to come back for another session. In his family his father had suffered from clinical depression, had become suicidal and was sectioned under the Mental Health Act. Alan's sense of hopelessness – in relation to himself and others – was his pervasive personal idiom and, as can be seen, related to all four domains as well as to a number of the areas highlighted above. The counsellor suggested an initial focus of helping Alan decide whether he wanted to return for a further session which symbolically also addressed the issue of whether to stay or leave the institution as well as the interpersonal dilemma which pervaded Alan's current and past life – whether anyone could be of help to him. Interestingly – Alan did return for a further four sessions – his personal idiom of hopelessness was closely related to an anxious identification with his father.

Alan demonstrates how a focus can be cumulative, incorporating past, present and the 'here and now' of the therapeutic process. The use of metaphor (with the issue of whether Alan wanted to return for another session) symbolically represented other areas of his life as well as speaking to his personal idiom. This can become a shared collaborative language between the client and the therapist to promote the construction of a focus and enable core conflicts to be addressed in a symbolic form. It also allows – as the case of Alan shows – defences to be circumvented without confronting them head on.

The important aspect of the core focus is that most relevant clinical material can be linked with it. This needs to be incorporated into the triangles of insight/persons and therapy described in Chapter 3. The client's idiom, narrative, and presenting complaint as they apply to the past, present, as well as the 'here and now' therapeutic relationship, become the focus of the therapy. It follows from this that when the focus cannot be determined (or if it is vague or diffuse), short-term therapy is contraindicated. Clients with vague, chronic difficulties, as well as clients who fluctuate between several different problem areas without the wish to settle on one focal area, are less likely to benefit from short-term therapy. Therapists need, however, to guard against the danger of assuming that no focal area exists when it is their own theoretical assumptions that prevents them discovering one. Not all foci need be Oedipal in nature. Clients whose predominant idiom suggests they are struggling with issues to do with separation–individuation and basic trust–mistrust may not lend themselves to discrete foci and may, as we have seen, require a more supportive, 'holding environment' where the focus consists of the continuous and ongoing recognition of the client's use of the therapist to monitor and regulate internal affects and states of mind. For others, a 'partial focus' may be more appropriate. This reinforces the need to ensure that wherever possible the client is encouraged to give examples of the context in which feeling states occur or inter-personal difficulties arise. This is particularly relevant with clients presenting with borderline difficulties. However, even with borderline clients, there are times when specific metaphors can be worked with as foci.

Chris

Chris was a highly impulsive, labile and attention-seeking young man whose father had been malignly neglectful and disinterested while his mother was experienced by Chris as more benign but as very intrusive. Chris has a history of taking regular overdoses leading to hospitalisation and regularly missed sessions. After one such occasion, shortly after beginning treatment, Chris thought he would apply to become an ambulance driver. Two issues dominated treatment. In relation to his missed sessions (and symbolically his overdose attempts): should the therapist intervene like his intrusive, if benign, mother, or not respond at all and risk becoming like Chris' neglectful, and malign, father? Equally the issue of Chris' interest in becoming an ambulance driver shortly after taking an overdose could be seen as reflecting two different parts of himself – a self-destructive one and a life-affirming one. Which of these were being brought to therapy? These were used as generic foci for the treatment and were able to be addressed by the use of a 'part object' (i.e. parts of the self) approach discussed in Chapter 3 which Chris found useful.

An exception to the reservation expressed above (that the absence of a focus is one of the contraindications for short-term work) would be adolescence where vagueness and confusion might be developmentally appropriate and the termination of therapy indicated when a focus has been gleaned or achieved (see Coren 1997). Failure to generate a focus may also be as informative as eliciting one; the process of the difficulty of yielding a focus may reveal a lot about the client's idiom and whether short-term therapy is likely to be helpful.

A further way of approaching the issue of how to set a focus is to have a hierarchy of foci.

Margaret

Margaret consulted her counsellor concerned that she was unable to complete her thesis despite being a few months from finishing her studies. Her sense of self was closely bound up with academic success and always had been. She was a gregarious and sociable young woman with many friends who spent week evenings socializing while at weekends would shut herself away, attempting to work, find she could not, and then be tormented with suicidal ruminations. When she recounted these to the counsellor, Margaret went to great lengths to reassure him 'not to worry' since she had no intention of acting on them. She came from a family where her parents had separated in Margaret's teens with her mother moving to India to lead a more contemplatory life. While mother was seen as vulnerable, unstable and somewhat flighty, father was academically demanding and expected a lot from Margaret. In the session, Margaret was tearful, emotional and overtly respectful towards the counsellor.

What to focus on? One way is to have a hierarchy of focus, along the lines of a hierarchy of need. What was Margaret's most pressing (symptomatic) problem and how was it maintained by historical/personality/dynamic issues? A hierarchy would read something like the following:

1. Margaret's difficulty with her thesis and a suggestion that she was uneasy with leaving the academic world with which her self-esteem was closely linked. By not working on her thesis she was subverting herself by staying the same.
2. Margaret's elaborate false self, where academic work is intrinsically linked with her self-esteem, can also be seen to be in evidence when her sociable self implodes at weekends and she considers self-destructive acts. Additionally, the need to please and appease her demanding father academically (which suggested compliance in the therapy may become an issue) and needing to look after a vulnerable and unresponsive mother (witness the reassurance offered to the counsellor in relation to the suicidal ruminations), could become possible foci.

3. Margaret's defence against any anger at her parents, especially her mother who had left the family to meet her own needs. This could elicit a third level of foci where Margaret's worry about her identifications with a vulnerable, selfish mother and a dismissive and demanding father were explored. Inevitably these would also be manifest in the therapeutic relationship.

The focus could initially be on (1) and progress via (2) to (3). This would be an example of how the focus could be developed cumulatively. Alternatively, the use of metaphor and symbols, might suggest by addressing (1) the counsellor was simultaneously addressing (2) and (3) as well. A hierarchy allows the therapist to start with the area of maximum pain – often the presenting problem – which is welcomed by the client and then generalise from there to other areas of the client's life.

For the therapist, it is helpful to keep a note of the focus and how it develops over time. Since the short-term therapist may well feel pressurised by the limited time, there is a danger of sticking very concretely to the initial focus and not allowing new material to modify and develop the focus.

One of the advantages of developing a discrete focus is that it reduces the possibility that short-term therapy (or the therapist) becomes an 'exciting object' (Fairbairn 1952; Stadter 2004). This is an object that excites but ultimately disappoints – a particular danger in short-term therapies where clients (and therapists) expect more from the experience than is possible. Repeated and constant attention to the agreed focus – or how potentially extraneous material may relate to it – has the effect of forcing the client – and therapist – to confront what can and cannot be done in therapy, and thus reduce the possibility of an exciting object transference becoming destructive.

Ideally the focus is a distillation of the client's core relational problem, incorporating both symptomatic and dynamic elements, and assists in providing both client and therapist with an overall conceptualisation of the problem, enables therapeutic drift (where the therapeutic dyad becomes sidetracked by possibly interesting but less relevant side issues) to be avoided, and guides the interventions of the therapist. Evidence suggests that treatment outcomes are enhanced by tracking the focus, modifying it as appropriate and avoiding being sidetracked by extraneous issues which may result from the therapist allowing his concentration to drift away from a focal state of mind. Focus drift can be reinforced by the client's interpersonal style (being vague and hard to follow), the client throwing up a smokescreen to circumvent difficult issues, or the appearance of a crisis often manifest close to the termination date (Binder 2004). The important point here is for both therapist and client to be aware when this is occurring and what function it may have in the treatment.

The ability to discover and articulate a core focus necessarily depends on the active participation of the therapist. This is a further challenge to psychodynamic short-term therapists.

The active therapist: a psychodynamic contradiction in terms?

Therapeutic activity contrasts with the more passive, exploratory, and leisurely model of time-unlimited therapies. Many clients in their pre-transference will expect a more conversational model of interaction with their therapists and are puzzled when this is absent without explanation. In focal time-limited therapy, an active therapist serves to maintain the focus and limit dependence as well as keeping the emotional tension high. This helps to link all material with the issue to be dealt with and prevents regression which may be untherapeutic and complicate the termination of therapy. The therapist models a therapeutic manner which, by its active engagement, indicates both therapeutic interest and hope as well as the expectation that the client will be similarly active in the attempt to master their problems or difficulty.

This active participation between client and therapist does not necessarily come naturally. As early as 1942, Sandor Rado drew attention to the need from the beginning of therapy for the therapist to attempt to 'counteract the patient's tendency to sink himself into a safe comfortable transference neurosis'. A similar danger confronts the therapist less used to working in a time-limited fashion. Alexander, when stressing the need for therapeutic activity, commented on the assumption that a passive therapist 'will solve everything as if by magic' and that this has the effect of 'prolonging many treatments unduly'. He went on to suggest that:

> Curbing the patient's tendency to procrastinate and to substitute analytic experience for reality ... (through careful manipulation of the transference relationship, by timely directives and encouragement) ... is one of the most effective means of shortening treatment. (in Barton 1971)

As we have seen, Alexander's emphasis on the active, engaged therapist rapidly became discredited and, in an effort to shield itself from Alexander's legacy, psychoanalysis retreated behind the belief that anything which was not 'interpretative' was likely to be 'suggestive' or in danger of 'influencing' the client. Anything that could not be classed as an interpretation was 'not psychoanalysis'.

However, even Freud had suggested that in the treatment of some cases (e.g. phobias) at some point, the analyst will have to encourage the client to engage in activities that he was avoiding. Therapy in this sense must be in the service of life, not the other way around. Freud was also aware of the problem of 'suggestion' although there were times when the analyst had to serve as 'mentor and guide'. This, more 'educative' function, is used selectively by contemporary short-term therapists as in the case study of William in the previous chapter. However, the use of words such as encouragement, manipulation, and direction ensured that the belief grew within the analytic tradition that, at worst, the client was going to be coerced, influenced and managed. Psychoanalytic suspicion of anything that approximates to 'influence and suggestion' can be traced back to these roots. In an effort to distance itself from the Freud of hypnosis and catharsis, psychoanalysis and dynamic therapies more generally, went to the other end of the spectrum; the concept of therapeutic neutrality and 'free floating attention'. At times, it seemed as though any intervention by the therapist was intrusive and, when not interpreting the transference neurosis directly, a failure on the part of the therapist. This led to psychoanalysis remaining non interactional and 'non-suggestive' so that the client's inner world could emerge in an uncontaminated and pure form. The worst that could happen to an analyst was to effect a 'transference cure'; that is, a cure by the 'personality' of the therapist. In passing, it is worth questioning whether there are any other forms of 'cure' in the dynamic therapies other than those achieved via the therapeutic engagement of the personalities of the therapist and the client. This is increasingly shown in efficacy studies where the skill, and personal attributes, of the therapist are the major variables affecting positive clinical outcomes. This is especially true of short-term therapy.

Short-term therapies are increasingly turning passive into active with respect to the therapist stance. This is particularly true of the more experiential therapies (Fosha 2000) but it must be noted that therapeutic activity does not imply manipulation or explicit guidance. An active therapist is, however, required to attend to the focus, reflect on here and now therapeutic interaction in clarifying and collaboratively exploring the client's material, making links between the therapeutic triangles and, at times, structuring sessions. It also implies a much more proactive use of self on behalf of the clinician which is very different from the more traditional models.

Therapeutic neutrality

The myth of therapeutic neutrality and the therapist's 'non-influential' posture has been challenged by, among others, Mitchell (1997). Talking from an open-ended, as opposed to a short-term, framework, Mitchell makes the point that it is less the interpretations made in the analytic setting which are mutative but more the client's discovery of 'a different kind of experience [in therapy] ... than they encountered in their childhood'. This is very similar to the notion of 'therapeutic surprise' discussed earlier. Since this is a central facet of therapy Mitchell implies that the therapist should seek to provide it more actively than analytic notions of 'neutrality' or 'abstinence' allow. There has been a belief, still widely held in therapeutic circles, that only therapeutic neutrality, passivity and abstinence can guard against intrusion, influence and suggestion. Mitchell, however, makes the point that a passive analytic stance can be experienced very differently by the client and be perceived in various differing ways by different clients. A therapist may think, through their non-intrusive passivity, that they are being neutral, while his client may experience him as being withholding, sadistic or seductive. Even silence is participation – Mitchell sees silence as being manipulative if its consequences remain unexplored in the ensuing therapy. It is, as Gill (1994) says, 'not the content of what the analyst does that makes it analytic; it is the curiosity and openness to explore the impact of one's own participation'. Seen in this light, therapeutic silence or reticence is just as potentially manipulative as activity; more so in the sense that it is rarely acknowledged or examined. Frustration is just as much a manipulation of the transference as activity or 'gratification'.

Mitchell tells an amusing anecdote to illustrate how therapeutic passivity can actually impede the progress of therapy. A client, who was in therapy with an analyst who adopted a 'withholding, blank screen' stance, became aware that after certain material the therapist's chair would squeak. In the absence of any explicit acknowledgement of this, she decided, believing that this 'betrayed some form of discomfort on his part', to use the squeaks to guide her contributions. The squeak, perhaps the most significant therapeutic material, was never analysed. This was, says Mitchell,

> ... ironic and tragic. The analyst was apparently convinced that he was protecting the patient's autonomy by not interacting, while that very denial created a secret, bizarre interaction that likely included some actual features of what the analyst thought and felt, expressed in an unintended fashion.

Neutrality, silence and passivity do not deal with the problems of influence and suggestion. They are as likely, if not acknowledged, to be as potentially coercive as therapeutic activity. The important point, whichever therapeutic stance is taken, is for it to be acknowledged, voiced and placed in the service of the client's therapy. Nevertheless therapeutic activity is still a problematic concept for many dynamic therapists in short-term therapy, not least since psychodynamic trainings still tend to be profoundly ambivalent and suspicious about departing from a more classic analytic stance. This is unfortunate since short-term dynamic therapists wish to start from valuing the client's strengths and adaptive qualities rather than starting from the elucidation of pathology or deficits – the bottle being half full rather than half empty – and this requires positive affirmation of the client's strengths and using them to address the client's problems. The therapist's responsiveness to, and encouragement of, the client's curiosity about themselves and how that can be harnessed to facilitate change, are central facets of the short-term therapist's stance and require an active engagement with the therapeutic process, making 'neutrality' (or, as it perhaps better termed 'unresponsiveness') untenable.

Therapeutic activity

In focal therapy the therapist and his contributions are there to be thought, and talked, about in relation to the client's core focal conflict. In time-limited focal therapies, silence can impede therapeutic progress by encouraging 'therapeutic drift' away from the focus, and, not infrequently especially with more concrete and borderline clients, raising anxiety to the extent that it threatens the therapeutic alliance. Silence or activity, in as much as they are interventions as any other, need to be used cautiously. All therapeutic interventions, including silence, need to be viewed in terms of how they answer the following question: How necessary is this intervention in the maintenance of the focus and how does it relate to the client's core relational difficulty? Therapeutic activity also means taking charge of the therapeutic frame and its boundaries. Therapeutic activity must not be confused with advice giving, confrontation, or directiveness. It does not mean coercing or influencing the client in directions more favoured by the therapist. The client needs to be heard rather than overwhelmed by the therapist's insights and suggestions.

While Freud (1912) advocated a suspension of 'judgment, and [giving] our impartial attention to everything there is to observe ... maintaining the same evenly suspended attention in the face of all one hears,' he also, in the case of Little Hans (1909), suggested that although 'it is not in the least our business to understand a case at once', this understanding can be achieved when 'we have received enough impressions of it'. These 'impressions', which come close to what we have termed contemporary 'idioms', are what form the focus of the therapy and can only be elicited by the active engagement of the therapist.

Therapeutic activity aids the formation of an early therapeutic alliance. The creation of a stable, safe environment, the establishment of a focus early in therapy and a balance between responsiveness and directness, all help engage the client in the joint undertaking of short-term therapy. Therapeutic activity also aids the swift response to any resistance.

Resistance

As we have seen in previous chapters, focal therapy can only succeed if any resistance, or negative feeling, however muted or disguised, is taken up promptly. Traditionally, resistance is viewed as that 'which keeps the unconscious unconscious' (Levenson 1995). Ideas and sensations which are potentially unpleasant are excluded from awareness via repression. This is a different perspective from that adopted by the short-term focal therapist who views resistance less as a rejection of awareness of some problematic or painful aspect of mental life, but more a response to the person of the therapist and what he may represent in the client's mind. Coming for counselling is often ambivalently experienced; it can be a risk becoming vulnerable and subjecting defences, which have worked reasonably well over time, to scrutiny. Consequently, therapy, or the therapist, may be seen as threatening by the client and it is this which must be understood. In all probability it will form part of the client's idiom, the understanding of which will contribute to the core focus.

Neophyte therapists tend to have clinical difficulty with the concept of resistance, and negative transference in general, fearing either that if the negative is acknowledged the client will not return or, conversely, that resistance is a stubborn refusal on the client's part to accept the truth of their situation and the therapist's insight. Focal therapy teaches us the opposite: that unless negative feelings are acknowledged and worked with from the beginning, the client will not return. Confrontation, or denial, is less helpful than attempting to understand what the negative transference – or pre-transference – may represent in the context of the emerging focus:

> ... the patient's manner of resistance usually has more implications for how that patient interacts with others than the original content he or she was avoiding expressing. The patient's way of resisting, to a large extent, determines his or her personality style. To escape what is feared, what is being defended against, becomes the person's characteristic mode of relating, which often leads to the dysfunctional interchanges with others. (Levenson, 1995, pp. 188–9)

Challenging and naming negative feelings and resistance in the first session can foster a stronger therapeutic alliance, not least since the client can see that you are not afraid to broach more difficult or painful subjects which he may be attempting to avoid. It also suggests that the therapy can safely incorporate difference, hostility and ambivalence, possibly unlike the client's other relationships. Resistance and the negative transference may, like other material in focal therapy, need to be approached from an 'at one removed', metaphorical level.

Jason

Jason, a 28-year-old Irishman, had recently arrived in Britain to begin a professional career. He made an appointment with a counsellor at the suggestion of his GP after collapsing in the street with chest pains for which no physical cause was found. This followed a long history of mystery ailments. Jason explained his background of being a 'worrier'. He was an only child of over-attentive parents who were themselves highly strung, socially withdrawn, and prone to stress-related illnesses. Although affable and sociable, he had not had any sexual relationships and acknowledged that he was confused 'about that whole area ... I don't really need a relation-ship; it's just another thing to worry about.' Jason could only worry about one thing at a time. The most striking thing about Jason's initial consulta-tion was his manner. He was pleasant and courteous while continually making reference to the fact that he knew what the problem was and had been able in the past to conquer his problems by 'talking myself out of my difficulties'; he knew he was a worrier and that his concerns about his health were ways in which he dealt with other possible worries but 'I don't want to become like Oprah ... no offence to you but I don't want counselling to become another thing to worry about.' Jason's idiom became apparent quite quickly in the opening meeting but dealing with his resistance needed some thought – merely confronting it head on (along the lines 'You are worried about your body as a way of avoiding worrying about your mind') would have led to Jason using his characteristic way of dealing with stressful mate-rial; a pleasant and polite denial coupled with a statement suggesting that it was a valid hypothesis which he had already thought about but, on reflec-tion, not one that he could subscribe to. Instead the counsellor took up Jason's statement that he did not want to add counselling to the things he had to worry about by saying that this was exactly what the counsellor thought could be helpful – after all by worrying about coming to see the counsellor, Jason might 'forget' about his other worries since, as he had earlier stated, he was the kind of person who 'could only worry about one thing at a time'. This also had the effect of linking the process of counselling with Jason's current anxiety about relationships and his parents' ambiva-lence about social relationships.

By promptly addressing negative feelings, one is likely to be addressing the client's core idiom as well as the triangles of persons and therapy. As we have previously noted, resistance can be central to the therapeutic process and present itself it disguised forms which require decoding (Becky in Chapter 2). A similar case is outlined in Binder (2004) of a client who talked constantly of her mechanic not repairing her car properly which functioned as a commentary on her therapy. The important aspect of resistance in short-term therapy is that it requires acknowledging as soon as it appears to enable it to be thought about and placed in the service of the core focus.

Transference interpretations

Similar modifications of technique are needed when thinking about transference interpretations. Traditionally seen as the sole curative factor in analysis, dynamic focal therapies tend to differ in the extent to which the personal transference needs to be directly interpreted as opposed to the necessity to address 'here and now' transference manifestations. Historically, the positions taken in relation to transference interpretations by time-limited therapists tend to differ along conservative and radical lines. Conservatives, believing brief therapies are more aimed at mild problems of recent onset, as opposed to characterlogical problems, have tended to avoid transference interpretations since they have been viewed as premature unless a transference neurosis has developed. The radical camp, believing that shorter-term therapies could address more severe problems, have suggested that transference interpretations, in addition to historical reconstruction, are appropriate and can lead to lasting characterlogical change. Here again the fault line tends to be between clients who are able to use transference interpretations and insight-orientated techniques, and those who cannot. Increasingly, however, the evidence suggests that therapists may need to be more radical than they imagine in who can be helped by short-term work, but this does not necessarily apply to transference interpretations which, if delivered without relevance to the focus, triangle of persons, or insensitively, are increasingly seen to be unhelpful and threaten the therapeutic alliance.

The emphasis in contemporary short-term therapy is less on the achievement of insight, than towards using the transference actively in the service of the core focus. It views interpretations (and perhaps linking or interventions aimed at the therapeutic process are better terms) as aiding the development of the dynamic focal hypothesis and helping a reformulation of the problem rather than seeing interpretations as leading to insight, leading to cure. Indeed, in short-term therapy, insight, or any change in perception, can occur during sessions, between sessions or a considerable time after therapy has finished and, although a welcome aspect of treatment, is not seen as solely responsible for any progress.

Interpretations in the area of transference, particularly ones that link feelings about the therapist with significant, current or past, others tend to be most successful. While many clients who can benefit from short-term, focal psychodynamic therapies do not need transference interpretations, Groves (1996) suggests that transference interpretations are appropriate in the following circumstances:

■ Transference feelings have become 'a point of urgency and/or a major resistance'.

- Transference 'distortions have disrupted the therapeutic alliance and interpretations are necessary to strengthen the alliance'.
- Conflicts in the transference 'directly reflect conflicts responsible for the presenting problem or maladaptive character traits'.
- The client is able to 'observe, understand or tolerate' transference interpretations.
- Where the 'length of the remaining treatment will allow sufficient exploration of whatever transference interpretations are made'.

In general, direct comments on the transference are more likely to be helpful when the therapeutic alliance is threatened with rupture or is in difficulties.

They are inappropriate or unnecessary when:

- Transference distortions do not develop.
- 'The point of emotional urgency and the related conflicts are fixed on current events and relationships outside the treatment situation'.
- A fragile therapeutic alliance will be further jeopardised by a distressing and unacceptable transference interpretation.
- The client is unable to 'observe, understand, tolerate or use transference interpretations'.
- Transference distortions are not clearly related to the presenting problem or 'significant maladaptive character traits'.
- The remaining time available is too limited to attempt 'even a partial analysis of transference material'. (Groves 1996, pp. 256–7)

A helpful distinction is the one mentioned earlier between the classical transference neurosis and the 'here and now' everyday more relational transference. The latter needs to be regularly interpreted in the area of the therapeutic triangle, while caution needs to be exercised in developing and interpreting the former. It needs to be remembered that many clients will hear transference interpretations as either a reproach or a form of criticism. This applies particularly to the more vulnerable or borderline client.

At some level, it depends on how clinicians define interpretations: are they interventions which make previously unconscious material amenable to consciousness, or can they be seen more on a continuum from complex formulations that are seen to facilitate insight to simple comments linking various aspects of here and now clinical material with the aim of developing a shared understanding?

Short-term therapists are more likely to find themselves on the latter end of this spectrum, and find it most helpful to begin with the 'here and now' in vivo therapeutic process and work backwards. As Scharff (1992) has suggested:

> Interpretation begins with linking and clarifying and proceeds all the way to understanding how whatever happened long ago in the patient's life influences current difficulties in relationships. The most effective interpretation begins with the current reenactment in the transference and counter-transference and proceeds to the reconstruction of repressed internal object relationship.

Increasingly, the more supportive short-term therapies make minimal use of transference interpretations as classically defined.

A useful way of teasing out the subtle difference between differing forms of transference manifestations, and the different responses required to each, is outlined by Stadter (2004). Drawing on Winnicott's distinction between the *environment mother* and the *object mother*, Stadter posits two forms of transference: the *contextual* and the *focused*. The contextual transference is related to the Winnicottian notion of the holding function of maternal ego support for the child's playful exploration of the world which facilitates the child's capacity to be alone and master his environment. This (environment mother) functions in the background providing a secure environment (or context) for development and growth. The focused transference is linked to Winnicott's 'object mother', who is in the foreground and with whom the child develops an intense bond incorporating 'love and hate, affection and aggression'. The contextual transference is 'prominent in the early phase of treatment and in brief therapy maybe predominant throughout'. Here the therapist is related to (and experienced) as a background supportive presence and, by definition, therapy, is not very interpretative, while, when the focused transference is paramount, the client relates to the therapist more as an 'object' mother where strong and powerful emotions are directed at the therapist. In the focused transference, interpretations play a larger part. This is a useful clinical distinction and can also apply to the nature of the short-term work which can be undertaken in different contexts and with different clinical populations (see Chapter 7).

It needs to be acknowledged that differing therapeutic traditions have different views of how change comes about. More dynamic therapies see interpretation as a way in which the client's self-under-standing can be facilitated giving him more control over his life, while more existential/humanistic therapies would see the mean-ingful therapeutic relationship and empathic attunement at the core of therapeutic change. More corrective therapies would seek change through direct therapist interventions.

We have seen that focal therapy demands that the opportunities for developing a transference neurosis are kept to a minimum. This is in keeping with Freud's warning about the dangers of transference gratification when the client's experience of the transference replaces the desire to be cured. Paradoxically one way of preventing the development of a transference neurosis is to interpret the transfer-ence, very early in therapy. This alerts the client to the dangers of regression and links transferential material with the relational focus.

One development in psychoanalytic theory with regard to trans-ference of direct relevance to short-term therapy is the importance placed on the client's reaction to the interpretation rather than the effect of the interpretation itself. Whether an interpretation is 'right' or 'wrong' is of less importance than the way it is experienced and internalised by the client. The client may have a 'relationship to the interpretation' (Racker 1968) which reveals much about their idiom and the way they are emotionally processing the therapeutic exper-ience. I recently suggested to a client, whose presenting problem was difficulty with her boyfriend, that she appeared somewhat hostile to me not unlike her description and experience of her partner. She refuted this saying 'hostile' was the wrong word; angry yes, but not hostile – 'hostility is what I feel towards my mother'! It is the emotional response to the interpretation or comment that illu-minates rather than the intervention *per se*.

Focal therapy sees what happens in the transference relation-ship as running in parallel to life experience outside the consulting room. The transference relationship is used by the client in the service of real life; it is less a repetition (although it is likely to be a recapitulation) of previous relationships than a rehearsal for future ones. Interpretations then are more in the area of what Levenson (1995) calls 'plausible possibilities based upon what the [client] is doing or saying' rather than reductive truths as 'known and uncov-ered by the therapist'.

It may well be that the emphasis which psychoanalysis has placed on what is seen to be the 'correct interpretation' has served to obscure what is centrally important in therapeutic change. A trans-ference interpretation can be technically correct but clinically inept.

Focal therapy teases out transferential patterns based on the client's experiences in therapy which are then concretely named, thus avoiding the danger of premature interpretations which are likely to be met with the client's hostility or confusion.

As with the topic of resistance, the importance placed by analytic orthodoxy on interpretations which are based upon the transference neurosis, make it more difficult for time-limited therapists coming from psychodynamic backgrounds to relinquish 'deep' interpretations. It is, says Mitchell, not unlike the old joke about 'the narcissist who suddenly says to his conversational captive, 'Enough about me. Tell me about yourself. What do you think of me?' In a similar vein, the therapist who can only oscillate between silence and transference comments is saying 'Enough of me making interpretative statements about what is going on in your mind. Let's talk about my mind. Here's what you think is happening in my mind'! (Mitchell 1997, p. 133). What would be unfortunate for the short-term dynamic therapist is the belief that interpretations in general, and transference interpretations in particular, are the core conditions for therapeutic change, and that they feel they are not working dynamically unless sessions include a substantive amount of interpretative work. Indeed, there is a suggestion that interpretations, as classically defined, are correlated with poor outcomes, especially with clients who have a history of poor relationships (Stadter 2004; Piper 1993). A useful concept here is Ogden's (1994) 'interpretation in action' which refers to way the therapy is conducted from the use of the frame to verbal interventions. If the client finds verbal interpretations problematic, then the therapy can focus more on 'interpretations in action' or Stadter's contextual transference. What the short-term therapist is looking to provide is a meaningful experience rather than 'uncovering the truth' (Mitchell 1993). Sometimes the transference cannot, or should not, be interpreted, (for example, when it might be experienced as persecutory by the client) but the short-term therapist can use his understanding of it (and the counter- transference) to better comprehend his client's difficulties and find other ways (metaphor, symbolic interaction) to address the issues represented by the transference. Binder (2004) terms this metacommunicating. Short-term therapy does not require every t to be crossed or i to be dotted.

Focal therapy demands that transference manifestations and feelings are responded to creatively and that comments are offered tentatively as material which the therapeutic dyad can jointly think about.

Sheila

Sheila consulted a therapist having recently started a new job in a new town. She felt friendless, depressed and experienced herself as boring, unable to keep a conversation going with potential new friends without slipping in to talking about her own problems. Sheila thought she 'started off alright' in company but found it difficult to maintain the interest of others. She had had two years of therapy some years previously which had helped but felt she was 'trapped' in the family myth that relationships outside the family were likely to be difficult and that family members were prone to low spirits. Both Sheila, her parents and elder brother, were quiet and tended towards introspection. She felt she could not 'sparkle' and, as a consequence, was not interested in going out with others. She had to be lively, charming and vivacious if she was going to be with others. If she could not capture their attention and interest, she would stay at home rather than be perceived as 'boring and depressed'.

In the opening session Sheila began by appearing thoughtful and reflective, saying 'interesting' and, at times, amusing things about herself and her life but as the session 'wore' on the therapist became aware of a feeling that the session seemed interminable. Glancing at his watch he was shocked to see that there was a further half an hour of the session left. He had to admit that he was bored. The more bored he felt, the more boring Sheila became, her voice frequently trailing off into a desultory murmur ... It came as no surprise that Sheila eventually asked the therapist 'I am not boring you, am I? ... I think my previous therapist got bored with me as the therapy just petered out towards the end ...' The therapist was now faced with having to metabolise his counter-transference of tedium and languor with Sheila's here and now transference. This conveyed, through the process of the session, Sheila's anticipatory hope and expectation which eventually turned to disappointment and annoyance turned against herself. It also gave a graphic account of her relational problem and that, however hard she tried, she was inevitably trapped in her family's depressive culture. The therapist felt that it was this 'here and now' transference, rather than a 'there and then' transference, which needed to be addressed. He did this by reflecting back to Sheila the process of the session (that she had begun brightly only to tail off) and that it seemed that Sheila's demand on herself to interest others only had the inevitable effect of making her experience herself as boring. The therapist said that he was aware of a stodgy and soporific quality that engulfed the session after the initial enthusiasm and wondered whether this showed just how problematic Sheila found new experiences.

This addressed the transference resistance and Sheila's idiom as well as the 'here and now' therapeutic process and would provide a focus for the ensuing work. One aspect of the focused work, during which the therapist suggested that perhaps Sheila needed to practise being 'more boring' (having established a therapeutic idiom where this form of playfulness was possible) was the recognition that the demand on herself to entertain or interest others was as impossible and absurd as the suggestion that she should be a better bore. This was a therapeutic breakthrough, leading to livelier sessions which was carried through into Sheila's daily life.

The short-term therapist cultivates a companionable, conversational therapeutic space, where the therapeutic relationship forms a central part of the experience for both therapist and client. The therapist must be emotionally engaged and enter openly into the client's subjective world since 'the patient cannot be expected to rapidly open up to a therapist who remains hidden and shielded' (Fosha 2000). In keeping with this, reconstructive transference interpretations are kept to a minimum, while the therapist offers himself as a transitory space for the client to explore different ways of being with themselves, others and the outside world. This necessitates a different approach to the issue of self disclosure on the part of the therapist. A distinction can be drawn between therapist's self -disclosure and the therapist's self-revelation where the former can sometimes be helpful while the latter invariably is not. This is related to the distinction made by Fonagy (1998) between the lending of one's subjectivity and disclosing facts about one's personal life. The former suggests a willingness on behalf of the therapist to be affected by the client's narrative and an active participant in the experiential therapeutic relationship (Howard 2008). While caution needs to be exercised in disclosing one's own personal life outside the consulting room, it is sometimes helpful (following Winnicott and Ferenczi) for the therapist to share internal affective states of mind or experiences with the client in the service of both the therapeutic alliance and to enable an attuned response to the client's material after it has been processed by the therapist. Counter transference feelings need to be made accessible in a cogent and swift fashion. So statements such as 'after you left last week I felt/thought' or 'that film you mention I have also seen and I am surprised you reacted to it in that fashion' by the therapist serve to place the therapist's subjective experience in the service of the client. Therapeutic self-disclosure, specifically 'self disclosure of the patient's impact on the therapist can be radical and dramatic [and] aid the patient's experience of the therapist's experience of them ... by disclosing her emotional response to the patient, [the therapist] acknowledges the patient's impact on her' which in itself can be therapeutic (Fosha 2000). This is very different from forms of self-revelation (e.g. 'yes, my mother died in similar circumstances and I felt …'etc.) on the part of the clinician, which are unlikely to be therapeutically helpful.

The short-term client may respond to a formal interpretation with either intellectual insight or agreement out of a wish to comply, which would be examples in which interpretations can be responded to defensively. It is generally more helpful that 'here and now' transferential comments are made which encourage an affective experience in the session. This can be facilitated by the therapist processing their own feelings and, where they are likely to be helpful in facilitating the focus, placing them at the disposal of the client. In this sense, limited, and prudent, self-disclosure can be used to 'short-circuit the patient's defensiveness and demonstrates the therapist's willingness to share difficult … affective experiences with the patient' (Alpert 1996). This clearly makes the concept of 'working through', as defined in open-ended therapies somewhat different in the shorter-term therapies.

The concept of working through

A further problematic area for those focal therapists trained in open-ended therapies is the concept of working through. It is another area in which briefer therapies challenge the beliefs implicit in more open-ended therapies. In time-limited therapies, there is little of this process which is thought central to longer-term therapies. Working through is in many ways one of the most diffuse psychoanalytic concepts. In open-ended therapies the process of therapeutic internalisation and assimilation – or less analytically stated, 'learning' – takes time and needs to be approached from very different angles. Personality is complex and time is needed to address the many differing aspects of the client. Working through generally addresses this:

> [By] pointing out to the patient how the conflicts and its defences are manifested in the various aspects of the patient's life both within and outside the transference. This process of repeating and deepening interpretations as the conflict shows itself in many diverse areas is known as working through. (Flegenheimer 1982)

The triangles of insight, persons, and therapy ensure that focal therapy attempts to address as broad an area of the client's life as possible. However, it does not involve the constant transferential repetition and interpretation which working through implies. One area where working through takes place in focal therapy is during and after its relational enactment in sessions with therapist. This is the affective component of therapy which ensures that it is not merely an intellectual exercise. The short-term therapist believes that therapy is a repetition: past relationships are replayed in the consulting room in relation to the therapist but in offering the client a new (and perhaps surprising) mode of relating in, and during, therapy, and responding in a manner that is different from important past objects or experiences, the therapist offers the client the possibility that new modes of relating are possible, and that these can be attempted in the 'here and now' of the therapy as well as in other areas of the client's life. However, it needs to be acknowledged that, limitations of time, and the briefer holding environment of short-term therapy, do mean there is less opportunity to consolidate therapeutic progress and support the client's external behavioural changes. Follow-up sessions may address this difficulty.

In keeping with the tenor of focal therapy, and the importance it places on its relational stance and the client's self-determination, the client is encouraged to continue working on the conflict after therapy is finished. An associated message that this implies is that it is not necessary or appropriate for the client to become too dependent on the person of the therapist or the process of therapy. The client may internalise the process rather than the clinician *per se* and it is this which becomes the agent of change and enables the client to develop an 'internalised therapeutic dialogue' after the treatment has ended. It is also assumed that the 'ripple' effect of therapy means that small changes brought about by a limited amount of therapy can lead to positive feedback, which, in turn, opens up the possibility of more major changes occurring. Since symptoms tend to be over-determined and interrelated, a shift in one area can lead to changes in another. In this sense, briefer therapies set a process in motion which is continued beyond the consulting room.

Alexander (in Barton 1971) had already drawn much hostility from the orthodox analytic community when he suggested that:

[Clients], having learned their therapist's predilections, bring seemingly interesting material to allay the analyst's impatience and give an impression of steady progress and deepening analytic insight. While the analyst may believe they are engaged in a thorough *working through*, in reality the procedure has become a farce.

While Mitchell (1997), postulating that working through is that 'most elusive, murkiest' of all Freud's technical concepts, suggests that it is a process during which the therapist

> [continues] to make the same interpretations or similar ones during stagnant periods when nothing seems to be happening in the hope and belief that something useful may happen if the therapist continues with his interpretation(s).

It may be that rather than mourning its absence in focal short-term therapy, the concept of 'working through' and its clinical application would benefit from further review in more open-ended therapies.

In focal therapy, the 'working through' begins after the therapy is finished. This may in practice be little different from the more open-ended therapies. The process of working through begins after the each session – we get on with the process of continually having to metabolise our emotional experiences. This is part of daily life rather than a specific aspect of the therapeutic setting. While arguably 'working through' continues after the therapy has finished, it needs to be pointed out that some clients will not acquire the capacity for self-reflection, or the internalization of the process, after a course of short-term therapy.

It must be accepted that briefer therapies lack the opportunity to rework, monitor and support therapeutic change over a longer period, and make it more durable, which open-ended therapies potentially can. One way of addressing this is to have follow-up sessions or set in place a form of intermittent therapy.

Finite time or topping up time?

A contentious area among time-limited therapists is whether the clinical contract allows the client to return, for 'topping up' sessions, or whether the time framework set for the treatment is such a central part of the process that it should not be extended. What most orientations agree on is that the suggestion that 'Let's meet for X weeks and see where we get to' should be avoided (since it conveys such ambiguity about the nature of the work and its likely future) although personally I find the 'Let's meet for X times and review' a useful approach to adopt particularly with clients who are profoundly ambivalent or for whom it is unclear at the outset whether short-term therapy is likely to be indicated.

The argument against allowing for a future review or topping up after the main course of therapy has ended is most forcibly put by those (e.g. Mann 1973; Shefler 2001) who believe that to offer a further session, or sessions, is to fudge or deny the reality of the ending thus making the work of termination less effective. Even the offer of a follow-up session is seen to be detrimental in working on the issue of individuation–separation. Smith (2005) draws on the work of Daniel Stern, Winnicott, and Mahler's (1985) concept of 'emotional refueling', or touching base, to suggest that, in contrast to Mann and Shefler, intermittent therapy can make a significant contribution to the client's struggle with separation/individuation.

Many time-limited therapists will defuse the issue somewhat by offering the client the opportunity to return on an 'as required' basis at the end of their contracted sessions. If one is offering intermittent treatment, says Mann, then the issue of termination does not arise and is consequently avoided. This might be as much a denial or evasion on the part of the therapist as of the client. It may also imply that offering follow-up, or topping up, sessions, suggests some doubt on the part of the therapist as to the current therapy's likely efficacy. Equally, and less charitably, clients who return could be seen to 'relapsing' or needing longer-term therapy which, in the competitive atmosphere of the current therapeutic environment, may not be welcomed by the more zealous short-term therapists.

One way of approaching this dilemma is to offer a finite number of sessions with the client choosing when to have them. Kutek (1999) describes a particularly inventive use of this method when talking about counselling in an Employment Assistance Programme for a large bank where the client chose to have a specified number of sessions immediately and 'bank' the rest for future use! When offering a finite number of sessions, encouraging the client to choose when to have them or how to space them out, is a particularly useful technique for learning something about the client's idiom of intimacy or dependence. Laurence, the young man described in Chapter 4, opted to have his sessions every fortnight which reflected his suspicion of intimacy and fear of intrusion. Agreeing to this, the therapist made frequent, if passing, references to this choice and what it may have represented for Laurence which he acknowledged and began to think about. In this way Laurence's core relational anxiety and idiom were named and addressed without Laurence experiencing this as persecutory or controlling or, indeed, it needing to be 'worked through'. Alternatively the scheduling of intermittent sessions over a prolonged period, rather than being a denial of the ending, may be helpful particularly for clients who have experienced traumatic losses or suffered from extensive emotional neglect.

The 'topping up' model of short-term therapy – also termed life-span intermittent therapy– speaks to the view of therapy as a process, which not only continues with the client after the contract has ended, but also enables the client to return at some future date when difficulties are encountered. Rather than see this as a failure of the previous therapy, this can be viewed as evidence that the client's initial experience of counselling was helpful and as a result, they are returning, for more of the same. Seen in this light, an individual block of short-term therapy can be seen as part of a process which may include short-term periodic episodes of therapy throughout the client's life. As Stadter (2004) – who terms this serial brief therapy – points out: 'Individual episodes of therapy can build on earlier episodes and – the whole is greater than the sum of its parts – the whole process takes on a power beyond each episode.'

An example of this is the case of Donald described below. Part of the problem for psychodynamic therapists is the belief that one can be 'fully analyzed' or treated when the truth, as Stadter points out, is that 'therapy, like life, is a process of becoming rather than a process of arriving' (2004, p. 125).

Donald

Donald consulted a therapist shortly after his eighteenth birthday concerned about his relationship with his girlfriend. Donald could not bear her smoking and his 'having to inhale such noxious fumes'. He showed an adolescent intolerance with the foibles and vulnerabilities of others and found his girlfriend's behaviour 'thoroughly objectionable and selfish'. The therapist saw Donald for six sessions focusing on Donald's fear of the contagion of others and the projection of his own vulnerability into others which he could then safely denigrate.

Donald returned to the same therapist three years later having separated from his (the same) girlfriend some weeks previously. To his surprise he found himself missing her, unable to concentrate or sleep, and noticing that 'I just start crying in the presence of other women.' The ostensible reason for their separation was that he did not think she was 'good enough for him'.

It turned out that Donald became frightened when his girlfriend started talking about a more serious commitment and, as a way of dealing with this fear, convinced himself that she was not good enough for him. Relationships did not matter, said Donald, since most significant historical figures who had left their mark on history had poor or non-existent personal lives. Donald might be the same.

He was an idealist and was increasingly aware that most things in his life fell short of his expectations. He thought that by splitting up from his girlfriend he 'could play the field' but to his dismay no one came close to her in his estimation and he was left tearful and morose wondering whether she had found someone else. Donald was seen for a further ten sessions and the focus, building on their previous work together, looked at his fear of intimacy, his defensive grandiosity and how he protected himself against feelings of loss.

Donald sought therapy on two further occasions. Once for four sessions, shortly before his marriage to a woman he had met some months previously and then for a total of 12 sessions prior to the birth of his first son. The foci in all the work with Donald was cumulative and developmental. While on the last two occasions Donald was seen by a different therapist, Donald himself outlined previous foci. Had he not, the clinic's notes were available which included brief notes as to the nature of the past work and focus.

This is an example of how a 'topping up' model can be linked to the various developmental stages of life; in Donald's case, leaving home and psychosexual confusion, issues surrounding intimacy versus autonomy, and getting married and becoming a parent. During these years of intermittent therapy the focus was progressively modified and developed to the extent that it formed a historical narrative which was 'held' by these therapeutic conversations.

The judicious use of time is not unlike any other intervention in focal therapy. It needs to be considered and applied in a thoughtful and flexible manner rather than in a rigid and unquestioning fashion. It may be that 'topping up' models are more helpful for some clients in some contexts than others. The model may well suit general practice since it is similar to the care offered by general practitioners to their clients, often seeing generations of a family over several years. It also needs to be acknowledged that if client's wish to use the therapist in an intermittent way over a period of time, then it is behoven on the therapeutic profession to find a clinically effective way of responding. Quite which clients in which contexts are likely to benefit from one method rather than another is closely linked to the issue of termination in focal therapy.

Termination in short-term therapy

Focal therapy revolves around the issue of termination and loss. Intermittent therapy – or follow-up sessions – may assist in addressing termination (or dependency) issues more gradually and allows more time for the process of therapy to be generalised to the client's functioning in the outside world. It may, however, function to 'dilute' the ending, and, in relation to follow-up sessions at least, need to be planned, rather than used reactively as a way of dealing with complications over the ending.

The short-term nature of the therapy will need to have been presented to the client from the first session – whether a termination date is set or not – in a positive manner stressing what can be achieved (and also what might not be able to be addressed although this is by no means clear at the outset of treatment) in the time available. Endings can be kept in mind either by counting down sessions as they occur or by linking any material about losses or endings with the ending of the therapy.

The manner in which clients deal with endings is a reflection of previous separations and the therapeutic response to termination needs to be sensitive to these issues. Given the interpersonal nature of short-term focal therapy, issues of loss and separation need to be interwoven in all phases of the therapy rather than merely worked on as the treatment nears its conclusion. It forms part of the ongoing narrative rather than necessarily a specific phase of treatment, although clearly more attention may need to be paid to it as the end draws closer. We have seen that the client's transference to the limited time available is likely to be linked to their personal idiom and by definition included, however peripherally, in the core focus. There is in all of us a general resistance to facing endings and loss and there is a danger, at one extreme, that the therapist, especially if trained in long-term therapy, will tend to insist – if not coerce – the client into 'facing the ending' (along the lines that the client is denying the ending), while at the other extreme they run the risk of colluding with the client and deny the ending completely. The therapist too must feel comfortable with separation issues since his idiom of separation will communicate itself to the client. The neophyte therapist may find any number of reasons for prolonging therapy which have more to do with his anxiety than any possible difficulty that the client has about ending. Examples here would include the need to be needed, not wishing to be 'cruel' or 'sadistic' to the client, therapeutic perfectionism or guilt.

Since issues involving separation are often related to the central focus, some therapists find it helpful to summarise the content and issues worked on at the end of each session which not only gives it structure but also has the effect of addressing endings and separations on a session-by-session basis. In that sense, the end of every session is a microcosm of the impending separation and keeps the issue of the time limitation on the agenda. Equally it is sometimes helpful for both therapist and client to count the sessions as they occur. A client who is discursive and concerned about time (possibly ignoring any time restraint) might find it helpful to have the sessions numbered or 'counted down' in every session (i.e. 'we must end there for today but we have another x sessions left'). This is another example of short-term therapy sessions requiring some degree of planning and preparation which is less necessary in time-unlimited therapies.

While many therapists differ on criteria for termination and techniques used in the ending of therapy, it is likely that where loss – or dependence – has been a significant issue in the therapeutic triangle and focus, this will be repeated in the therapy and require active attention as termination issues are addressed. This is more likely with clients struggling with pre-Oedipal issues. Where the focus has been more Oedipal in nature, loss and separation may be less pressing issues, and consequently need less therapeutic attention. For these clients, endings may not be experienced as painful losses with the associated feelings of abandonment and anger. Termination then becomes one of a number of possible variables which may relate to the core focus.

Indeed, many contemporary short-term treatments would not regard termination as needing extra attention although significantly these tend to be therapies that do not use specified termination dates (Della Selva 2004). Conceiving of the ending as a potential difficulty or a crisis may at times be a reflection of the therapist overestimating its significance (Binder 2004). Alternatively, some clients may experience relief at the ending perhaps reflecting their ambivalence over intimacy and dependency. Whether therapy is finite, includes follow-up sessions, or is intermittent, the therapist's aim is to make the therapeutic process 'portable and lifelong' (Stadter 2004) so that the client has access to it between sessions and after they have ended. What needs to be internalised is the therapy as a process which makes it akin to a transitional object, which, in Winnicottian terms, does not necessarily need to be mourned. Since different clients will have different ways of dealing with the ending – aligned to their personal idioms – the therapist needs to be guided by the individual needs of the client and the unique quality of the specific therapeutic relationship. For some clients, six sessions might be an eternity while for others it will not be enough to accomplish even limited therapeutic goals. Whether termination is a central part of the core focus or not, short-term therapy, by its very nature, places time, and its limitations, in the centre of the therapeutic frame. The ending is anticipated from the beginning and must be factored into the whole treatment process.

As with so many other facets of short-term therapy, termination can be addressed in the context of regular, careful and empathic supervision.

Summary

In this chapter we have ranged widely over the similarities and differences between short-term and open-ended psychodynamic work. Central to the short-term frame are the fact that therapy is relatively brief, and the transference to time and what it represents assumes great importance, as does the establishment and maintenance of a therapeutic focus. We have discussed how the short-term therapist needs to be proactive in relation to the therapeutic frame, content and process. This leads to a therapeutic stance that is companionable, where sessions are structured like a conversation, with the therapist offering tentative hypotheses and linking all material to the focus and triangle of persons. We have looked at how the transference interpretations of traditional longer-term psychodynamic therapy are modified by the short-term therapist so that they speak to the therapeutic process rather than necessarily solely to the person of the therapist. The agent of change in short-term therapies differs from the notion of working through in that it speaks to setting a process in train which does not require the person of the therapist to facilitate. We have seen how intermittent – or topping up – models of short-term therapy are becoming increasingly popular and discussed how they might speak to a developmental perspective of clinical practice. We now move on to look at how this can be taught and the nature of supervision required for the short-term therapist.

6

TRAINING AND SUPERVISION

Training matters

The central tenets of short-term focal therapy – brevity, activity, focus, selective attention, benign neglect – pose problems for psychodynamic therapists as they run counter to the fundamental assumptions of many psychodynamic orientated trainings. In a sense the psychodynamic therapist who is interested in short-term work has to transcend, or unlearn, many of the theoretical and clinical values and approaches of his training.

Freud recognised that psychodynamic treatments might need to be made more available and accessible for a larger section of the population. In 1919, at the fifth International Psychoanalytic Conference in Budapest, the heavy demand on psychoanalysis was discussed and it was suggested that Ferenczi's active technique was a possible way for psychoanalysis to develop to meet the anticipated large-scale requests for treatment. This was before the Ferenczi–Freud split. Freud, however, aware of the danger of psychoanalysis becoming a treatment for the privileged few, had talked of having psychoanalytically based outpatient clinics and making treatment free of charge. Few, however, took up this challenge.

At the same Budapest conference, Freud made his famous statement that 'It is very probable, too, that large-scale application of our therapy will compel us to alloy the pure gold of psychoanalysis freely with the copper of direct suggestion.' While Freud was not suggesting that briefer therapies were 'copper' and thus less valuable (he was referring to his old hypnosis and catharsis methods), his words have subsequently been misinterpreted to suggest that the 'applied psychoanalysis' of short-term therapy was less valuable, and a second choice, after 'pure' psychoanalysis. This has bedevilled attempts to develop short-term treatments based upon psychoanalytic principles ever since. Freud, in the same paper, went on to say:

But whatever form this psychoanalysis for the people may take, whatever the elements out of which it is compounded, its most effective and important ingredients will assuredly remain those borrowed from strict and untendentious psychoanalysis.

Freud was throwing down the gauntlet for others to devise a form of short-term therapy, based on psychoanalytic principles, which could be made widely available, effective and accessible. However, he had also, perhaps inadvertently, given rise to the belief that whatever form of therapy this might entail, it was likely to be second best to the 'pure gold' of psychoanalysis. Balint (1973), in discussing why the initial Focal Workshop at the Tavistock Clinic failed, gives a graphic example of the threat that psychoanalytically trained practitioners felt at the suggestion of briefer treatments. To this day, trainings in psychodynamic therapy and counselling are hampered by this belief and it represents a major hurdle in the training of psychodynamic short-term therapists.

Contemporary issues in the training of time-limited therapists

One of the problems is the widespread belief within the psychodynamic community that short-term therapy is just a modified and compressed form of psychoanalysis. There is a very real danger that the profession assumes that competence in long-term work can easily transfer to briefer interventions. This has been reinforced by the relative dearth of trainings in psychodynamic short-term therapies as well as the fact that the majority of dynamic short-term practitioners are clinicians whose formative training was in open-ended treatments. We have seen in previous chapters how short-term dynamic therapy, although selectively using psychoanalytic insights and their clinical applications, is very different from psychoanalysis. Short-term dynamic therapy cannot be a concentrated version of psychoanalysis. Short-term dynamic therapy is increasingly developing a knowledge base of its own, for which psychoanalytic theory provides the foundation. Its clinical application is, as we have seen, very different from psychoanalytic methods and requires of the clinician different skills and a flexible, more pluralistic, mind set or framework

If time-limited therapy is to be the treatment of choice for certain clients, then it has to be the choice of treatments for the therapist. A treatment with which the therapist does not feel comfortable is unlikely to be very helpful for the client. Resistance on the part of the neophyte therapist is a major difficulty in trainings. If, as Flegenheimer (1982) suggests, a client says, 'Can I be helped in such a short space of time?' and the therapist, for whatever reason, shares this ambivalence, then the prognosis will be bleak. Training needs to address this ambivalence towards short-term therapies which is unconsciously fostered by the training itself and then internalised by the trainee therapists.

While there are trainings, and trainees, wary of seeing their clients forever, there are many negative attitudes and resistances that face those teaching and learning short-term psychodynamic therapy. Among these are some we have already come across and some we have not mentioned: the guilt at not offering the client enough, including feelings that the therapist is rejecting or abandoning the client; anger at 'the system' for not allowing enough to be provided; the difficulty of accepting limitations and conveying the therapist's feeling that focal therapy is second rate, leading to the danger that the client enacts the therapist's ambivalence, and the therapist's need to mourn not being wanted. Since the short-term therapist is confronted with the limitations of time and outcome (in terms of what realistically can be achieved), his own narcissism and professional identity may be challenged. There is also the possibility that the clinician will harbour ambivalent feelings about having to work in settings and contexts where they have to implement an exclusively short-term frame under restrictive managerial guidelines. This can reinforce the split where short-term is seen as bad and long-term as good. We will consider this further in the next chapter. Many of these difficulties stem from the value systems of open-ended trainings and reflect the ambivalence that psychoanalysis has always felt towards briefer approaches. Longer-term therapists are often slow to adapt to the philosophy of short-term therapies – transference to a body of knowledge can be a major problem – and may find themselves drifting into old habits of attending to everything that comes up in a session without sticking to the focus. Therapeutic activity and structure may require them to have to replace the ideal of entering each session without 'memory or desire' with the need to prepare for sessions by reading up last week's case notes to ensure that the narrative themes – and the focus – are remembered for the ensuing session. Conversely, those with little experience of longer-term work are in danger of missing metaphors, idioms, the subtleties of the therapeutic process, and unconscious communications.

These issues have led to a lively debate in training circles over whether, to learn short-term therapy, the trainee needs an initial experience in open-ended longer-term therapy, or whether, given the amount of unlearning that the therapist has to do after his open-ended training to become comfortable with more focal approaches, trainees would be better advised to train in briefer methods from the beginning of their training. This would address the difficulty of having to modify, adapt or change the skills and beliefs inherent in longer-term open-ended treatments. The former view suggests that in order for therapists to be able to properly assess for short-term treatments, and to feel comfortable and competent with transference, counter-transference, resistance, strategies for intervention as well as being receptive to metaphors, idioms, symbols and unconscious communications, they require the in-depth knowledge and experience that only open-ended long-term psychodynamic work provides. The experienced therapist is potentially more able to make a rapid assessment, identify and link various dynamic processes and to make a formulation which straddles the presenting problem, intra- and inter-personal material. To discern, and keep to, the focus may require knowledge, sensitivity and ease on behalf of the therapist with psychoanalytic theory and its clinical applications. Mann and Goldman (1994) advise that:

> Time-limited therapy is not for the beginning therapist. The best preparation for it is extensive experience in long term psychotherapy so that one can gain full appreciation for the unconscious functioning of the mind, the ego defences, transferences and resistance.

Others believe that the preconceptions fostered by long-term treatments (for instance, that it is impossible to be both brief and deep, active and not influence) are such that it is preferable to train therapists in short-term therapy without them having learnt and internalised the 'bad habits' of long-term therapies. Sifneos at one point abandoned training experienced therapists in short-term work since he experienced considerable resistance from therapists who had trained only in long-term therapy, and concentrated on the training of volunteers or people early in their training who were less likely to be set in their clinically rigid ways. Habitual ways of thinking are difficult to modify or adapt. In this sense:

> The novice comes to [brief psychodynamic therapy] with fewer preconceived ideas about what constitutes good practice and

with enthusiasm and high motivation that are great assets for learning. (Messer and Warren 1995, pp. 54–5)

Budman and Gurman (1983) have suggested that the value systems and goals of the long-term and short-term therapist are different. This is encapsulated in the 'state of mind of the therapist and client' rather than specifically the length of treatment or number of sessions. Among these differences are the suggestions that short-term therapists tend to be more pragmatic, less preoccupied with notions of 'cure', believing more in developmental change (as opposed to static pathological descriptions) and that psychological change can occur outside, or after, therapy. Many therapists, trained in long-term work, see short-term therapy as a prelude to getting the client into longer-term therapy rather than an end in itself. The danger exists that this preoccupation with further treatment may blind the therapist to the 'here and now' focus of short-term work (and what can be achieved in a short space of time), and can function as a defensive avoidance on the part of the therapist.

This point of view is expressed most forcibly by those short-term therapies which lend themselves to either manualised or explicitly technical approaches and tend to assume that the therapist can slip in and out of therapeutic modalities almost at will. They tend to place minor emphasis on the use of self as a therapeutic vehicle (or the use of 'the therapeutic process') and thus differ from the more dynamic approaches which place more emphasis on counter-transference. The danger with the more manualised short-term therapies is that the therapist becomes technically competent but the therapy becomes overly mechanical in its application and lacking in sensitivity. The manualised therapist is also likely to be less able to deal with the unexpected, arguably apparent in most, if not all, therapeutic encounters. An example from the current clinical climate would be the client who, worried about a swelling in his leg which needed an X-ray, was faced with a physician who, under the guise of transparency and client empowerment, went through a protocol-driven manual with the client, listing the most likely outcomes of the investigation from the most minor to the most severe. As the physician moved towards the possibility of a tumour, the client became progressively more anxious. The physician, unable to emotionally 'attune' to his client, or skilled in any form of self-reflective practice, continued with the manualised intervention, much to the distress of the client.

Both these points of view with regard to training express valid differences in approach. However, there is currently little in longer open-ended dynamic trainings that are necessarily helpful (in terms of applying the process/dynamic issues of short-term therapy to the contexts in which it is practised) for the short-term therapist, this despite the fact that models of focal therapies which form the basis of this book are heavily reliant on psychodynamic insights and their applications. The danger exists that open-ended therapists will lack the specific skills required by, or possess frames of mind that preclude the ability to use, short-term approaches. This is of some concern since at present most therapists practising short-term dynamic therapy have had little training in this modality and allow their core training to dictate how they work as short-term therapists.

To overcome this difficulty, Messer and Warren suggest that trainings need to recognise the differences between the novice therapist (who needs to learn the clinical skills required for short-term therapy) and the psychodynamically experienced therapist who needs more attention paid to emotional resistances and intellectual preconceptions (Messer and Warren provide interesting training blueprints for both groups, 1995, pp. 54–8). The open-ended therapist has considerable unlearning to do which is frequently more problematic than learning new skills. What has become clear is the need for the clinician trained in open-ended therapy to abandon any perfectionist goals and embrace more realistic ones.

Some consideration also needs to be given to the specific therapist competencies for short-term therapy. Just as not all clients are necessarily suited to a short-term approach, the same applies to clinicians. Some clinicians are more temperamentally suited to briefer interventions than others. Shefler (2001) suggests that 'immense curiosity regarding emotional phenomena' should be the foremost quality of the short-term therapist as well as being able to be comfortable with attaching and separating relatively quickly. Additionally, clinicians with separation difficulties 'or with passive or dependent tendencies' (2001, p. 278) are likely to be less suited to short-term work. The obverse may equally be an issue – clinicians who are ambivalent about forms of attachment may be attracted to briefer clinical encounters as would those with more 'active tendencies'.

Negative attitudes to short-term therapy and its value systems need to be addressed early in trainings for psychodynamic therapists practising short-term therapies. This parallels the central importance in the therapy of working actively with the client's negative feelings early in the treatment. Preconceived beliefs are unhelpful for trainees learning focal therapies. If psychoanalytically informed short-term therapy is to have any future, ways must be found for trainings to incorporate the teaching of briefer treatments in a manner which prevents the assimilation of long-term treatments as the norm from which short-term therapy can only deviate. Short-term values and a focal mind set must be assimilated without losing that which is fundamental to psychodynamic thinking. This is assuming greater contemporary importance, not least since trainings need to prepare their students for the workplace which is increasingly focal in character. Trainings which prepare their students to become 'pure' open-ended psychotherapists and counsellors are unlikely to have much to offer public sector clinical services. Roth and Fonagy (1996) have pointed both to the importance of training, which they state becomes increasingly important the more severe or chronic the problem presented, and also to the fact that therapists are likely to achieve better outcomes the more they are able to adapt their technique to match the client's problem, which may mean a more flexible approach to treatment modality.

However, given that it is now widely accepted that time-limited therapy is a specialised form of treatment requiring its own methodology and clinical application, specific trainings in short-term psychodynamic therapy are needed. At present, a great deal of short-term therapy is being done but on the basis of very little training. The crucial problem trainings in psychodynamic short-term therapy face is how to preserve that which is essentially psychodynamic (knowledge of unconscious processes, transference and countertransference, the symbolic nature of much therapeutic communication) and is the cornerstone of the idiomatic form of short-term therapy described in this book, while at the same time ensuring that the clinician maintains the flexible and open mind set to recognise the values of the more plural and active clinical modality which focal therapy entails. Flegenheimer (1982), believing that prejudices about length of treatment and method need to be put aside, has suggested that the preferred trainees for short-term psychotherapy are those who have some grounding and background in psychodynamic theory but are 'not yet habituated to the particular techniques of long term therapy'. This would suggest that psychodynamically oriented trainings that wish to incorporate shorter-term treatments need to ensure that their trainees are expected to treat at least one client using a short-term, focal approach. Similarly, when working within an institution, it is often suggested that the therapist has at least one long-term client in treatment. This ensures that the therapist is in touch with the process issues which arise in more open-ended treatments but carries the danger that this client will be over-valued at the expense of other more short-term clients. This forms the baseline from which time-limited work may be judged rather than being viewed as something similar but very different. Briefer treatment modalities need to be placed on a par with the more open-ended approaches not merely added as an afterthought as the trainee reaches the end of their course and faces the world of paid clinical work.

In the same vein, clinical supervision of time-limited therapy needs to recognise that this is a different modality from the supervision of open-ended treatment not merely an adjunct to it or a modified and concentrated version of dynamic psychotherapy supervision.

Just as short-term therapies see, as part of their outcome goals, the enabling of their clients to develop some form of mentalisation or self-reflective practice, it may be that the competencies for the short-term clinician need to be similar.

> The learning experiences to develop [short-term] therapist's competencies are not that much different from the learning experiences for …a patient to improve his or her relational skills. (Binder 2004)

A premium is placed on both the therapist and client to be able to self-monitor and self-regulate their experience. Binder is particularly exercised by what he terms 'inert 'knowledge in psychodynamic trainings. This is conceptual or theoretical knowledge that does not necessarily easily lend itself to practical or skilful application in the consulting room. The clinical difficulty is how to help the novice clinician with when and how to implement these concepts and procedures. It is here that good quality of supervision can help.

Support and supervision

Time-limited therapies are stressful for the therapist. The discipline involved in making and ending therapeutic relationships, the high turnover of clients, sticking to the focus, and the need for therapeutic activity are emotionally draining. Therapists have to continually deal with their own separation anxiety; they have to continually separate from people with whom they have been quite intimate. Focal therapists need to be well supported if they are to remain sensitive to the individual client's problems. There are dangers in becoming either overly technical or vulnerable to burnout as a result of the demands of working in such an active and brief fashion. There is some evidence that without regular supervision short-term therapists are likely to become mechanical, authoritarian, tend to have difficulty sticking with the focus, vulnerable to offering more sessions, and find it more difficult to deal with 'here and now' process material.

Supervision

Access to regular high quality supervision is imperative. Although individual supervision is recommended, short-term work is also well suited to group supervision. Malan (1963) recommended team supervision and case conferences where members can support each other in formulating a focus, dealing with therapeutic anxiety or guilt, and diminishing the chances of therapeutic drift. Without adequate supervision, planned short-term therapy is likely to be unsuccessful since the therapist is likely to become unfocused, anxious or confused and the client more likely to drop out.

The functions of regular clinical supervision include support, guidance, positive and negative feedback and suggestion, the articulation of alternative views and the continuing stimulation of professional curiosity and learning for both supervisor and supervisee. It also functions to link theory and practice so Binder's 'inert' knowledge can be applied to real-life clinical encounters. Since supervision is relationship-based, a good supervisory relationship is vital for effective supervision to take place. In short, supervision provides a secure base from which learning and clinical practice can develop. This is not unlike the establishment of a good therapeutic alliance. Given this, it is clear that the attachment patterns for both supervisor and supervisee will be a feature of supervisory relationships. This holds true for both short-term and open-ended therapies but clearly is more intense and immediate for the short-term supervisory couple.

What form supervision takes is in some measure dependent on the particular orientation of the short-term therapist. The more 'manual-driven' therapies rely more on direct guidance while others use audio and video tapes. There is considerable evidence that technical strategies and therapeutic tactics, which have a place in short-term therapy, can be effectively taught via these methods (Binder 1993; Henry et al. 1993).

This differs, however, from the traditions in psychodynamic supervision which involve the observation of, and reflection on, the therapeutic process as it unfolds. Traditionally, psychodynamic supervision has been heavily reliant on the process recording (the verbatim exchange between client and therapist) of each session which is then discussed in detail in supervision. Psychodynamic supervision has sought to incorporate the twin roles of 'the supervisor as educator', a reflection of the one person drive/structural model of psychoanalysis, and 'the supervisor as therapeutic facilitator' who, among other things, can point out the supervisee's 'blind spots'. The latter form of supervision is linked more with the relational, object relations, model of therapy. Integrating these two differing paradigms, as in other areas of dynamic psychotherapy, has not been easy.

Binder and Strupp (1997) propose a paradigm for psychotherapy supervision which distinguishes between *'declarative'* knowledge (theories, principles, concepts and facts – in danger of becoming Binder's 'inert' knowledge without good supervision) which can be directly taught and *'procedural'* knowledge (when and how to implement and apply declarative knowledge). This is a useful distinction in the supervision of idiomatic short-term work which lends itself to both the more didactic skills-based supervision, and the use of intuition, based on the therapeutic process, in making short-term, focus-related, interventions. In supervision, the short-term therapist needs to have some didactic input that assists in the development of technical competence, as well as an opportunity for the development of the capacity to think intuitively in clinical settings which is more closely linked to procedural knowledge. These different forms of learning can then be incorporated into clinical supervision leading to what Schön (1987) has termed *'reflection in action'* – the ability to intuitively improvise where standard principles may not apply. This is different from *'reflection on action'* which is more characteristic of the supervisory practice of the open-ended therapies where time limitations are less of an issue. Reflection on action involves past 'action' (clinical material or sessions) or stopping in the midst of action (as in many 'live' supervisory settings, particularly family therapy) while reflection in action is more intuitive where 'deliberation occurs in the midst of action, without interrupting whatever is ongoing … leading to a reshaping (of the process) while it is occurring' (Schön 1983, 1987). Reflection in action enables the short-term therapist to incorporate Casement's (1991) 'internal supervisor' with a personal intuitive style which can respond to the moment-to-moment vagaries of a therapeutic session. The supervisory relationship needs to be sufficiently internalised so that the therapist can go on from there to arrive at a distinctive personal style of practice based on both declarative and procedural knowledge. This provides the foundation of reflective practice that only good supervision can provide and, while 'reflection on action' is also part of the short-term supervisory framework, 'reflection in action' is required for the 'thinking on one's feet' aspect of short-term work where material might require an immediate response in that particular session.

Current psychodynamic supervision theory suggests that a form of parallel process is at work in any supervisory relationship (Ekstein and Wallerstein 1972; Jacobs 1996; Bramley 1996b). This proposes that in any discussion of clinical process and material, important issues from the treatment relationship are enacted in the supervisory relationship. While it would be unwise to hold this as a hard and fast rule, it is a useful way of thinking about the supervision of short-term therapy where the demands of the treatment modality may well be a reflection of, or acted out in, the supervisory relationship. However, the parallel process supervisory paradigm of open-ended therapy needs to be kept in proportion in the shorter-term therapies where, in keeping with the nature of the clinical work, the supervisor is more 'a co-participant who helps [the supervisee] create useful meanings for understanding the clinical material and facilitates their development of a personal technical style' (Binder 2004).

Consequently, as in short-term focal therapy, short-term therapeutic supervision requires a modification of the traditional supervisory relationship. While short-term supervision aims, like open-ended supervision, at the benign internalisation of the supervisor or supervisory relationship, there are a number of significant differences between open-ended and short-term supervision. There can be little of the free association to the client's material or discursive reflections on the therapeutic process in focal supervision. While all good supervisory relationships should allow the supervisee the safety to 'play', an aspect of the parallel process is that short-term supervision needs to be framed in a similar fashion to short-term focal treatments, incorporating the specific discipline, for both supervisor and supervisee, of working within a short-term model.

In this sense the supervisory relationship needs to model the central tenets of short-term work – activity, focus, brevity and curiosity. Included in this is the discovery of the idiom of both supervisor and supervisee. Prompt attention needs to be paid to the early manifestations of the therapeutic process. The initial counter-transference may point to aspects of the time-limited intervention which may be problematic for the therapist. The supervisee's antici-patory hopes, fears, and expectations need to be voiced. The super-visor needs to model an active agency and confidence that something of value can be achieved in a short space of time. This is particularly important since it is likely that at some stage in the treatment the supervisee will doubt the efficacy of their work. The ripple effect of short-term work may take some time to be evidenced, and the neophyte therapist may become despondent. The supervisor needs to hold on to therapeutic hope as well as modelling for the super-visee a specific therapeutic stance of speed and decisiveness.

The supervisor needs to keep a close eye on the meaning of state-ments like 'this client needs long-term work' particularly if it appears early in therapy. Unless obviously apparent (in which case it is likely to have been evident at the assessment stage), it is likely to represent either anxiety or guilt on the part of the supervisee. Arguably, the briefer the therapy, the more structured the supervisory relation-ship needs to become. Specific idiomatic relational patterns, as manifested in client–therapist interactions, need to be highlighted rather than non-specific intra-psychic dynamics. Attention needs to be paid to the temptation for the therapeutic and supervisory dyad to drift away from the focus. The supervisee needs to be encouraged to carefully prepare for the next sessions. Keeping the therapist to the task in hand is a major supervisory function while the selection and tracking of a focal theme throughout the therapy (and by defin-ition in the supervision) needs to be encouraged. Supervisory feed-back needs to be concise, succinct and promptly formulated. Both negative and positive feedback needs to be specific rather than framed in generalities.

The supervisor needs to be aware of the possibility of therapeutic collusion whereby the therapist will, albeit unconsciously, indicate to the client that long-term work would be more enjoyable and useful for both parties, making termination more problematic. This can be helped by the careful monitoring of transference and counter-transference. In short-term therapy supervision, the timing and spacing of supervision (although not the framework or boundaries) can be flexible, reflecting what happens clinically. It need not be weekly or individual – group supervision can offer a diversity of views and the group can be mobilised in helping to stick to the focus. However, it needs to be noted that close monitoring of the therapeutic relationship, process and client material is imperative, particularly in very brief short-term contracts, where the scope for more leisurely and discursive reflection is limited.

The need to establish a speedy therapeutic alliance with a client is mirrored in supervision. Any negative feelings toward, or ambivalence about, time-limited work needs to be actively acknowledged and worked through. Both supervisor and supervisee may have pre-transferences to short-term work which need to be aired. These may be reflections of what is happening in the therapy.

Didactic teaching and clinical practice can and should be combined in the supervisory relationship. It may appear paradoxical but some process-led idiomatic short-term therapy can be taught (e.g. how to respond to and use metaphors, and the linking of apparently diffuse narratives). Given that a positive therapeutic alliance is intimately connected to treatment outcome, the relational skills of the therapist need to be addressed particularly if they are early signs of difficulty in this area. There is urgency about short-term work that needs to be reflected in the supervision – one has to think and respond inventively since time is limited.

The supervisor needs to be constantly aware of the developmental sequence of short-term therapy and to assist the supervisee to bear in mind that therapy is always in one of three stages – beginning, middle or end. The differing stages require different supervisory – and clinical – input, and failure to recognise this can lead to a unsatisfactory outcome. In recognition of this, Mander (2000) suggests a three-stage supervisory input. The supervision moves from the beginning of treatment where a focus is formulated and strategies planned; a middle phase where anxieties about attachment and separation are in evidence and an interim assessment of what has and has not been achieved can be made, and a final stage before the last session where a review of the therapy can be made, and thought given to whether a follow-up is indicated.

The externalising of 'third party blame' ('if only the uncaring employing agency would allow a few more sessions') needs to be discouraged. While there is room to allow space for the meaning of the clinician's frustration since it may affect their clinical work, a preoccupation with any third party's shortcomings functions to take the supervision outside the room and defensively avoid the need to attend to the task at hand. This is true of the supervisory as well as the therapeutic relationship. Explicit supervisory attention needs to be paid to the specific intensity of short-term work. The high turnover, the constant making (and breaking) of therapeutic relationships, the frustrations of the time limitation, and the discipline of adhering to the central focus are all likely to make intense emotional demands on the short-term clinician which need to be constantly borne in mind in supervision. Issues of loss for the supervisee are never far from the surface and need to be acknowledged in supervision since difficulty with separation may complicate an otherwise successful treatment. Supervising short-term therapy is 'like watching people travel up an escalator; they are off and on in a flash and you catch no more than a glimpse of them' (Mander 1998). Both supervisor and supervisee might find not knowing what happens next frustrating. The need for mourning on the part of the supervisee may need to be articulated.

Finally, it may be that not every therapist is temperamentally suited to practise time-limited focal therapy and this will require sensitive handling on the part of the supervisor.

Intuition in short-term therapy

Before leaving supervision, a word about intuition, that most elusive quality that can lead to the therapist's most helpful and liberating insights. Does it have a place in time-limited therapy or is it merely a vehicle for unprocessed self-indulgence? In short-term idiomatic therapy, the therapist must allow himself an imaginative inner play. Intuition, derived from the Latin 'to look', is essentially a way of looking and seeing. As defined by Webster, it is 'the direct knowing or learning of something without the conscious use of reasoning, immediate apprehension or understanding'. In short-term therapy, intuition, while appearing as 'immediate knowing' and consequently in its unprocessed form potentially unhelpful, serves to direct attention to areas that might not be logical but have idiomatic significance. The dynamic short-term therapist requires an intuitive sense of 'where to look, what to look at and how to look at it' (Bollas 1992). Binder (2004) had added 'what to do about it' to Bollas' list of intuitive senses. This enables the 'acquisition of the ingrained, extensive procedural clinical knowledge that serves as a foundation for the capacity to understand clinical situations deeply' to be used in order to improvise in a productive way in short-term therapy. Bollas views intuition as form of desire on the part of the clinician which, when successful, allows the clinician to explore 'lines of investigation that would meet with incredulous disapproval' if subjected to the laws of evidence or logic.

It follows that intuition cannot be taught but results from respecting the vagaries of transference, and most especially counter-transference, as manifested in sessions and brought to supervision. Without some sense of intuitive response, the time-limited idiomatic therapist is left not knowing 'where and how to look' or indeed 'what to do about it'. Ideas, feelings and 'hunches' need to be used to gauge their idiomatic and focal significance. Intuition is, in some senses, a development of the synthesis of declarative and procedural knowledge. The ability to use intuition as an aid in improvisation in clinical situations is, as can be seen in the case studies in this book, an important aspect of the short-term therapist's skills. This is closely linked to Malan and Della Selva's (2006) definition of emotional intelligence as the ability to accurately identify and adaptively express one's own feelings as well as with the ability to read other's emotions and respond empathically. Clients can always disagree if our intuition is wrong but it is surprising how often an initial intuitive response leads to something of significance.

The reflective practitioner

Training and supervision have, as their aim, enabling the clinician to ally technical (academic/research) knowledge with knowledge derived from practitioner experience leading to the form of reflective practice discussed above (Schön 1983). The concept of the reflective practitioner implies that the skilled therapist will make use of therapeutic intuition. Using counter-transference and supervision can aid in intuitive responses to the client's material which can assist in making tentative hypotheses, or quests enabling them to be tested out with the client. The therapist has the freedom to get it wrong and models a form of speculative intelligence to the client. In this way, the essential foundations for practice and supervision (thinking, feeling and intuition) can be combined. Psychological intuition, defined as 'the ability to process evidence before it has properly manifested itself in the session ... that second sight that therapists must innately possess' (Bramley 1996b) differs from empathy. The therapist must learn to maintain some emotional distance from the client, and not to be overwhelmed or identified by the client's pain, to be able to allow intuition to play its part.

It follows from this that experienced clinicians are likely to be able to make more direct use of their intuitive responses to their clients than practitioners starting out on their short-term therapy careers. Perhaps the last word on the subject of the relationship between technique and intuition should be left to Winnicott (1971):

> It cannot be avoided that changes ... [in] my work do occur in the course of time and on account of experience. One could compare my position with that of a cellist who first slogs away at *technique* and then actually becomes able to *play music,* taking technique for granted. I am aware that doing this work more easily and with more success than I was able to do it thirty years ago ... and my wish is to communicate with those who are still slogging away at technique, at the same time giving them the hope that will one day come from playing music.

Intuition can be a valuable tool for the time-limited therapist when it is harnessed to the central beliefs which underpin focal treatments; developmental theory derived from psychoanalytic observation, and the concept of lifespan development. These are brought to bear on every clinical encounter. They provide a means of understanding complex problems in a non-pathologising manner and enable difficulties to be viewed as developmental challenges rather than enduring personality characteristics which have their origins in childhood. It follows from this that problems which may have their origin in the past, and are maintained in the present are able to be addressed in a wide variety of therapeutic contexts.

We now address the clinical implications of using a short-term dynamic model in various clinical settings.

Summary

In this chapter we have discussed the issues of training and clinical supervision. Short-term therapy is stressful for a number of reasons, not least the large number of people that the short-term therapist is asked to treat. The need to maintain therapeutic activity and focus add to the pressure of practising time-limited therapy. Training needs to accept that short-term therapy is not merely a concentrated version of psychoanalysis or dynamic psychotherapy, but drawing on psychodynamic theory, has its own methodology and clinical application. We have looked at the debate between those who believe that short-term therapy can only be practised after some experience of open-ended therapy and those who contend that the ambivalence and resistance likely to be apparent after a training in long-term therapy lead to rigidity and hamper training in briefer, more focal, therapies. We have discussed the advantages, and disadvantages, of short-term dynamic practitioners coming from long-term, open-ended trainings. The need to combine the declarative knowledge of psychodynamic theory and the procedural knowledge of therapeutic practice has been highlighted with the aim of arriving at a model of short-term practice where clinicians are able to intuitively deal with clinical situations that demand 'reflection in action' as well as 'reflection on action'. The place that intuition can play in the development of the reflective practitioner has been discussed.

Models of the supervisory relationship, and how they differ in short-term work, have been highlighted. The supervision of focal work mirrors the process of short-term dynamic therapy and imposes its own discipline on supervisor and supervisee.

TIME-LIMITED THERAPY IN DIFFERENT CONTEXTS

It is the contention of this book that short-term focal therapy is applicable to a wide range of clinical settings. Furthermore, that the insights and clinical skills of psychoanalysis and psychodynamic psychotherapy can be applied to briefer therapies. Open-ended dynamic psychotherapy is a costly undertaking and inappropriate for many clients. Therapists working in public, voluntary and institutional/corporate sectors are increasingly recognising the need and potential benefits of working within a more limited time frame. It needs to be acknowledged, however, that it is increasingly the case that financial considerations are as much in evidence as therapeutic ones in many clinical services and contexts. This is likely to be an increasingly important variable as initiatives such as Improving Access to Psychological Treatments (IATP), and the need for a comprehensive evidence base for specific treatments, begin to dictate the nature and content of public sector mental heath provision. Resource allocation and the issue of teasing out those clients suitable for short-term interventions (and which form of intervention; emotionally supportive or expressive, reflective or structured, etc.) from those that are not, are likely to be issues that will demand increasing attention. As we saw in earlier chapters, the client's specific idiom, motivation, ability to reflect, and tell their story and relational history, need to be placed at the centre of therapeutic assessment and decision-making rather than crude issues of resource allocation or the individual clinician's specific preferences.

A useful distinction can be made between settings where 'topping up' or 'intermittent' models of short-term interventions are appropriate and those more suited to strict adherence to a circumscribed time limit. 'Closed' institutions (e.g. educational organisations) where people are likely to be part of the organisation for some time and experience a number of developmental transitions during the course of their membership (joining, being part of and leaving the institution), may lend themselves to an 'intermittent' model, while others (employee assistance programmes or those that have a 'single issue' remit, e.g. bereavement counselling, etc.) may benefit from a more circumscribed time limit.

Primary care

General practitioners, recognising the high levels of psychological and emotional problems with which their clients are presenting, are increasingly using counselling skills or employing counsellors to respond to these clients. The pioneering work of the Balints (Balint, E. 1973 and Balint, M. 1955, 1964) in this area has enabled many to recognise what can be achieved with minimal intervention and shown how optimum use can be made of the doctor–patient relationship. They enabled the recognition that it was not necessarily the doctor's prescription that was helpful but the clinical relationship offered by the doctor himself. More recent work (Burton 1998; Wiener and Sher 1998; Stiles et al. 2007) has also helped define and evaluate the nature of the therapeutic interventions which are applicable to primary care settings. Close collaboration between the doctor and the therapist underpins all therapeutic work in these settings. This is not without problems and issues such as confidentiality, competition and the split of transferences to GP and therapist need careful attention and management. Clients tend to have long-term transferences to their GP or Health Centre practice, which, in a paradoxical fashion, can facilitate the fleeting transferences required for short-term therapy. The method of referral within the practice needs careful attention since the client has to move from a medical (often including medication) to a psychological (requiring a therapeutic dialogue) framework. Medical and psychotherapeutic models may not be congruent and the counsellor may need to spend considerable time and energy in attempting to bridge the gap in understanding. Much will depend on the collaboration between the doctor (as well as other practice staff – often the reception staff are crucially important in facilitating a smooth referral) and the counsellor since the client's primary positive transference may be to the practice or doctor and the potential for splitting (good doctor–bad counsellor or vice versa) is great. The potential for competitive or rivalrous relationships (another example of the Oedipal constellation – GP/practice, counsellor and client) is subsequently increased with a danger that they will be acted out by one, if not all, of the participants. In this setting – and the others described below – there can be transient and shifting transferences to various people or contexts which need holding and understanding. It helps if the other practice staff have some understanding of, and sympathy towards, the nature of therapeutic counselling so that the possibility of counselling being undermined is reduced. Similar considerations would apply for the counsellor who may feel isolated, misunderstood and, at times, under siege. All these factors may come to be acted out in the therapeutic relationship with the client. Conversely, the positive transference towards the practice may act as a 'secure base' for the client which encourages him to enter into a short-term emotionally demanding talking treatment

In this setting, the counsellor may well need to be suitably flexible in deciding which form of therapeutic intervention to pursue. With many 'heart-sink' referrals to counsellors in primary care, a more attuned supportive approach maybe indicated. Smith (2005) has outlined an intermittent supportive/expressive form of short-term treatment, grounded in psychodynamic understanding, which lends itself to primary care settings, and uses the setting to facilitate the establishment of a therapeutic focus. Involving minimal use of transference interpretations and maximal use of notions of attachment, attunement, self-esteem, client ego strengths and their relation to external environment, a holding therapeutic environment is created in the primary care setting for substantive change to take place for clients with very damaged internal worlds, few external resources and limited capacity to make use of a more reflective approach. Bravesmith (2004) describes a collaborative way of working with a borderline client in general practice where the dynamic (and systemic) understanding of the context and setting is used to facilitate a short-term intervention. Inevitably, in general practice, the counsellor is likely to be referred (and be expected to take on) a wide range of clients with very different problems and levels of chronicity and complexity. In this way, work that has previously seen to be 'merely supportive' can lead to substantive change within a context which may have a number of therapeutic constraints.

The specific difficulties, often in evidence in these settings, which surround those clients who are recommended or 'sent' for therapy or counselling, are particularly amenable to the approaches described in this book which place a premium on the active engagement with ambivalence and resistance. It is in this area that one is likely to locate, and work with, the client's specific idiom. Henrietta is an example of a client with multi-faceted problems seen in this setting and treated within a dynamic framework as described in this book.

Henrietta

Henrietta was a 50-year-old married woman, who, depressed and 'trapped' in a loveless marriage, was referred by her general practitioner for counselling to 'find out why I have put up with the situation for so long and what to do about it'. Henrietta was increasingly desperate about her 28-year-old marriage. Overweight, suffering from high blood pressure and chest pains and prone to bouts of hyperventilation, she had suffered from poor physical and mental health for some time. She had a number of admissions to psychiatric hospitals when her concern about being able to cope with her four children as well as looking after her own elderly and sickly mother and brother had precipitated severe depressions, leading to suicidal thoughts and behaviour. An initial response to Henrietta's history and presentation may well have been one of some scepticism as to whether she could be helped within a short-term framework.

Her husband, described by Henrietta, as solitary and anti-social, was not one to discuss problems. He did not appear to acknowledge any problem although Henrietta subsequently acknowledged that she did not confide in him 'since I know he will ignore me'. He was very close to his elderly mother and there appeared to be some competition between Henrietta and her mother-in-law over who was better able to 'mother' him. She was on the point of applying for teacher training, now that her own children were older, and her main source of concern was that her husband would not agree to this step towards independence and consequently refuse to help finance her studies. This was a reflection of her perception of the lack of concern that he showed towards her. This was an early idiomatic communication – ambivalence and competition over the issues of mothering and nurture, as well as a lack of concern about (and ambivalence towards) making her own needs known and her own independence. This was also evidenced in the therapeutic relationship (i.e. the present 'here and now' of the therapeutic triangle).

She came from a small tightly knit rural community 'where people stay married'. Her father became disabled as a result of a farming accident when Henrietta was aged 12 and died after a slow and degenerative illness when Henrietta was 15. She had helped nurse her increasingly irritable and volatile father and 'knew what it is like to be one-parent family'. Her mother had struggled after the death of her father and would not hear of Henrietta's thoughts about leaving her husband. This could be seen as a communication about the past. A history of ambivalently having to care for others, as well as an internalisation of the sense of not leaving situations no matter how desperate they may be.

This all poured out disinhibitedly in the assessment session which, coupled with her concern for the robustness of the therapist (mentioned below) was evidence of the 'here and now process' aspects of the therapeutic triangle. It was not too difficult to ascertain 'why Henrietta had put up with the situation for so long'. Her own background and experience as a one-parent family ensured that separation or divorce were not seen as realistic options. Using the therapeutic triangle, and Henrietta's idiom of being trapped in a situation which was beyond her control, doubting whether men would want to (or could) care for her, and her need to mother others (reflected in the assessment session by anxious enquiries as to the therapist's robustness in relation to Henrietta's anxious and breathless presentation), a formulation was made along the following lines. The therapist tentatively shared this with her as a hypothesis for them both to consider.

Henrietta did not want to leave her husband. This was partly a result of her experience in her family of origin but also because she did actually care for him. How else could one understand the extent of her anger at his seeming lack of affection or attention? In the absence of any evidence, she was, however, unsure of whether he cared for her although it was pointed out that it was difficult to know what evidence Henrietta would require as she did not want to talk to him about it, 'knowing' what his response would be. Her experience of looking after her ailing father with her mother was currently replicated by the competition between Henrietta and her mother-in-law in mothering her husband. It was very important for Henrietta to be able to give and 'mother' others as evidenced in the therapeutic process; Henrietta would begin and end every session enquiring as to the therapist's welfare. This limited the ability of the therapist to 'nurture' Henrietta. It also reflected her ambivalent response to allowing her husband to show any nurturing qualities towards her; witness Henrietta's refusal to talk to him about her problems or resentments. Additionally, despite the overwhelming nature of her presentation, it was difficult for therapist to nurture her since she was much more comfortable giving, rather than receiving, nurture.

These issues formed the focus of the six sessions. They incorporated the present complaint, the historical antecedents and the 'here and now' process. The central organising metaphor for the treatment was the issue of offering and accepting nurture. What evidence would one need to know that someone cared? Being 'looked after' and making her needs known became the central organising focus which could be addressed in most of the material presented either directly or metaphorically. Central to this was whether husband would accept her wish to train as a teacher and contribute to her course fees. Since Henrietta remained determined not to approach her husband with her grievances, wanting to silently nurture them as it appeared she had done with her dying father, this issue had to be approached in a roundabout way.

Henrietta mentioned that her eldest daughter was both aware and concerned at the lack of communication between her parents but had been sworn to secrecy by Henrietta. Eventually Henrietta acknowledged that this might not be helpful for all concerned, not least her daughter, and gave the girl permission to talk to her father about how she felt about life at home. In the penultimate session Henrietta revealed that without discussing it with her, her husband had signed a cheque for her first year's course fees. This was some evidence of his affection and suggested that Henrietta's reluctance to speak to him was a reflection of her own ambivalence about her own independence. This could be seen as evidence of Henrietta's uneasy identification with her mother whose independence was compromised by devoting all her life to her husband and family

This intervention cannot be said to have cured Henrietta's vulnerability to depression or her problematic marriage. It did, however, give Henrietta a framework for understanding her difficulties, through narrative and metaphor, made sense out of her previously random and irrational feelings, and helped her to discover ways of recognising and dealing with situations where her self-esteem was under threat. It also enabled her, without confrontation, to see the ways in which, because of her own unresolved issues, she was instrumental in contributing to situations which she experienced as both painful and as originating from outside herself. In this way she was able to regain some control over her life.

Counselling in business and industrial contexts

Similar considerations apply to the burgeoning field of Employee Assistance Programmes (EAPs), where the therapeutic time frame is frequently dictated by the employer. A debate exists as to whether these programmes are aimed at their clients' developmental needs or merely directed at 'patching people up' to return to the workforce, helping people feel better about losing their jobs, or an excuse for poor management. The number of sessions is frequently dictated by the service provider on the basis of negotiation with the counsellor who, in turn, will have discussed this with the client. Issues of therapist and client suitability and length of treatment are open for negotiation and the close involvement of the service provider ensures that a further (Oedipal) threesome is set up which will need careful processing. Assessment is not dissimilar to other contexts ('sounding out what is on offer, what the client's expectations are, where the client is emotionally and developmentally, whether they can tell a plausible life story, engage in dialogue, what their emotional baggage is and what in particular has ...brought them', Mander

2005) and needs to be undertaken promptly since the client may not take up the offer of more sessions. Frequently, workplace issues (relationships with colleagues, etc.) need to be linked to personal or relational issues which might not be immediately apparent and the counsellor needs to have a clear sense of the organisational dynamics which may provide the context of the problems. The client who presented with anxiety attacks soon after being moved to a department where he was asked to respond to customers who were frequently critical of the organisation for which he was working, was able to discover the link between the present and his experiences at school when his parents were mocked and criticised by his peers. The use of the triangle of persons and idiomatic triangle may be particularly useful here as the notion, which has pervaded this book, that it is the quality of the engagement, rather than its quantity, which is paramount. Issues of boundaries, contracts and confidentiality (not least in the cases of workplace drug or alcohol abuse and absenteeism) need particularly close attention and require delicate negotiation with all those involved. However, much creative short-term work can be achieved in this setting (Mander 2000). Trevor is an example of this.

Trevor

Trevor was a 42-year-old executive in a software company who came to counselling via an EAP. He sought therapeutic help after the company he was working for expressed concern over whether Trevor was suffering from burnout. Indifferent towards most things, he clung to his working life which was 'always there and predictable' but felt he had no motivation to do anything 'for anyone even myself'. He had been meaning to seek help for some years but had 'never got round to it'.

Needing some prompting he explained that he could take little pleasure from his young child and found his relationship with his wife lacked vigour and spontaneity.

He had grown up as an only child in the north of the country. This was described as safe and secure until the age of 7 when his parents separated. This came as a complete shock to him since he had no indication that his parents did not get on; subsequently it transpired that both parents had other partners whom they married within a year of the separation. Trevor lived with his easy-going and relaxed mother and her new husband until age 12 when his mother, whose increasing depression Trevor had mistakenly seen as a reflection of her easy going-ness, separated from her husband and Trevor went to live with his father in a town some miles away. His father's new family, which included two step-siblings, was one where emotions were not discussed which he found very difficult. Trevor dealt with this disruption by becoming a fretful and anxious teenager, developing a range of psychosomatic illnesses, while spending all his spare time in his room with his computer which he had brought from his previous home. Trevor had been a passive child who had feigned illness in order to avoid going to school where he felt he did not fit in well. He felt under-stimulated by school preferring to spend the time at home on his own with his computer. By his own admission, he had become sad and lost 'no one really caring what I do'. He had always found relationships with women difficult and married his first girlfriend who was the first female to take notice, or take an interest, in him. He was not sure how counselling might help and was unable to articulate any version of what a more fulfilled life for him might consist of; he lacked the motivation even to think about this. During the session he frequently looked at his watch and twice needed to consult his pocket electronic notebook to confirm where he next needed to be. The session had a desultory flavour where time passed slowly as Trevor attempted to address the questions his counsellor put to him.

Trevor's idiom was one of withdrawal and suspicion of his active agency. For Trevor, not being noticed, having no opinions was preferable to risking being spontaneous or active. We could see how his history, particularly parental separation, could have led him to be passively and anxiously identified with his son which defensively manifested itself as indifference. To be active or spontaneous in the present would risk his marriage as it had the parental marriage; far better to withdraw into software where one could feel safe. The result was an uneasy compromise; family life was safe but dull. Trevor's suspicion of others, and the world of emotions, could be linked with memories of his relaxed and emotional mother (which masked a significant depression) and his emotionally withdrawn father. His yearning for the safety of the life prior to the parental separation led him to withdraw into the world of objects which were more under his control than people who could suddenly, without warning, separate and cause such turmoil. Despite, or perhaps because, of his indifference, Trevor appeared sad and lost in relation to his present and past families as well as in the encounter with the therapist. He had never got round to living and had no sense of active mastery; this was also in evidence in the triangle of his family of origin, current family and the session. His passivity ensured that no one actually cared what he did which fuelled his belief that others were not interested in him. The process in the session added to this impression – here was a man appearing not interested in counselling; wanting, via technology, to escape contact with the therapist in a similar fashion to past attempts to escape from the world of relationships which were experienced as too painful or uncertain. He had, however, turned up for the session of his own volition and the fact that his company had expressed their concern/interest did perhaps suggest that he was more ambivalent about receiving help than his resistant manner implied.

In Trevor's case, more sessions than the prescribed six were required, given his suspicion of, and lack of trust in, the value of relationships. This was discussed and approved with both Trevor and the EAP. What would need to be addressed initially was the lack of motivation – his idiom of passivity – as it manifested itself in the therapy. The sad and lost little boy behind the indifference needed to be spoken to, understood and acknowledged. Trevor's therapy – like his life – needed meaning and direction. By focusing on, and where appropriate challenging, Trevor's passivity and withdrawal and what it represented, a time-limited intervention could address the central conflicts in Trevor's past and present life via the microcosm of the therapeutic process.

Education

Similarly, adolescents, young adults and those in education are likely to benefit from short-term active interventions which stress the necessity of being aware of the developmental context of psychotherapy with these client groups (Coren 1997, 1998). Identity formation, the task of separation, and areas of sexuality and competition, are crucial developmental obstacles at this stage of life and are influential in personality formation. Intervention at this time offers the possibility of a much more profound outcome over and above the number of sessions offered. In education, short-term therapy captures the developmental fluidity of the process of being a student and parallels the student's experience of learning. This is also true for young adults. Many young people at a time in their lives when they need to go out and actively master the world are – unless open-ended therapy is specifically indicated – unlikely to be helped by a regressive relationship in long-term therapy. Ambivalent about intimacy, adolescents (traditionally difficult to engage in all forms of therapy) and young adults are likely to experience the form of third party/oblique role of the therapist in focal therapy more helpful. Similarly, the developmental process is helpful in working, using a short-term model, with children where short-term interventions can remove developmental obstacles. With all these groups, short-term therapy, because of the importance of developmental progression, is unlikely to be merely superficial, but able to influence the course of development in a more substantive fashion. Dinah is a student who shows how an idiomatic short-term frame can be used in an educational setting.

Dinah

Dinah was a 26-year-old graduate student training to be a teacher. She reluctantly came to see a counsellor having acknowledged a similar behavioural pattern repeating itself. She would embark on projects but then convince herself that she was not up to them and find ways of sabotaging herself. On this occasion she was tempted to 'run away' from the course and 'throw everything up'. In these opening statements we already can see how a personal idiom was being articulated; it was highly likely that attempts would be made to 'sabotage' the project of counselling, possibly via an attempt to 'throw everything up', not being able to metabolise the counselling experience. It would be important for the therapeutic framework to incorporate and use this idiom.

Dinah's family background and idiom of being mothered confirmed this view. She came from a farming family where mystery surrounded her mother who was not available to her as a small child. Dinah believed that her mother was in hospital during this period 'suffering from a form of epilepsy' but this was never spoken about either at the time or subsequently. Her parents separated when Dinah was aged 6 and father, with whom she lived, remarried soon after. This liaison brought two other children into the family which Dinah found difficult since 'I was Daddy's little girl'. Sharing became difficult for her and it was through her undoubted, if personally brittle, academic success that she learnt that she did not have to share. She hated boarding school, having been 'sent' there aged 11 and by her account spent most of her time there in tears (as she did in the opening session). On reflection, though, Dinah speculated whether it wasn't home rather than school which had been 'so awful'. Dinah's mother now worked locally and they saw each other frequently ... 'she seems fine now but at times gets very hyper'. Dinah said that nothing of any importance from the past – or present – was ever discussed in these meetings.

Dinah was offered five sessions focusing on her tearful wish to run away from things that she might succeed at or enjoy. Within a personal idiom of 'sabotage' and lack of ability to complete projects (although they were generally completed, it did not lead to a personal feeling of 'completeness'), we can see how, using Dinah's own phrases and language, the therapeutic triangle could be addressed simultaneously. The experience of teaching had touched on her own childhood experiences and was forcing Dinah to review her assumptions, or narrative, about her past. An idiom of parenting and being parented (alive in the counselling relationship) her functioning in loco parentis in relation to the small children in her class, and her experience in her family of origin, all contributed to her need to 'sabotage' herself. There were two parts of her: the 'on paper' confident and successful woman and the 'sabotaging' little girl. Who were these two and where did they come from? How did the person who was confident and excited about new projects turn into the one who sabotaged things and wanted to run away? Could they be related to aspects of the therapeutic triangle?

Dinah was a thoughtful and introspective person who studied diligently at school with considerable success. She worried that she could not teach since she was preoccupied with the 'naughty children' whom she felt she had nothing to offer although they held a strange fascination for her. For Dinah, it was as though being naughty was very brave. Dinah identified with these 'naughty' children since she wished as a child that she had been able to 'rebel and be heard.' No one had noticed her distress but perhaps, despite her solitary tears, Dinah had not been 'brave enough' to acknowledge her misery to others. She did not like sharing 'things' with others since 'it just makes me angry'. Personal confidences to others merely underlined the fact that her mother was absent mirroring her reconstituted family of origin. A maternal presence had not been available and contributed to Dinah's doubt whether she was able to succeed or see things through. Her father's praise was suspect since he needed to 'make up for the fact that my mother was not there'. Indeed, his praise just made her weep – angry tears – since it reinforced the continued absence of her mother, the one person whom she felt could confirm her worth. Dinah speculated that she may be like her mother; she too could get very excited about a project but all that dissipated when the project needed to be worked at and completed. Dinah did not have confidence in herself to see it through. Amidst this was considerable anger – how could one expect to feel confident and good about oneself when mother was 'mysteriously' absent?

Dinah completed her course of study not without a great deal of soulsearching. She also completed her short-term therapy which had faced her with the temptation to 'throw it all up'. Her yearning for some form of maternal approbation, defended against since it seemed disloyal to her father who had brought her up, led her to entertain the thought of talking to her mother about both the past and the 'sabotaging' present. In short, this narrative of a missing attachment and its sequel, provided Dinah with hope for the future and a framework within which she could begin to think – and feel – differently about herself.

We can see that for Trevor, Dinah and Henrietta, a dynamic formulation can be made which incorporates the past, the present, including the reason for seeking help, and the here and now process, or transference. These factors, combined with Trevor, Dinah and Henrietta's personal idioms, could be linked to understand their difficulties and to identify a therapeutic focus which the therapist could share and discuss with them; dynamic focal therapy is nothing if not collaborative This, then, becomes central to a time-limited conversation, to some extent irrespective of the context in which it occurs, although the clinician needs to be sensitive to the contextual factors which may influence the form, if not the nature, of the therapeutic conversation.

Bereavement and the elderly

At the other end of the life-span, short-term work with the elderly is also becoming more recognised and models appropriate to this population are being articulated (Hildebrandt 1995; Gorsuch 1998; Terry 2008). Recognising that there are special issues, both symbolic and real, in relation to loss, and that limited time has a special meaning for older clients, the idea of a therapeutic time frame has a powerful impact in work with older people. Mortality, loss, the absence of meaning and the creation of a new, or modified, narrative all provide foci for the elderly client. Time is literally running out, thus

> the time limit in psychotherapy is a vehicle for the work that must be done ... therapy becomes a microcosm, a symbolic space in which certain experiences are made possible and certain affects can be borne ... the time limit represents the therapist's faith that something of value can happen within the frame, *within this moment*. (Messer and Warren 1995, p. 319)

The client's capacity to mourn and relinquish, often ambivalent, relationships with those they have lost, may lend itself to a short-term intervention based around the 'counting down' of sessions model (mentioned earlier) where the working towards an agreed ending becomes a metaphor for the stages necessary for mourning (Mander 2005). Affirmation and mirroring may be of particular importance to the elderly client, thus lending weight to short-term approaches which adopt a self-psychological framework (Lazarus 1988). Similarly, bereavement lends itself to a short-term approach particularly to phase-oriented treatment models with specific goals and tasks for each stage which run parallel to the different aspects of a grief reaction.

However, as we noted with Tina in Chapter 3, particular attention needs to be paid to the client's idiom when considering phase-linked treatment models. There is increasing evidence that when working with the medically or terminally ill and HIV Positive clients, a time-flexible focused approach is helpful (Guthrie 1993;

Levenson and Hales 1993; Pollin and Kahaan 1995; Levenson 1995, pp. 222–31; Eimer and Freeman 1998). An expanding literature is appearing on the use of short-term therapy in community mental health provision (Mynor Wallis and Gath 1992; Brech and Agulnick 1996, 1998; Hudson-Allez 1997; Carter 2005; Gabbard et al. 2007; Paley et al. 2008) and in psychiatric services (Macdonald 1997; Guthrie et al. 1999; Moorey and Guthrie 2003) which highlights the importance of client assessment and therapist training in the practice of short-term therapies.

Similarly, forms of crisis intervention and the treatment of post-traumatic stress disorder, while perhaps more in the nature of de-briefing than therapeutic process-led counselling, have always lent themselves to the discipline of a more focused approach (Bisbey and Bisbey 1998).

The fundamental beliefs in short-term therapy of activity, focus, careful selection and assessment together with the client's idiom and relational past and present, form the basis of short-term focal therapy. These hold true, irrespective of the setting or context in which the therapy occurs. A general rule of thumb would be that the shorter the therapy, the more the therapeutic variables need to be kept to a minimum. Changes of room during therapy, a less than secure framework and therapeutic boundary, the distinction (and referral) between the assessor and the clinician who will carry out the therapy, and an ambivalent therapist or clinical setting, are likely to add to the variables that may make treatments less brief. In addition, in contrast to the open-ended psychodynamic tradition, the short-term therapist needs to explain the treatment to the client to avoid false expectations and to ensure that the client shares responsibility for the therapy.

Working with cultural, ethnic or religious difference

Every clinical encounter is one where the clinician engages with difference. We are always engaging with the (an)other. As clinicians, we need to discover the idiom of our clients to enable a therapeutic alliance to be established. From our discussion of the concept of idiom, and its importance in short-term therapy, we can see how a personal idiom is formed, in part, through cultural transmission. Idioms are built up from internalisations and introjections from the external world including language, culture and social relationships. Idiomatic concepts of affect, language and emotional vocabulary (and the culturally laden idea of 'psychological mindedness') evolve through the assimilation of environmental conditions making the clinician's initial task to discover and enter the client's personal and cultural idiom, of primary importance. As clinicians, we are privileged in some contexts and disadvantaged in others, according to different aspects of our identity and idiom. Of course, this applies to our clients as well. It is a feature of the society in which we live that we are powerfully – and often unconsciously – influenced by it. Ideas of self are powerfully influenced not merely by contemporary culture but also by past events that have shaped that society (Wheeler 2006). Transference then becomes a much deeper, complex and potentially richer therapeutic tool.

Salient features of working with difference have been highlighted (Burham 1993; Palmer 2002; Laungani 2004). These may centre on the individual's view, or belief system, about individualism versus collectivism, where the latter gives primacy to the group rather than the individual. Other dimensions of cultural difference include cognitivism (primacy given to rationality, logic) versus emotionalism (feelings, intuition, relationships), free will (proactive freedom of choice) versus determinism (limited choice and a reactive approach to the world), and materialism (belief in science and the reality of the external world) versus spirituality (external world is illusory and reality is internal to the individual). As a basis of this, attempts have been made to arrive at competencies for the cross-cultural clinician. These include cultural awareness, cultural knowledge, skill in conducting a culturally sensitive assessment and treatment, and a desire and curiosity to encounter and engage with clients from diverse backgrounds and avoid stereotyping. All involve listening for, and hearing, the client's idiom

Short-term therapy may be more acceptable to ethnic, social, cultural or religious minorities than more traditional open-ended psychodynamically informed interventions. Western philosophical and cultural tradition, which emphasises forms of introspection including the capacity to reflect, may well be alien to those from other cultures and backgrounds, making open-ended longer-term reflective psychotherapy less amenable or appropriate to these clinical populations (Coren 1997, Chapter 5). Western tradition, shared by psychoanalytic theory and practice, values autonomy, self-direction and agency, individual choice and control. Mind, illness, emotional distress and healing are culturally very relative concepts. Types of communication for one culture ('self disclosure in a hierarchical relationship, or interaction in a group setting', Bhugra and Bhui 1998) may not suit another. Societies and groups with predominantly religious views may well have very different therapeutic approaches based more on healing and religious rites – therapeutic passivity 'may well be interpreted as incompetence by some ethnic minority groups whose model of a healer is a traditional one' (Bhugra and Bhui 1998). Arguably, 'psychological mindedness', a cornerstone of the assessment process for open-ended treatments, could be viewed as a defensive action on behalf of the clinician which functions to avoid engagement with another's difference. We need to allow our clients to teach us their culturally specific idioms.

Fatima

Fatima was a 40-year-old British Muslim woman who presented for counselling as a result of finding herself losing her temper with her husband and getting increasingly anxious in her daily life. Presenting in headscarf and hijab, Fatima described herself as a devout Muslim. She felt her faith was very important to her and, as a result, the counsellor encouraged her to talk about what that represented for her and how if affected her daily life. She had grown up in a secular Muslim family in the north of England; her father, the proprietor of a small shop, and her mother, a housewife prone to becoming very stressed and anxious. Her parents had separated when she was small – much to Fatima's shame and distress – and Fatima grew up in an impoverished household with her mother, maternal grandparents and younger sister. Fatima had converted to a more strictly religious sect when she was 18 and married her husband – a marriage arranged by her mosque – when she was 20. Through talking about her religious, social and cultural beliefs it became apparent that Fatima had substituted her family of origin for that of her husband and was discovering that it felt as though she had escaped from one dysfunctional family to another. Her husband's family lost no opportunity to denigrate Fatima and her contributions to the marriage. As a stay-at-home wife, she was also becoming increasingly aware that she was becoming as anxious and dissatisfied as her own mother had been in her marriage. In some ways Fatima had hoped that she had dealt with her unhappy childhood by becoming more religious only to find she was repeating aspects of her past in her current marriage. During the six sessions of counselling, during which Fatima teased out the importance of religion in her life from the psychological and social pressures on her – often involving her 'educating' her counsellor as to the cultural and religious idioms important to her – she decided that she would attempt to train as a nurse and become more involved in her mosque and in that way find a solution that respected her faith yet also challenged her feeling that she was replicating something unresolved from her childhood in her marriage.

Thus, the short-term therapist, through therapeutic activity, curiosity, focus and collaboration, enables the construction of a mutually shared language and therapeutic idiom.

One useful question for the clinician to bear in mind is asking the client a version of 'How will you let me know if I get it wrong or if my own views about (religion, culture, etc.) are unhelpful to you?' This proved a helpful frame of reference when working with Fatima. Assessment, focus and treatment must be formulated within the client's cultural frame of reference, social networks and belief system which may involve 'counsellors [being] open to hearing a world view which is outside their experience or alien to them' (Wheeler 2006). This is particularly important in short-term therapy where the omission of a cultural dimension may serve to prolong the treatment and lead to an unsatisfactory outcome.

I have written elsewhere (Coren 1997) about the use of metaphor when working with psychosomatic problems but metaphor is also important when working with clients from different cultural, religious or ethnic backgrounds. Short-term therapy, because it values the external world (and the client's wish to exert some active agency on it) and stresses the importance of the client's idiom, and its metaphoric or symbolic manifestations, may well be particularly welcome for clients who do not share ideas about individual autonomy, self-disclosure or insight more akin to the Western philosophical tradition.

Organisational aspects of time-limited therapy

Institutional factors are also likely to play a part in the satisfactory practice of short-term therapy (Towler 1997). The context, history, assumptions and societal meaning of the institution where the therapy is practised will all impact on the therapeutic process. Professional and administrative staff in the agency should be committed to short-term therapy. The implementation of a time-limited policy on a therapeutic service which has not offered this in the past is likely to provoke administrative and professional ambivalence. Anxiety about change will coexist with a hopeful anticipation for service development and individual therapist growth. Institutions which adopt a short-term approach as a result of fiscal restraints or administrative diktats are likely to need to ensure that the feelings and issues which are evoked by having to work in this fashion are not enacted in the treatment or between individuals in the team.

Equally, services which operate short-term therapy under these conditions are more likely to adopt an 'us and them' approach; the tendency to project hostile or negative feelings onto administrators or budget holders which can result in a half-hearted or ambivalent approach to short-term clinical work. This is frequently evidenced by claims that administrators do not recognise how 'disturbed' or 'needy' the service's population is and as a result 'they' are cruelly preventing these clients getting the longer-term or open-ended treatment which they need. The result is a grudging and reluctant implementation of a short-term framework by therapists who are at best ambivalent about working briefly and often have little specific training in more short-term approaches. In these situations, the unconscious (or subconscious) wish that the short-term treatment should fail, proving the clinician's initial doubts correct, is generally in evidence.

Summary

In this chapter we have looked at a variety of settings and contexts in which short-term therapy is practised. The setting, and aim of treatment, can dictate the form of treatment offered although it needs to be noted that the fundamental beliefs underlying short-term dynamic therapy hold true in all contexts. We have discussed how this applies in working with difference. (Nevertheless, it is important to acknowledge that the therapeutic process is affected by the context in which it occurs.) Much psychoanalytic theory was generated from private practice. This needs to be modified in order to be applied to diverse contemporary institutional settings. Since institutional structures and organisational goals are apparent in consulting rooms, they need to be both worked with and addressed by time-limited dynamic therapists. Time-limited therapy practised from an institutional base, or paid for by a company, implies that there is always a third presence in the room. The challenge for short-term therapy is to harness this third presence to facilitate creative therapeutic change.

8

DOES IT WORK?

Therapeutic outcome and the effect of managed care on time-limited therapy and its practitioners

Since Freud's time, dynamic psychotherapy has struggled with the twin issues of treatment outcome and evaluation. At one level, it is relatively straightforward: you ask the client whether they feel better after a course of treatment and their answer provides you with the success or failure of your treatment. Unfortunately, however, it is not that simple. Are successful outcomes linked to symptom relief, personal development or life 'domains', such as the quality of life or the ability to cope with certain previously stressful events? Should it measure the process of treatment or merely focus on the end result? How can one control for therapist (and client) variables and limit the concern that any research tool will interfere with the process of the therapy? This last factor in particular has bedevilled research in dynamic psychotherapy. Psychodynamic therapists have in the past been emotionally dependent on (and defensive of) single, process-led, case studies and resistant to objective, verifiable and replicable evidence of therapeutic outcomes. This position has been reinforced by the belief that open-ended dynamic psychotherapy seeks more diffuse ends, affecting both process and outcome, which may include self-exploration or personal development and growth (although it could be argued that this is a hoped-for consequence of time-limited therapies as well) which do not lend themselves to easily quantifiable research. However, as we are now living in an age of evidence-based practice, where the purchasers of counselling and mental health services want proof that a treatment works before committing funds to it, the onus is placed on specific treatments to show evidence of their efficacy. Those unable to do this will not be recommended to the purchasers of mental health services.

However, there are a number of difficulties with the current research paradigm used for the allocation of mental health provision. We need to distinguish between efficacy research (those involving 'pure' or highly selected client groups, which may not reflect the clinical populations which present at mental health agencies) and effectiveness research (which, while having less internal validity and consistency – the clients are more varied – are more representative of clinical presentations). A further distinction needs to be drawn between outcome research and process research. The former addresses whether therapy has any effect at all, which forms of therapy work for whom, and whether the outcomes last over time. Process research, which traditionally has been the favoured area for psychodynamic investigators, focuses on how change occurs with particular emphasis on looking at therapeutic processes occurring between the therapist and client during treatment. Early research into short-term treatments was deeply flawed in both their sampling and control methods. The short-term clients included in the studies did not receive planned short-term therapy but were often people who terminated what were intended to be longer-term treatments. The short-term treatments were frequently carried out by people with little or no training in briefer methods of therapy who often used truncated techniques borrowed from the long-term therapies.

Roth and Fonagy (2005) have looked at the effectiveness of psychological treatments across the field of mental health. While this provides welcome evidence that psychological treatments do help, there are still fewer controlled studies of brief dynamic treatments than more protocol led therapies, although Roth and Fonagy give useful pointers to the nature of short-term interventions with specific disorders. For example, given the prevalence of relapse in clients suffering from depression, a more intermittent/topping up, maintenance-based, therapeutic regime may be indicated.

Allowing for the difficulties of controlling for client and therapist variables, there is currently a great deal of research into short-term treatment. The increasing popularity of manualised therapies, particularly in the United States, where the therapist is guided through the stages of therapy with the aid of a manual, has made more rigorous evaluation possible as well as focusing more closely on the client–therapist dyad via audio and video taping of sessions.

Clinical descriptions of short-term dynamic therapy are now plentiful and reports of treatment outcome are encouraging. It is suggested that most clients who have been through an episode of short-term therapy have received significant benefit (Crits-Christoph

1991; Stadter 2004). Considerable research in the field of short-term therapy suggests that various forms of short-term therapy are efficacious with specific client populations (Koss and Shiang 1994). Current research suggests that most therapeutic benefits occur early in treatment for the majority of clients (Smith et al. 1980; Lambert et al. 1986; Howard et al. 1986;). For up to 75 per cent of clients the law of diminishing returns applies. However, for a small number of clients with entrenched problems, longer-term, although not necessarily open-ended, therapy is likely to be more helpful.

Research evidence points to planned short-term therapy as being most successful with the less severe problems. Clients presenting as depressed or anxious are likely to improve faster than those considered to be borderline. More severe problems (personality disorders or borderline personalities, psychosis and substance abuse) may need more time and find a more flexible use of the time frame, including 'intermittent' therapy, more helpful. It will come as no surprise that clients who come to address circumscribed problems (loss, interpersonal relationships, depression, and anxiety) do best and that one of the main benefits of short-term treatments is that they help accelerate positive change. Given the more structured nature of focal therapies they are likely to avoid the dangers highlighted by Roth and Fonagy (2005) in their review of the differential effectiveness of various therapies. They suggest that non-specific, poorly structured treatments such as generic counselling, non-focused psychodynamic psychotherapy and a variety of experiential therapies are likely to be less effective the more severe a client's presentation and problems are.

Comparative studies of short and time unlimited therapies show no significant difference in results between the two in outcome although research here is hampered by the lack of well-designed evaluation research for open-ended therapies. In general, it can be said that short-term therapies do as well as the longer-term therapies with which they are compared (Koss and Shiang 1994; Garfield 1998). Given the time and resource implications, this is a not inconsiderable finding. There is some evidence to suggest that premature terminations, or drop-out rates, are reduced when clients were offered a circumscribed time-limited therapy (Sledge et al. 1990).

An area of difficulty centres on which factors lead to good outcomes of treatment – these may not be for the reasons supposed by either the therapist or the theory underlying the treatment (Bateman et al. 2000). In general, no consistently significant differences emerge in outcomes between different short-term models

(Luborsky et al. 2002; Lambert and Ogles 2004), an outcome termed the 'dodo bird effect' from *Alice in Wonderland* – 'everybody has won and all must have prizes', although this proposition is contentious (Norcross 2005). While there a number of specific techniques that are linked with successful outcomes (many of them discussed in Chapter 5 – formulation, focus, activity, termination, etc.), it is the specific qualities of the therapeutic relationship which appear to have most bearing on successful treatments (Messer 2001). While previous research has focused on either process or outcome of therapy, current findings heavily point to the therapeutic alliance as the single most predictive measure of a successful outcome (Hartley and Strupp 1983; Frieswyk et al. 1986; Crits-Cristoph et al. 1988; Gaston 1990; Koss and Shiang 1994). This non-specific factor appears more crucial than either theoretical orientation or clinical technique. The therapeutic alliance, and therapist variables, are increasingly seen as predicators of good outcome, whichever short-term orientation is used. Therapists' contributions to any clinical encounter can be loosely grouped into three categories: their techniques, their skills and their personal qualities (Schafer 1982), although teasing out which of the three qualities are paramount has proved very difficult (Roth and Fonagy 2005). The discrete fit, and interaction, between clients and their therapists, will affect, positively or negatively, the process and outcome of therapy. The therapeutic relationship, rather than the theoretical model or style of therapy, will have the major impact on the success of the therapy. This holds true across varying therapeutic orientations and reinforces the belief that it is common factors in therapy, rather than the specific techniques or the clinical approaches of each therapeutic orientation, that are most helpful to clients. This is welcome news for those who believe the relational style of both client and therapist is at the centre of the therapeutic project but also suggests, as we have discussed, that specific attention needs to be paid early in therapy to the working alliance, particularly where it appears not to be working. These findings have helped the debate over outcomes to move on from the fraught and sterile question 'Does this therapy work?' to the more clinically helpful 'Which factors make this treatment model succeed or fail?' The next step would be to ask, 'Which factors make this therapist more successful with his clients than that one?' The debate needs to move on from attempting to identify empirically supported treatments to attempt to identify empirically supported clinicians (Lambert and Ogles 2004). It is frequently assumed that most therapists believe that outcomes 'are as dependent on a therapist's competence and personal qualities as the techniques they practice' (Gabbard 2007) but hard evidence for this is difficult to elicit.

There is now a substantive body of research into short-term psychodynamic therapy which supports its efficacy and suggests that the changes last over time (Gelso and Johnson 1983; Lambert et al. 1986; Hoglend 1988; Anderson and Lambert 1995; Shefler 2001; Stadter 2004; Malan 2006; Abbas 2008). Further research is still needed in the area of 'what works for whom?' in time-limited treatments but we are seeing increasingly sophisticated attempts to look at specific aspects of therapist interventions (e.g. interpretations) and relate them to successful client outcomes (Hoglend 1996, 2003; Piper 2002) as well as looking at successful client–therapist matching and specific types of interventions irrespective of type of therapy. Arguably, a therapist's ability to successfully implement an intervention is, in part, a consequence of the client's trust in the therapeutic relationship and of their therapeutic engagement. The effectiveness of short-term interventions may depend as much on the skills of the clinician, and the quality of the therapeutic alliance, as on the nature of the therapeutic intervention.

A fruitful area for further research is the question of how much therapy is required for significant and lasting change especially for borderline personality disorders. Equally, research is beginning to address the question of which clients benefit from an emotionally expressive/interpretative approach and which are likely to be helped by a more explicitly supportive model (Piper 2002).

Cognitive behavioural interventions have been systematically evaluated for several disorders, and shown to be highly effective (Roth and Fonagy 2005), although, when comparisons have been made, cognitive therapy has not been shown to be more effective than other psychotherapies.While it is the case that cognitive behavioural therapy has published a great deal of research data, and is thus favoured by the purchasers of mental health services, psychodynamically based short-term therapies are beginning to provide evidence of empirical efficacy and have an increasingly large evidence base (Guthrie et al. 2001; Messer 2001; Stiles et al. 2007; Abbas 2008).

It needs to be acknowledged that 'while short treatments can be offered with no less of efficacy for some disorders, for others, longer therapies, though more costly, are more effective' (Roth and Fonagy 2005) and that advocates of short-term treatments need to be mindful of the importance of making judgements of treatment length on clinical rather than explicitly resource criteria. However, there is now increasing evidence that significant change is possible for many presenting problems within 16 sessions and significantly less for clients with more circumscribed or developmental problems. Treatment lengths are likely to be linked with treatment aims (Gabbard 2007) while, for the more severe difficulties, a 'topping up' or serial/ intermittent therapy model may be indicated. There is, however, the danger, in the rush to 'prove' the efficacy of short-term treatments, that these will be tailored to the wishes of the purchasers of therapeutic services rather than the wishes and needs of their clients.

Managed care or does the piper call the tune?

It currently remains unclear whether the interest in short-term focal therapies represents a breakthrough, particularly for psychodynamically based therapies, in therapeutic techniques and efficacy, or whether it heralds the beginning of the disappearance of concepts such as clinical autonomy and professionalism. In an age where fiscal pressures push for shorter treatments, there is enormous pressure to prove the efficacy of one treatment over another and for therapies to compete for public and private funding on grounds which owe much to financial audit and the market place rather than clinical need. There is considerable incentive for therapies not only to compete with one another but also to assert their potency by making claims as to their efficacy which suggest that treatment can be successfully completed in the shortest possible time using the minimum of resources. Therapy is in danger of becoming a commodity or product, much like any other in our society, rather than a discrete form of relationship which may not readily lend itself to the discipline of the market. The 'marketisation' or 'privatisation' agenda can have (and some would say already has) a devastating effect on clinicians. Having to compete and tender against each other in order to win 'business' for their services, short-term clinical contracts and agreements, and a managerial culture, can all contribute to a sense of uncertainty and demoralisation within the helping professions. Concepts such as 'winning' and 'losing' and fighting to survive in the marketplace become commonplace and can lead to an extremely detrimental effect on clinical services and individual clinicians.

While it has been the norm that the individual clinician – or clinical service – has, together with his client, decided on the duration, goals, and methods of treatment, contemporary developments are leading to these decisions being taken by health service managers or insurance administrators. The American 'managed care' industry, beginning to be evidenced in Britain by, among others, employee assistance programmes and insurance-driven health care, whereby industry or insurance companies pay for, or reimburse, the cost of therapy, has meant that they, rather than clinical need or opinion, define which (and what forms of) problems are treated and how long that treatment should last. Often this leads to a specific number of sessions allocated to all problems irrespective of any clinical assessment – the one size fits all approach – and to the growth of telephone or computer counselling. The latter, in itself, can have many advantages in enabling those who would not take up face-to-face therapeutic help, to access psychological services and, via the triage system, ensure that the resources of highly trained clinicians are concentrated on the more serious problems. However, many of these services now tend to be time-limited and frequently managed and evaluated by non-clinicians. Whether this can be called planned short-term focused psychotherapy, based upon therapeutic ethics and values and taking its lead from the needs of the client, is debatable. Arguably, managed care or employee assistance programmes are likely to affect the process of therapeutic counselling and in turn influence the way the general public, and the therapeutic professions, view the therapeutic task. While there are a number of potential benefits (including innovation, the accountability of both the profession and the individual clinician in ensuring that therapies do not go on interminably, and a cost reduction to the public purse), there are also a number of problems. Some clients may well seek therapy for personal growth, self-knowledge or educational reasons, and these, often termed somewhat dismissively 'the worried well', are unlikely to be funded for counselling by the service funders. The need to frequently, if not constantly, renegotiate the length of treatments, creates an unstable and potentially unsafe, therapeutic environment for both therapist and client while the preoccupation with costs can mean that quality is sacrificed. Therapy can be excessively hurried and can lead to the 'deprofessionalisation' of the professions with the public viewing very brief, often crisis, interventions, as the norm (Stadter 2004). Under an insensitive managerial agenda, the danger exists that professional autonomy will be compromised – with a detrimental effect on the morale of clinicians – and the standing of the profession in the wider community will also be questioned. Evidence is growing that the popularity of manualised therapies – often it must be said very helpful with straightforward problems – is leading to the danger that they are being implemented by poorly trained clinicians who have little knowledge of therapeutic process and, as we have discussed, are unable to deal with unexpected clinical manifestations.

Managed care demands that clinicians demonstrate that their treatments are both necessary and effective. Concrete and identifiable gains need to be seen to be achieved in the shortest possible time, with minimum financial outlay and with the minimum of professional support. This favours highly structured brief forms of therapy with goals that are tightly circumscribed, easily measurable and observable. At best, these can be seen to speak to the needs of the client rather than the preference of the therapist. Clinical preference on behalf of the therapist has, in the absence of consideration of other therapeutic alternatives, frequently been unhelpful for clients and an indulgence on behalf of the therapist. Vague attempts to help 'clients feel better', idiosyncratic or amorphous clinical judgements based more on subjective feelings on the part of the therapist than objective evidence, and therapists who know rather better than their clients what their clinical material represents and when clients are 'cured', are becoming endangered species. At worst, however, brief managed care interventions, which are manual-led and highly technical in their execution, can fail to acknowledge subtle differences between seemingly similar client groups and represent a bureaucratic form of social control, a crushing of clinical freedom, and a means of denying psychic pain and emotional distress. This is very different from the forms of short-term focal therapy which we have been discussing.

Therapy as a corporate commodity

Short-term therapies are in danger of, willingly or otherwise, becoming part of what has been described as the 'corporatization of psychotherapy' (Pingitore 1997). This entails the disappearance of psychotherapy's libertarian, subversive, questioning or radical potential at the expense of a therapy which is based on the use of technology, techniques which can be easily learnt by lay people, and aimed at the rapid adjustment to the mores of society as defined by employer, insurance company or provider of health care. The danger exists that short-term therapies which allow themselves to be incorporated into the managed care industry without any clinical safeguards become merely means of social control; attempts to change behaviour which an employer, say, finds difficult. In that context it can become an alternative to good management where 'difficult' employees are told to seek counselling to 'correct' their attitude or increase their productivity to the organisation. Psychotherapy, which at best is about personal growth and empowerment, is in danger of becoming a 'cost effective treatment for individuals with socially disruptive behaviours' (Kutek 1999). A further effect of this corporatisation is the tendency to discriminate between different problems or ailments; alcoholism may qualify for treatment while personal alienation or confusion may not. Additionally, clients may need to be defined as 'ill' to become eligible for treatment. Managed care, in many parts of America, demands that the client be given a DSM number based upon a psychiatric definition in the Diagnostic and Statistical Manual of the American Psychiatric Association where each DSM number is authorised a fixed number of sessions, independent of the client's individual needs. Managed care, and fiscal prioritised resource management, can also represent a form of 'invisible rationing of treatment' in the absence of any more open public debate in the wider community (as well as by users of any particular service) as to what the underlying philosophy of thera- peutic help and its aims may or should be. This industrialisation of therapy, which values cost effectiveness above all, involves a high degree of standardisation of procedures and protocols, and the interchangeability of clinicians and service providers, is a very different creature to the more humanistic foundations of the various therapeutic traditions. Treatment manuals and specific protocols do not in themselves guarantee minimal therapeutic competence. The idiosyncrasies of any particular therapeutic dyad create a dynamic unique to that dyad – which cannot be replicated – resulting in complex challenges for the manualised therapist (Binder 2004). A skilful therapist needs to be able to adapt flexibly to the immediate clinical circumstances in any given session and be able to improvise when necessary. These are not skills available to the manualised – or the globalised (see below) – therapist.

This form of 'social engineering' potentially has more subtle influences on both the therapeutic profession and the wider culture in which it is promogated. Pingitore sees corporatisation increas- ingly leading to the non-clinical management of psychotherapy where the therapist's 'jurisdiction over diagnosis [and] treatment is under attack by health care administrators and entrepreneurs'. The risks are that treatments will require standardisation and be heavily dependent on rigid diagnosis and outcome evaluation research. Resources will follow the most recent research findings. If ten sessions of a specific therapy are found helpful in the latest outcome evaluation, then everyone will be funded for ten sessions of that treatment, irrespective of the problem or the wish of the consumer. Since health insurance tends to place a limit on the number of sessions they are willing to reimburse, this will lead to attempts to ensure that therapy will not continue beyond what the administrators think is the minimum necessary length. One of the outcomes of this will be the need for more technical flexibility on the part of clinicians. This may prove increasingly problematic for those trained in 'pure' models of therapy with no experience of, or exposure to, alternative therapeutic methods. The therapeutic relationship will be influenced by the fact that there will always be third parties in the room, be they funding bodies or non-professional 'review personnel'. The net effect is that therapy is potentially in the service of the employer or insurance company as much, if not more, than the client.

Since the aim of therapy under managed care, and increasingly in the public health care system, is not personal growth or fundamental shifts in personality, but 'symptom reduction and behaviour adjustment' (Kutek 1999), the psychodynamic therapist's professional autonomy and skill base are immediately challenged. Since corporate-applied therapy tends to be symptom- and goal-orientated, an insidious effect of this is that the more reflective, explorative, personal developmental therapy is sidelined at the cost of the more functional adaptive, coping strategies model. In this scenario, the therapist, feeling unable to influence the course of his professional work and whose judgement is always under scrutiny, potentially becomes more and more deskilled, if not disaffected. Ethical problems may arise if the clinician thinks his client needs longer treatment while the funding body does not (Small and Barnhill 1998). As the content and length of treatments are increasingly dictated by third party service providers, clinicians, and psychotherapies in general, face a number of difficult ethical, clinical and political questions (Kupers 1981; Messer and Warren 1995, p. 330; Binder 2004). A consequence may be a growing cynicism over the use of short-term treatments on the part of the clinician which may give scope for the therapist to act out his discomfort with funding decisions in the therapeutic relationship to the detriment of his client.

A contemporary outcome of this may well be in evidence in the 'globalisation effect' of therapies. The combined pressures of standardisation, the need for an evidence base and the managerial culture described above, can lead to one therapy being seen as applicable 'to everyone everywhere'. While we have seen that many short-term therapies are currently addressing similar areas, this is very different from the hegemony of one therapy over all others. Arguably, currently cognitive behavioural therapy (and to a certain extent, manualised therapies) occupy that position – this is very different from having a plurality of approaches on offer designed to speak to the diverse and complex problems confronted by people today.

'Making a virtue out of necessity'

Clinicians need to practise short-term therapy because of choice, based on therapeutic criteria, rather than being coerced into offering treatments against their professional judgement. The danger exists that in this economic climate many therapists may be asked to use time-limited focal therapy as a result of institutional resource limitations, poor line management in organisations, and lengthy public health sector waiting lists. The industrialisation of forms of psychotherapy, often combined with a wary and increasingly cynical clinician's belief that he has 'to make a virtue out of necessity' and practise 'brief therapy', is a reflection of the dangers inherent in a system where fiscal and administrative necessity rather than clinical discourse or research based upon psychological theories of personality and human development are given pre-eminence.

The pressure will mount for focal therapy to be offered to inappropriate clients. Our discussion of assessment has shown that some clients are likely to benefit more than others from time-limited therapy; it is incumbent on therapists and their employers, or those paying for clinical services, to recognise this. It would be extremely unfortunate, and bring all therapies into disrepute, if more and more clients were offered short-term therapy because of resource limitations and a vague hope that 'it is better than nothing' and 'may help' as a result of there being little other therapeutic help on offer. Focal short-term therapy needs to be part (albeit an important one) of a continuum of provision, rather than something that is offered to all as an administrative or fiscal convenience. Time-limited short-term therapy should never be the only therapeutic option. Difficult clinical decisions will still need to be made to avoid clients being offered short-term therapy inappropriately. Time, as we have seen in focal therapy, needs to be used flexibly based on the clinical needs of the client; a blanket provision of, say, ten sessions for everyone will not speak to the need to carefully tease out how many sessions are required for any individual client.

Additional problems are likely to arise since funding decisions based on over-prescriptive purchasing or reimbursement policies by health service managers and insurance companies may well stifle clinical innovation and development. Few clinicians will feel safe to innovate in the absence of any encouragement from funding bodies. If funding is available only for tried and tested therapies, where will clinical innovation and development come from? (See Roth and Fonagy 2005 for further discussion of how genuine evidence-based practice may be delayed as a result of administrative funding decisions.) Similar concerns affect clinical trainings; who will take responsibility for trainings if those funding services decide that only one narrow form of treatment is to be made available?

Whither exploratory psychotherapy?

An unhelpful dichotomy has been drawn between the belief that open-ended psychotherapy is leisurely, reflective, exploratory and discursive, and short-term therapy which is thought to be hurried, superficial, and lends itself to didactic or authoritarian tendencies. While, as we have seen, this polarity is both unhelpful and untrue of both forms of therapy, its hold on, at least the clinician's imagination, is perhaps a reflection of how far the emphasis in contemporary culture and society on active agency, speed and immediacy goes against the grain of many of the central tenets of the more exploratory psychotherapies (Shipton and Smith 1998). There appears at times to be a devaluing of the relational in contemporary society, that goods are more important than people, a preoccupation with the peripheral and fleeting, a constant wish for new and exciting experiences with the attendant low attention span, which add to the concerns that certain forms of 'brief therapy' merely mirror the less attractive or thoughtful aspects of contemporary culture. Although, as we have seen, focal therapy is both thoughtful and reflective (and open-ended therapies can be both active and focused), these stereotypes are difficult to relinquish. This poses problems for the profession of psychotherapy and counselling. Short-term therapists in particular need to be aware that they are practising focal therapy for the right clinical reasons.

At times, it appears that the debate has become clouded by an inability to distinguish between clinical necessity and administrative or fiscal demands. Health service administrators will always be more informed by financial imperatives than theories of personality and human development. The reverse will be true of clinicians. The language of these two worlds is difficult to reconcile yet attempts to do so must be encouraged.

The retreat into grandiosity

Hubris, in the trumpeting of the efficacy of short-term therapies in the hope of favourable funding, is likely to be short-lived since there will always be a minority of clients for whom short-term focal therapy is contraindicated. It is also reminiscent of the founding fathers – and mothers – of psychoanalysis who argued vociferously in favour of psychoanalysis as the cure for many of the world's ills. Those who claim that short-term therapy can help everyone can be seen as retreating into a form of grandiosity. The opposite of grandiosity, denigration, is also in evidence in contemporary therapeutic debates. A stigma is attached to weakness or vulnerability which are traits to be hidden or placed in others and then denigrated or disparaged. Therapists too can denigrate what it is they are offering (short-term therapy, say) as a way of defensively avoiding the effective active engagement with both their client and employing agency.

In a world that puts a premium on competence, effectiveness, efficiency and control, the idea that every problem has a rational and immediate solution is particularly attractive, however erroneous it may be. Contemporary culture has great difficulty with aspects of existence that are beyond our control and imply human limitation. There appears to be little place in society for helplessness, weakness and dependency. It would be tragic if focal short-term therapy, which has so much to offer to so many, were to be co-opted into a corporate vision of life which seeks to deny, or minimise, the existence of emotional suffering.

These are very real difficulties for the short-term therapist to consider but one effect of living in the real external world means that some accommodation needs to be found between clinical autonomy and professional (and lay) accountability. Even without these external constraints, there are other professional dilemmas which the short-term therapist faces.

Is clinical rigour being replaced by administrative sadism?

As we have seen, the danger exists of fitting all clients into a narrow range of therapeutic modalities. This is made more acute since in many areas it is increasingly difficult for short-term therapists to refer on those clients who require longer-term treatment since these resources are either not available or have long waiting lists. Only having one treatment modality available runs the risk of reinforcing the belief among clinicians that it is not the best that they can offer and less than the client needs. The emphasis then becomes more on technique than exploration or reflection.

Looking at some of the more prescriptive short-term therapies, one is struck by the technical onslaught against resistance employed by some clinicians; these have the flavour of indoctrination rather than therapeutic 'play'. Indoctrination leads to compliance; clients can incorporate their therapists in a manner analogous to pets resembling their owners. Arguably this is as much a danger in open-ended therapies but the premium placed on therapeutic activity and focal attention in short-term therapy makes it more vulnerable to accusations that it can lead to a submissive compliance. However, it is the case that some short-term therapies have aroused discomfort out of a sense that their therapeutic techniques appear to be at best insensitive, or at worst sadistic. This is particularly true of the more analytic drive/structural approaches employed by, among others, Davanloo and Sifneos, who have been accused of authoritarianism akin to religious fundamentalism where only compliance with the therapist's view of reality is acceptable (Messer and Warren 1995, p. 109). While these reservations are being addressed in the more recent work of Della Selva, Malan, and Osimo (2003), critics have suggested that there is little of reflective exploration, open and spontaneous dialogue in these therapies, merely compliance to the therapist and his view of reality. Therapeutic process is pre-empted by therapeutic zeal while it is the provocative stance of the therapist which arouses the client's intense feelings and anger rather than historical transferences. The therapist elicits affect rather than observes affects, in that sense repeats the original trauma, while resistances are battered down rather than respected.

One consequence of this is that clients may not be heard. Clinicians only hear what they are able to hear. All clients will pick up ways in which their therapists can or cannot tolerate or hear their pain. 'Brief' clients may not feel free or safe to tell the whole story. They too may feel the need to select their contributions on the basis of what they feel comfortable telling a therapist from whom they may shortly separate. 'Brief' clients may tell 'brief' stories in the same way that focal therapists may only hear stories that can be related to the focus. In this way, the concept of time will affect (and potentially limit) the process. The pressure on the therapist to 'cure quickly' will parallel the pressure on the client to 'get better' quickly. The therapist may get irritated by the client who does not improve quickly. The dangers of selective material and compliance are all too obvious. Focal therapists need to be aware of the danger of never hearing of, or encouraging their clients to reveal, the full extent of the client's suffering. This can also be a potential area where therapeutic sadism can be in evidence. The therapist may avoid, or not respond, to painful, or difficult, material. The focus in short-term therapy needs to be in the area of the client's most painful conflict – it must never function to exclude painful or problematic clinical material.

A further objection to focal short-term therapy is that, unlike open-ended analytic therapies, which because of their intensity and rigour are 'deep' and consequently the results are profound and long-lasting, time-limited therapy can only be superficial and the results temporary. According to this school of thought, the depth of therapy is proportional to its length; open-ended intensive analytic psychotherapy can reach parts of the personality which other therapies cannot. Associated with this is the belief that the true nature of any individual's problems will only be discoverable over time. This is what Wolberg (1980) has termed the 'prejudices of depth'. While it is true that briefer therapies are more modest in their aspirations than long-term psychotherapy, there is little empirical evidence to back up the claim that some therapies are deeper than others or that it takes a long time to ascertain the true nature of a client's difficulties. It would appear that these claims are related to the need to justify more intensive and long-term therapies on the basis of their rigour. There is increasing evidence that core conflictual relational themes can be observed very early in therapy (Crits-Cristoph et al. 1988; Silberschatz and Curtis 1986). The equation of length of treatment with depth and rigour is one that many clinicians have questioned. Ferenczi (Stanton 1990, p. 33) is quoted as saying that therapeutic progress is not related to the depth of either an interpretation or the client's insight. Alexander believed that daily sessions, rather than making therapy more intensive and therefore rigorous, merely made therapy more routine and superficial while Winnicott thought depth was unrelated to intensity or length of treatment.

Rigour and depth are problematic and diffuse concepts for the psychodynamic therapist.

Beverley

Beverley, a 30-year-old woman, had been seen for some five years employing a 'topping up' model of focal therapy. She was first seen on her arrival in the UK and sessions focused on aspects of cultural dissonance, familial conflicts and her own professional and relational aspirations. These had been reflective and explorative sessions during which the therapist felt they had come to know each other quite well, had a positive therapeutic alliance, believing he had a good understanding of Beverley and her concerns. The therapist was surprised when, during his fifth year of seeing her (and during a period when she had become depressed after the failure of a professional venture), she asked him whether they could engage in some 'short-term' cognitive work since 'although our work together has really been helpful, it has not really addressed the innermost me'. She now needed 'something deep which could affect the way I think and behave'. The implication was that their work together (stretching over a number of years and focused on transitions, relationships, family and culture), although helpful, had in some respects been 'shallow'. What Beverley thought was 'deep' were her cognitive thought processes and she now wondered whether they might be able to be accessed in a shorter time.

Clients may be able to define what is deep and what is superficial for their therapists and these definitions may bear little relationship to the therapist's fantasies of what constitutes rigour and depth. Issues of depth versus superficiality are historical legacies of the disputes within the psychoanalytic profession. 'Superficial' has served to determine all that is 'not psychoanalysis' or intensive psychotherapy and has become a term of abuse. 'Supportive' therapy has, as we have seen quite unjustifiably, had similar evaluative overtones. Similarly, short-term therapy has been dismissively termed a 'band aid' or 'plaster' but this may be exactly what is required when someone is hurt – as Messer and Warren (1995) suggest, it provides the 'antiseptic protection to enable healing to take place'.

However, the focal therapist must ensure that therapy is not carried out in a crudely mechanistic and unempathic manner. This could be a danger given the sheer volume of clients that might be seen in short-term therapy.

Short-term therapy: the easy option?

It has been said that short-term therapy, because it is brief, is less demanding than more open-ended therapies. These beliefs still linger in the mind of therapists partly as a result of the harsh psycho-analytic superego with its equation of intensity, length and rigour. Therapists who have been trained in psychodynamic open-ended therapies and then practise (or are placed under pressure to adopt) a more time-limited model are likely to have an ambivalent transfer-ence to short-term therapy. They are likely to view focal therapy as an abbreviated and superficial (and therefore less demanding) form of psychoanalysis and view the undertaking as 'second best' as a result of the hierarchy that exists in dynamic psychotherapy: 'psychoanalysis is the best form of treatment available, long-term psychotherapy has merit if psychoanalysis is not possible, and lesser forms of therapy are makeshift at best' (Flegenheimer 1982). This is made more acute if therapists are made to undertake time-limited therapy by their employers and leads to the combination of profes-sional ambivalence and practical cynicism felt by psychoanalytic practitioners towards focal therapies. All this fosters the belief that short-term therapy is easier (i.e. less intense or demanding) than longer open-ended therapies.

The need to work within a short-term framework places the ther-apist under a great deal of pressure. In some ways it is as, if not more, intense than open-ended therapies. The therapeutic demand of constantly dealing with beginnings and endings (with little of the more leisurely middle bit in between), the high activity level, and the need to be constantly actively present in every minute of every session, ensures that focal therapy is emotionally very demanding for the therapist. One of the difficulties is the seemingly promis-cuous nature of short-term work; seeing so many people in such a short space of time imposes its own discipline and demands. In researching this book I was struck by how, in many clinical vignettes in the short-term therapy literature, clients are not given a name, merely a function or symptom (e.g. 'the case of the man with the headache' or 'the case of the masochistic statistician'.) It may be that this is a reflection of the short-term therapists' need to defend against any personal or more intimate therapeutic contact with their clients given the sheer numbers they are being asked to treat. Given that contemporary short-term therapies are focused on making intense emotional contact between therapist and client to strengthen the therapeutic alliance and working relationship, this can become a potential difficulty. One of the consequences of the more cost-effec-tive nature of short-term therapies is that clinicians will come under pressure from their employers to see more and more people, with a consequent danger of clinical fatigue or burnout. This places increased importance for short-term therapists to have access to regular supervision and support, as discussed in Chapter 6, as well as for their employers to recognise the stresses inherent in the high turnover of clients.

Summary

In this chapter we have discussed research into, and the evidence base for, short-term therapies and highlighted some of the difficulties in process led research. There is a difference between the efficacy of a therapy in a research trial and its effectiveness in clinical practice. The single most important factor appears to be the quality of the therapeutic relationship, whichever therapeutic tradition or protocol is used. The effect of an increasing 'corporatisation' of therapy, and the influence of the market place, have been seen to pose a number of ethical and professional dilemmas for clinicians, which short-term therapists in particular, need to reflect on. The place of the 'relational' in contemporary culture, the focus on 'quick fixes', and the denigration of an idiom of thoughtfulness and reflection, carry the dangers that short-term therapy is seen as a reflection of the culture in which we live and lead clinicians to be ambivalent about their practice. Alternatively, hubris in championing short-term therapy can equally be problematic in failing to be suitably humble – a cornerstone of any therapeutic practice.

CONCLUSION

Psychoanalysis began as a short-term therapy. We have seen how dynamic therapies gradually became longer and open-ended. Describing the various time-aware contemporary therapies has enabled us to highlight the common features of each. From this, a model of short-term psychodynamic therapy has been articulated and its application discussed. The challenges this poses to counsellors and therapists trained in open-ended therapies have been addressed. Attention has been drawn to specific difficulties associated with short-term therapies in contemporary society with the premium it places on the quick fix.

We have focused in this book on a number of discrete features of time-limited practice. Client selection with an emphasis on interpersonal – or object relations – development; an individualised clinical focus incorporating the triangle of persons and how this is replicated in interpersonal patterns including in the consulting room; a time frame, whether limited or intermittent, which adds a sense of intensity to the experience for both members of the therapeutic dyad; a sense of active agency on the part of the clinician and an emphasis, where appropriate, on issues of attachment, separation, loss, and endings. These provide the scaffolding onto which idiom, metaphor, symbols and affects can be added to provide an effective short-term intervention.

Rather than promising miracle cures in unrealistically few sessions, time-limited dynamic therapies need to articulate models of treatment which are applicable to a large number of people in various different settings. Central to this is the ability to differentiate those who can be helped by short-term focal interventions from those who cannot. I hope this book has contributed to this process. For many years, to stand any chance of success, psychodynamic psychotherapy was viewed as a long-term undertaking. Short-term therapy was seen as essentially brief and superficial. As short-term psychotherapy has become more acceptable, these views are being challenged and briefer approaches are being seen as treatments in their own right rather than modifications or diluted versions of the real thing. Time-aware short-term treatments can be the treatment of choice for many psychological problems. While some people may wish to enter into open-ended, time-unlimited, therapies, many do not. Despite being the preference of many therapists trained in open-ended models, long-term therapy is more expensive, requires a great investment of time, and the outcomes have not been demonstrated to be superior to shorter forms of therapy. Time-limited therapy proposes that people continue to grow throughout their lives and that limited interventions can assist this development. Its focus is on the obstacles to development rather than disease or deficits. In this way, it can assist even those deemed to be severely damaged. However, it remains the case that not everyone can be helped by focal interventions. What is required is a plurality of provision based on a thorough assessment of an individual's needs.

For psychodynamic therapists, the difficulty has been how to preserve that which is unique and of value in psychoanalytic theory and clinical practice. What makes the therapeutic conversations described in this book psychodynamic? I would contend that the central paradigm of time-limited therapy is the use and understanding of the therapeutic relationship, which outcome studies have shown to be the single most reliable predictor of therapeutic success. The awareness of unconscious processes in the transference and counter-transference and how these can be identified and utilised with the use of symbols, metaphors and personal idioms within the treatment relationship, together with knowledge of developmental theory, makes these short-term encounters possible and productive. Many time-aware therapies are focusing increasingly on the therapeutic alliance and relationship and particularly on the feelings associated with this. Psychodynamic short-term therapies place importance on the here and now therapeutic process as this is evidenced in the consulting room and how this is understood in relation to the client's past and present experiences. This might not be psychoanalysis but it is psycho-analytic. The debate is not about whether short-term dynamic therapy is better or worse than longer-term psychotherapy, but about the difference between these two models.

People in distress lose track of who they are and wish to be. At best, time-aware conversations, offering alternative scripts and construc-tions of the client's problems, can help both therapist and client unravel the mystery of how the problem has originated and is currently maintained. It offers an active relationship with the therapist, the discovery of a shared narrative and a way of overcoming problems (Holmes 1993). For the clinician, what is of most import is that short-term therapy becomes a state of mind where a time-aware and time-sensitive framework forms the basis of any therapeutic encounter and one that 'puts the mental processes and actions that characterise a proficient therapist in the foreground, and puts the theory bound technical strategies in the background' (Binder 2004). The increasing technical emphasis on forms of therapy that adopt a somewhat rigid, manualised approach to therapy, is in danger of producing a protocol-led therapeutic culture which, in essence, is an attack on the relational. The relational, quixotic and unpredictable as it is, cannot be trusted, and so protocols ensure that is negated, if not denied. The protocol-driven therapist cannot deal with the unexpected in any therapeutic encounter – this is problematic since it is the unexpected that defines any clinical encounter and, arguably, is what has most therapeutic value.

There are, however, dangers. Increasingly, we are seeing psychological therapies becoming a form of social engineering which may well have the effect of diluting psychodynamic therapies' subversive and radical culture, making adaptation, as opposed to, say, personal liberation, a therapeutic aim or outcome. Since time-limited therapies appear to sit comfortably with contemporary market forces, are they in danger of losing that which is distinctively therapeutic and libertarian? Or are they the best form of commodity currently on the therapeutic market? Does focal time-limited therapy comply with our culture or is it the best product of our culture since, in contemporary life, time is both limited and valuable? In a curious way, this returns to the fundamental rule of psychoanalysis: free association. Does it inevitably lead to therapeutic drift? Is it the means or the obstacle to cure? For psychodynamic therapists, the jury is still out yet time-limited dynamic therapy offers the profession a means of creatively harnessing the profound insights of psychoanalysis with the contemporary demand for empirically driven treatments. In this, it may realise Freud's wish that psychoanalytically informed therapy can become a therapy for the people.

BIBLIOGRAPHY

Abbass, A., Hancock, J., Henderson, J. and Kisely, S. (2008) *Short-Term Psychodynamic Therapy for Common Mental Disorders*. Cochrane Database of Systematic Reviews.

Adler, A. (1958) *What a Life Should Mean to You*. New York: Capricorn.

Ainsworth, M., Blehar, M., Waters, E. and Wall, S. (1978) *Patterns of Attachment: Assessed in the Strange Situation and at Home*. Hillsdale, NJ: Erlbaum.

Alexander, F. and French, T.M. (1946) *Psychodynamic Therapy*. New York: Ronald Press.

Alpert, M.C. (1992) 'Accelerated empathy therapy: a new short term dynamic psychotherapy', *International Journal of Short Term Psychotherapy*, 7(3): 133–56.

Alpert, M.C. (1996) 'Videotaping psychotherapy', *Journal of Psychotherapy Practice and Research*, 5(2): 93–105.

Anderson, E. and Lambert, M. (1995) 'Short-term dynamically orientated psychotherapy: a review and meta-analysis', *Clinical Psychology Review*, 15: 503–14.

Anstad, C. and Hoyt, M. (1992) 'The Managed Care Movement and the future of psychotherapy', *Psychotherapy; Theory, Research, Practice, Training*, 29(1): 109–18.

Aron, L. (1990) 'One person and two person psychologies and the method of psychoanalysis', *Psychoanalytic Psychology*, 7: 475–95.

Aveline, M. (1995) 'How I assess for focal therapy', in C. Mace, *The Art and Science of Assessment in Psychotherapy*. London: Routledge.

Azim, H.F. *et al* (1991) 'The quality of object relations scale', *Bulletin of the Menninger Clinic*, 55(3): 323–43.

Baker, H. (1991) 'Shorter-term psychotherapy: a self-psychological approach', in P. Crits-Christoph and J. Barber (eds), *Handbook of Short-Term Dynamic Psychotherapy*. New York: Basic Books.

Balint, E. (1973) *Six Minutes for the Patient*. London: Tavistock.

Balint, M. (1955) 'The doctor, his patient and his illness', in *Problems of Human Pleasure and Behaviour*. London: Maresfield Library.

Balint, M. (1964) *The Doctor, His Patient and His Illness*. London: Pitman.

Balint, M., Ornstein, P. and Balint, E. (1972) *Focal Psychotherapy: An Example of Applied Psychoanalysis*. London: Tavistock.

Barber, J.P. (1994) 'Efficacy of short-term dynamic psychotherapy', *Journal of Psychotherapy Practice and Research*, 3(2): 108–21.

Bateman, A., Brown, D. and Pedder, J. (2000) *Introduction to Psychotherapy*. London: Routledge.

Barkham, M. (1989) 'Exploratory therapy in 2 + 1 sessions: rationale for a brief psychotherapy model', *British Journal of Psychotherapy*, 6: 79–86.

Barkham, M., *et al.* (1999) 'Psychotherapy in two plus one sessions: outcomes of an RCT of cognitive behavioural and psychodynamic interpersonal therapy for subsyndromal depression', *Journal of Consulting and Clinical Psychology*, 62.

Barton, H.H. (ed.) (1971) *Brief Therapies*. New York: Plenum Publishing.

Beck, A.T. (1976) *Cognitive Therapy and the Emotional Disorders*. New York: International University Press.

Beck, A.T. and Freeman, A. (1990) *Cognitive Therapy of Personality Disorders*. New York: Guildford Press.

Beinart, H., Kennedy, P. and Llewellyn, S. (eds) (2009) *Clinical Psychology in Practice*. Oxford: OPS/Blackwell.

Bergin, A. and Garfield, S. (1994) *Handbook of Psychotherapy and Behaviour Change*. Chichester: John Wiley & Sons, Ltd.

Berne, E. (1963) *Games People Play*. New York: Grove Press.

Berne, E. et al. (1973) 'Transactional analysis', in J. Groves (ed.) *Essential Papers on Short-Term Dynamic Therapy*. New York: New York University Press.

Bhugra, D. and Bhui, K. (1998) 'Psychotherapy for ethnic minorities: issues, contexts and practice', *British Journal of Psychotherapy*, 14(3).

Binder, J.L. (1993) 'Is it time to improve psychotherapy training?' *Clinical Psychology Review*, 13: 301–18.

Binder, J.L. (2004) *Key Competences in Brief Dynamic Psychotherapy*. New York: Guildford Press.

Binder, J.L. and Strupp, H.H. (1991) 'The Vanderbilt approach to time-limited dynamic psychotherapy', in P. Crits-Christoph and J.P. Berber (eds), *Handbook of Short-term Dynamic Psychotherapy*. New York: Basic Books.

Binder, J.L. and Strupp, H.H. (1997) 'Supervision of psychodynamic psycho-therapies', in C.E. Watkins (ed.), *Handbook of Psychotherapy Supervision*. New York: John Wiley & Sons, Ltd.

Bisbey, S. and Bisbey, L.B. (1998) *Brief Therapy for Post Traumatic Stress Disorder: Traumatic Incident Reduction and Related Techniques*. Chichester: John Wiley & Sons, Ltd.

Bloom, B.L (1992) *Planned Short-Term Psychotherapy: A Clinical Handbook*. London: Alleyn & Bacon.

Bollas, C. (1992) *Being a Character: Psychoanalysis and Self Experience*. London: Routledge.

Bowlby, J. (1953) *Child Care and the Growth of Maternal Love*. London: Penguin.

Bowlby, J. (1980) *Attachment and Loss*, Vol. 3, *Loss, Sadness and Depression*. New York: Basic Books.

Bowlby, J. (1988) *A Secure Base: Clinical Applications of Attachment Theory.* London: Routledge.

Bramley, W. (1996a) *The Broad Spectrum Psychotherapist.* London: Free Association Books.

Bramley, W. (1996b) *The Supervisory Couple in Broad Spectrum Psychotherapy.* London: Free Association Books.

Bravesmith, A. (2004) 'Brief therapy in primary care: the setting, the discipline and the borderline patient', *British Journal of Psychotherapy,* 21, 1.

Brech, J. and Agulnick, P. (1996) 'An audit of a brief intervention strategy on the waiting list of a community counselling service', *Counselling,* 7(3): 322-6.

Brech, J. and Agulnick, P. (1998) 'The advantages and disadvantages of a brief intervention strategy in a community counselling service', *Psychodynamic Counselling,* 4(2): 237-58.

Brunning, H. (1998) 'Working briefly with meaning', *Changes,* 16(4): 274-84.

Budman, S.H. and Gurman, A.S. (1983) 'The practice of brief psychotherapy', *Professional Psychology: Research and Practice,* 14: 277-92.

Budman, S.H. and Gurman, A.S. (1988) *Theory and Practice of Brief Psychotherapy.* New York: Guildford Press.

Brunner, J. (1986) *Actual Minds, Positive Worlds.* Cambridge, MA: Harvard University Press.

Burham, J. (1993) 'Systemic supervision: the evolution of reflexivity in the context of the supervisory relationship', *Human Systems,* 4: 349-81.

Burton, M. (1998) *Psychotherapy, Counselling and Primary Mental Health Care: Assessment for Brief or Longer Term Treatment.* Chichester: John Wiley & Sons, Ltd.

Cameron, C. (2007) 'Single session and walk in psychotherapy', *Counselling and Psychotherapy Research,* 7(4): 245-9.

Carter, M.F. (2005) 'Time limited therapy in a community mental health team setting', *Counselling and Psychotherapy Research,* 5(1): 43-7.

Casement, P. (1991) *Learning from the Patient.* New York:. Guildford Press.

Clarke, D.M. and Fairburn, C.F. (1997) *Science and Practice of Cognitive Therapy.* Oxford: Oxford University Press.

Coren, A. (1996) 'Brief therapy: base metal or pure gold?', *Psychodynamic Counselling,* 2: 22-38.

Coren, A. (1997) *A Psychodynamic Approach to Education.* London: Sheldon Books.

Coren, A. (1998) 'Brief psychodynamic counselling in educational settings', in J. Lees and A. Vaspe (eds), *Clinical Counselling in Further and Higher Education.* London: Routledge.

Creed, J. et al. (2003) 'The cost effectiveness of psychotherapy and parotoxene for severe irritable bowel syndrome', *Gastroentorology,* 124(2): 303-17.

Creed, R. et al. (2002) 'Depression and anxiety impair health related quality of life and are associated with increased costs', *Psychosomatics,* 43: 302-9.

Crits-Christoph, P. and Barber, J. (eds) (1991) *Handbook of Short-Term Dynamic Psychotherapy.* New York: Basic Books.

Crits-Christoph, P., Luborsky, L., Dahl, L., Popp, C., Mellon, J., and Mark, D. (1988) 'Clinicians can agree in assessing relationship patterns in psychotherapy','*Archives of General Psychiatry*, 45: 1001–4.

Davanloo, H. (ed.) (1978) *Basic Principles and Techniques in Short Term Dynamic Psychotherapy*. New York: Medical and Scientific Books.

Davanloo, H. (ed.) (1980) *Short Term Dynamic Psychotherapy*. New York: Jason Aronson.

Davanloo, H. (1990) *Selected Papers*. New York: John Wiley & Sons, Ltd.

Davanloo, H. (1994) Personal communication to J. Groves, quoted in J. Groves, *Essential Papers on Short Term Dynamic Therapy*. Albany, NY: New York University Press, p. 378.

Della Selva, P. (2004) *Intensive Short Term Dynamic Psychotherapy*. New York: Karnac.

De Shazer, S. (1982) *Patterns of Brief Family Therapy*. New York: Guildford Press.

De Shazer, S. (1985) *Keys to Solution in Brief Therapy*. New York: W.W. Norton & Co.

Deutsch, F. (1949) *Applied Psychoanalysis*. New York: Grune & Stratton.

Dryden, W. and Feltham, C. (1998) *Brief Counselling: A Practical Guide for Beginning Practitioners*. Maidenhead: Open University Press.

Dupont, J. (1988) *The Clinical Diary of Sandor Ferenczi*. Cambridge, MA: Harvard University Press.

Dziegielewski, S.F. (1997) 'Time limited brief therapy: the state of practice', *Crisis Intervention*, 3: 217–28.

Ekstein, R. and Wallerstein, R. (1972) *The Teaching and Learning of Psychotherapy,*. 2nd edn. New York: IU Press.

Egan, G. (1994) *The Skilled Helper*. Pacific Grove, CA: Brooks/Cole Publishing Company.

Eimer, B. and Freeman, A. (1998) *Pain Management Psychotherapy: A Practical Guide*. New York: John Wiley & Sons, Ltd.

Elbstree. L. (1982) *The Rituals of Life: Patterns in Narrative*. New York: Kennikat.

Ellis, A. (1973) *Humanistic Psychotherapy: A Rational Emotive Approach*. New York: McGraw-Hill.

Erikson, E.H. (1980) *Identity and the Life Cycle*. New York: Norton.

Erikson, M. (1980) *Innovative Hypnotherapy: Collected Papers of Milton H. Erikson on Hypnosis*, Vol. 4, ed. E. Rossi. New York: Irvington.

Eron, J.B. and Lund, T.W. (1996) *Narrative Solutions in Brief Therapy*. New York: Guildford Press.

Fairbairn, W.R.D (1952) *An Object Relations Theory of the Personality*. New York: Basic Books.

Feltham, C. (1997) *Time Limited Counselling*. London: Sage.

Ferenczi, S. and Rank, O. (1925) *The Development of Psychoanalysis*. Madison,, WI: International University Press.

Flegenheimer, W.V. (1982) *Techniques of Brief Psychotherapy*. New York. Jason Aronson.

Fonagy, P. (1991) 'Thinking about thinking: some clinical and theoretical considerations in the treatment of a borderline patient', *International Journal of Psychoanalysis*, 72: 639–56.

Fonagy, P. (1998) 'An attachment theory approach to the treatment of the difficult patient', *Bulletin of the Menninger Clinic*, 62: 147–69.

Fonagy, P. (2001) *Attachment Theory and Psychoanalysis*. New York: Other.

Fonagy, P. et al. (1991) 'The capacity for understanding mental states: the reflective self in parent and child and its significance for security of attachment', *Infant Mental Health Journal*, 12: 201–18.

Foote, B. (1992) 'Accelerated empathic therapy: the first self-psychological brief therapy?' *International Journal of Short Term Psychotherapy*, 7(3): 177–92.

Fosha, D. (2000) *The Transforming Power of Affect: A Model for Accelerated Change*. New York: Basic Books.

Frances, A. and Clarkin, J.F. (1981) 'No treatment as the prescription of choice', in J. Groves, *Essential Papers on Short-Term Dynamic Psychotherapy*. New York: New York University Press, pp. 449–61.

Frances, A. and Perry, S. (1983) 'Transference interpretations in focal therapy', *American Journal of Psychiatry*, 140: 405–9.

French, T. (1952) *The Integration of Behaviour*, Vol. 1, *Basic Postulates*. Chicago: University of Chicago Press.

Freud, S. (1909) *Analysis of a Phobia in a Five Year Old Boy, Standard Edition*, Vol. 10. London: Hogarth Press.

Freud, S. (1912) *Recommendations to Physicians Practising Psychoanalysis, Standard Edition*, Vol. 12. London: Hogarth Press.

Freud, S. (1917) *Mourning and Melancholia. Standard Edition*, Vol. 14. London: Hogarth Press.

Freud, S. (1923) *The Ego and the Id. Standard Edition*, Vol. 19. London: Hogarth Press.

Freud, S. (1955) *Studies in Hysteria. Standard Edition*, Vol. 2. London: Hogarth Press.

Friedman, S., and Fanger, M. (1991) *Expanding Therapeutic Possibilities: Getting Results in Brief Psychotherapy*. Lexington, KS: Lexington Books.

Frieswyk, S.H., Allen, J.G., Colson, D.B., Coyne, L., Gabbard, G.O., Horowitz, L. and Newsome, G. (1986) 'Therapeutic alliance: its place as a process and outcome variable in dynamic psychotherapy research', *Journal of Counselling Psychology*, 54: 32–8.

Fromm-Reichman, F. (1950) *Principles of Intensive Psychotherapy*. Chicago: University of Chicago Press.

Gabbard, G., Beck, J. and Holmes, J. (2007) *Oxford Textbook of Psychotherapy*. Oxford: Oxford University Press.

Gardner, J. (1991) 'The application of self psychology to brief psychotherapy', *Psychoanalytic Psychology*, 8(4): 477–500.

Garfield, S. (1998) *The Practice of Brief Psychotherapy*. Chichester: John Wiley & Sons, Ltd.

Gaston, L. (1990) 'The concept of the alliance and its role in psychotherapy: theoretical and empirical considerations', *Psychotherapy: Theory, Research and Practice*, 27: 143–53.

Gelso, C.J. and Johnson, D.H. (1983) *Explorations in Time-Limited Counselling and Psychotherapy*. New York: Teachers College Press.

George, E. *et al.* (1990) 'Problem to solution', in *Brief Therapy with Individuals and Families*. London: B.T. Press.

Gill, M. (1994) *Psychoanalysis in Transition*. Hillsdale, NJ: The Analytic Press.

Gorsuch, N. (1998) 'Time's winged chariot: short term psychotherapy in later life', *Psychodynamic Counselling*, 4(2): 191–202.

Greenberg, J.R. and Mitchell, S.A. (1983) *Object Relations in Psychoanalytic Theory*. Cambridge, MA: Harvard University Press.

Greenson, R.R. (1981) *The Technique and Practice of Psychoanalysis*. London: The Hogarth Press and Institute of Psychoanalysis.

Groves, J.E. (1996) *Essential Papers on Short Term Dynamic Psychotherapy*. New York: New York University Press.

Gustafson, J.P. (1986) *The Complex Secret of Brief Psychotherapy*. New York: Norton.

Gustafson, J.P. (2005) *Very Brief Psychotherapy*. London: Routledge.

Guthrie, E. (1993) 'Psychological management of patients with irritable bowel syndrome', in M. Hodes and S. Moorey (eds) *Psychological Treatment in Disease and Illness*. London; Gaskell, Royal College of Psychiatrists.

Guthrie, E. (1999) 'Psychodynamic interpersonal therapy', *Advances in Psychiatric Treatment*, 5: 135–45.

Guthrie, E., Kapur, N., Mackway-Jones, K. et al. (2001) 'Randomised controlled trial of brief psychological intervention after deliberate self poisoning', *British Medical Journal*. 323: 135–8.

Guthrie, E., Kapur, N., Mackway-Jones, K., Chew-Graham, C., Moorey, J., Mendel, E., Francis, F.M., Sanderson, S., Turpin, C. and Boddy, G. (2003) 'Predictors of outcome following brief psychodynamic interpersonal therapy for deliberate self poisoning', *Australian and New Zealand Journal of Psychiatry*, 37: 532–6.

Guthrie, E., Moorey, J., Barker, H., Margison, F. and McGrath, G. (1998) 'Brief psychodynamic interpersonal therapy for patients with severe psychiatric illness which is unresponsive to treatment', *British Journal of Psychotherapy*, 15(2): 155–66.

Guthrie, E., Moorey, J. and Margison, F. (1999) 'Cost effectiveness of brief psychodynamic interpersonal therapy in high utilisers of psychiatric services', *Archives of General Psychiatry*, 56(6): 519–26.

Hartley, D.E. and Strupp, H.H. (1983) 'The therapeutic alliance: its relationship to outcome in brief psychotherapy', in J. Masling (ed.), *Empirical Studies of Psychoanalytical Theories*, Vol. 1, Hillsdale, NJ: Analytic Press, pp. 1–37.

Hawton, K. *et al.* (1989) *Cognitive Behaviour Therapy for Psychiatric Problems*. Oxford: Oxford University Press.

Hayes, S.C. and Strosahl, K.D. (2004) *A Practical Guide to Acceptance and Commitment Therapy*. New York: Springer.

Heard, D. and Lake, B. (1986) 'The attachment dynamic in adult life', *British Journal of Psychiatry*, 149: 430–8.

Henry, W.P., Schacht, T.E., Strupp, H.H., Butler S.F., and Binder, J.L. (1993) 'Effects of training in time limited dynamic psychotherapy: mediators of therapists' response to training', *Journal of Consulting and Clinical Psychology*, 61: 434–40.

Hildebrand, P. (1995) *Beyond Mid-Life Crisis*. London: Sheldon Press.

Hobson, R.F. (1982) *A Conversational Model of Psychotherapy: A Training Method*. London: Tavistock.

Hoglend, P. (1988) 'Brief dynamic psychotherapy for less well adjusted patients', *Psychotherapy and Psychosomatics*, 49: 197–204.

Hoglend, P. (1996) 'Long term effects of transference interpretations' *Acta Psychiatrica Scandinavica*. 93: 205–11.

Hoglend, P. (2003) 'Long term effects of brief dynamic psychotherapy', *Psychotherapy Research* 13: 271–92.

Holmes, J. (1993) *John Bowlby and Attachment Theory*. London: Routledge.

Holmes, J. (1997) 'Attachment, autonomy, intimacy: some clinical implications of attachment theory', *British Journal of Medical Psychology*, 70(3).

Holmes, J. (2001) *The Search for a Secure Base*. Hove: Psychology Press.

Holmes, J. (2008) 'Mentalisation: a key skill for psychiatrists and their patients – in 100 words', *British Journal of Psychiatry*, 193: 125.

Hopkins, L. (2006) *False Self: The Life of Masud Khan*. New York: Other Press.

Horowitz, M.J. (1986) *Stress Response Syndromes*. Northvale, NJ: Jason Aronson.

Horowitz, M.J. (1991) 'Short-term dynamic therapy of stress response syndromes', in P. Crits-Christoph and J. Barber (eds) *Handbook of Short-Term Dynamic Psychotherapy*. New York: Basic Books.

Horowitz, M.J. (1997) *Stress Response Syndromes: PTSD, Grief, and Adjustment Disorders*. Northvale, NJ: Jason Aronson.

Howard, K., Kopta, S., Krause, M. and Orlinsky, D. (1986) 'The dose-effect relationship in psychotherapy', *American Psychologist*, 41: 159–64.

Howard, P. (2008) 'Psychoanalytic psychotherapy', in S. Haugh and S. Paul (eds), *The Therapeutic Relationship: Perspectives and Themes*. Ross-on-Wye: PCCS Books.

Hoyt, M.F. (1985) 'Therapist resistances to short-term dynamic psychotherapy, *Journal of the American Academy of Psychoanalysis*, 13: 93–112.

Hoyt, M.F. (2000) *Some Stories Are Better Than Others: Doing What Works in Brief Therapy and Managed Care*. Hove: Psychology Press.

Hudson-Allez, G. (1997) *Time Limited Therapy in General Practice*. London: Sage.

Jacobs, M. (1988) *Psychodynamic Counselling in Action*. London: Sage.

Jacobs, M. (1996) 'Parallel process-confirmation and critique', *Psychodynamic Counselling*, 2(1).

Jerry, P.A. (1994) 'Winnicott's therapeutic consultation and the adolescent client', *Crisis Intervention and Time Limited Treatment*, 1(1): 61–72.

Kelly, G.A. (1955) *The Psychology of Personal Constructs*. New York: Norton.

Kernberg, O. (1975) *Borderline Conditions and Pathological Narcissism*. New York: Jason Aronson.

Klerman, G.L. *et al.* (1994) *Interpersonal Psychotherapy of Depression*. New York: Jason Aronson.

Kohut, H. (1971) *The Analysis of the Self*. New York: International University Press.

Kohut, H. (1977) *The Restoration of the Self*. New York: International University Press.

Kohut, H. (1984) *How Does Analysis Cure?* Chicago: University of Chicago Press.

Koss, M.P. and Shiang, J. (1994) 'Research on brief psychotherapy', in A. Bergin and S. Garfield (eds), *Handbook of Psychotherapy and Behaviour Change*, 4th edn. Chichester: John Wiley & Sons, Ltd.

Kraemer, S. and Roberts, R. (1996) *The Politics of Attachment: Towards a Secure Society*. London: Free Association Books.

Kupers, T. (1981) *Public Therapy: The Practice of Psychotherapy in the Public Mental Health Clinic*. New York: Free Press.

Kutek, A. (1999) 'The terminal as a substitute for the interminable', *Psychodynamic Practice*, 5(1): 7–24.

Lambert, M.J. and Ogles, B.M. (2004) 'The efficacy and effectiveness of psychotherapy', n A. Bergin and S. Garfield (eds), *Handbook of Psychotherapy and Behaviour Change*, 5th edn. New York: Wiley.

Lambert, M.J., Shapiro. D.A., and Bergin, A.E. (1986) 'The effectiveness of psychotherapy', in A. Bergin and S. Garfield (eds), *Handbook of Psychotherapy and Behaviour Change*, 3rd edition. New York: Wiley.

Langs, R. (1976) *The Bipersonal Field*. New York: Jason Aronson.

Laungani, P. (2004) *Asian Perspectives in Counselling and Psychology*. London: Routledge.

Lazarus, L. (1988) 'Self psychology: its application to brief psychotherapy with the elderly', *Journal of Geriatric Psychiatry*, 21(2): 104–25.

Lees, J. and Vaspe, A. (1999) *Clinical Counselling in Further and Higher Education*. London: Routledge.

Leibovich, M.A. (1996) 'Why short-term psychotherapy for borderlines?' in J. Groves, *Essential Papers on Short-Term Dynamic Therapy*. New York: New York University Press, pp. 437–47.

Levenson, H. (1995) *Time Limited Dynamic Psychotherapy*. New York: Basic Books.

Levenson, H. and Hales, R.E. (1993) 'Brief psychodynamically informed therapy for medically ill patients', in A. Stoudemire and B.S. Fogel (eds), *Medical Psychiatric Practice*, Vol. 2. Washington, DC: American Psychiatric Press.

Levenson, H., Speed, J., and Budman, S.H. (1995) 'Therapist's experience, training, and skill in brief therapy: a bicoastal survey', *American Journal of Psychotherapy*, 49: 95–117.

Litrell, J. (1998) *Brief Counselling in Action*. New York: W.W. Norton & Co.

Luborsky, L. *et al.* (2002) 'The dodo bird verdict is alive and well – mostly', *Clinical Psychology: Science and Practice*, 9: 2–12.

Lynch, G. (1998) 'The application of self psychology to short term-counselling', *Psychodynamic Counselling*, 473–485.

Macdonald, A.J. (1997) 'Brief therapy in adult psychiatry: further outcomes', *Journal of Family Therapy*, 9(2): 213–32.

Mace, C. (1995) *The Art and Science of Assessment in Psychotherapy*. London: Routledge.

Mace, C. (1999) 'Socratic psychotherapy', *Changes*, 17(3): 161–70.

Magnavita, J. (1997) *Restructuring Personality Disorders: A Short-Term Dynamic Approach*. New York: Guildford Press.

Mahler, M., Pine, F. and Bergman, A. (1985) *The Psychological Birth of the Human Infant*. London: Karnac.

Main, M. (1995) 'Recent studies in attachment: overview with selected implications for clinical work', in S. Goldberg et al. (eds), *Attachment Theory: Social, Developmental and Clinical Perspectives*. New York: Academic Press.

Malan, D. (1963) *A Study of Brief Psychotherapy*. London: Tavistock.

Malan, D. (1976) *Toward the Validation of Dynamic Psychotherapy: A Replication*. New York: Plenum Press.

Malan, D. (1979) *Individual Psychotherapy and the Science of Psychodynamics*. London: Butterworth.

Malan, D. (1992) 'The most important development in psychotherapy since the discovery of the unconscious', in H. Davanloo (ed.), *Short Term Dynamic Psychotherapy*. New York: Jason Aronson.

Malan, D. et al. (1975) 'Psychodynamic changes in untreated neurotic patients: apparently genuine improvements', in J. Groves, *Essential Papers on Short-Term Dynamic Therapy*. New York: New York University Press, pp. 461–506.

Malan, D. and Della Selva, P. (2006) *Lives Transformed: A Revolutionary Method of Dynamic Psychotherapy*. New York: Karnac.

Mander, G. (1998) 'Supervising short-term psychodynamic work', *Counselling*, November, 9(4): 301–5.

Mander, G. (2000) *A Psychodynamic Approach to Brief Therapy*. London: Sage.

Mander, G. (2005) 'Suitability and contexts for brief therapy', *Psychodynamic Practice*, 11(4).

Mann, J. (1973) *Time-limited Psychotherapy*. Cambridge, MA: Harvard University Press.

Mann, J. (1992) 'Time-limited psychotherapy', in P. Crits-Christoph and J.P. Barber (eds), *Handbook of Short-Term Dynamic Psychotherapy*. New York: Basic Books.

Mann, J. and Goldman, R. (1994) *A Casebook in Time-Limited Psychotherapy*. Cambridge, MA, Harvard University Press.

Marx, J.A., and Gelso, C.J. (1987) 'Termination of individual counselling in a university counselling centre', *Journal of Counseling Psychology*, 34: 3–9.

Messer, S.B. (2001) 'What makes brief psychodynamic therapy efficient?' *Clinical Psychology: Science and Practice*. 8(1): 5–22.

Messer, S.B. and Warren, S.W. (1995) *Models of Brief Psychodynamic Therapy: A Comparative Approach*. New York: The Guildford Press.

Mitchell, S.A. (1993) *Hope and Dread in Psychoanalysis*. New York: Basic Books.

Mitchell, S.A. (1997) *Influence and Autonomy in Psychoanalysis*. Hillsdale, NJ: The Analytic Press.

Model, A. (1968) *Object Love and Reality*. New York: International Universities Press.

Molnos, A. (1995) *A Question of Time*. London: Karnac Books.

Moorey, J. and Guthrie, E. (2003) 'Persons and experience: essential aspects of psychodynamic interpersonal therapy', *Psychodynamic Practice*, 4.

Mynor Wallis, L. and Gath, D. (1992) 'Brief psychological treatments', *International Review of Psychiatry*, 4: 301–6.

Norcross, J. (ed.) (2005) *Handbook of Psychotherapy Integration*. Oxford: Oxford University Press.

O'Connell, B. (2005) *Solution Focused Therapies*. London: Sage.

Ogden, T.H. (1994) *Subjects of Analysis*. Northvale, NJ: Jason Aronson.

Osimo, F. (2003) *Experiential Short-Term Dynamic Psychotherapy: A Manual*. Bloomington, IN: First Books.

Paley, G., Cahill, J., Barkham, M., Shapiro, D., Jones, J.P., Patrick, S. and Reid, E. (2008) 'The effectiveness of psychodynamic-interpersonal therapy (PIT) in routine clinical practice: a benchmarking comparison', *Psychology and Psychotherapy: Theory, Research and Practice*, 81(2): 157–71.

Palmer, S. (2002) *Multicultural Counselling: A Reader*. London: Sage.

Peterfreund, E. (1983) *The Process of Psychoanalytic Therapy: Models and Strategies*. Hillsdale, NJ: Analytic Press.

Pingitore, D. (1997) 'The corporatization of psychotherapy: a study in professional transformation', *Free Associations*, 6(1): 101–26.

Piper, W.E. (1993) 'Concentration and correspondence of transference interpretations in short-term individual psychotherapy', *Journal of Consulting and Clinical Psychology*, 61(4): 586–95.

Piper, W.E. (2002) *Interpretive and Supportive Psychotherapies: Matching Therapies and Patient Personality*. Washington, DC: APA.

Pollin, I. and Kanaan, S. (1995) *Medical Crisis Counselling: Short-Term therapy for Long Term Illness*. New York: Norton.

Racker, H. (1968) *Transference and Countertransference*. New York: International Universities Press.

Rado, S. (1942) 'The relationship of patient to therapist', *American Journal of Orthopsychiatry*, 12(3).

Rank, O. ([1929] 1973) *The Trauma of Birth*. New York: Harper & Row.

Ricoeur, P. (1984) *Time and Narrative*, Vol. 1. Chicago: University of Chicago Press.

Ross, P. (1999) 'Focussing the work: a cognitive behavioural approach', in J. Lees and A. Vaspe (ed.) *Clinical Counselling in Further and Higher Education*. London: Routledge.

Roth, A. and Fonagy, P. (2005) *What Works for Whom? A Critical Review of Psychotherapy Research*, 2nd edn. New York: The Guildford Press.

Rutter, M. (1985) 'Resilience in the face of adversity: protective factors and resistance to psychiatric disorder', *British Journal of Psychiatry*, 147: 598–611.

Ryle, A. (1995) *Cognitive Analytic Therapy: Developments in Theory and Practice*. Chichester, Wiley.

Ryle, A. (1997) *Cognitive Analytic Therapy and Borderline Personality Disorder: The Model and the Method*. Chichester: John Wiley & Sons, Ltd.

Ryle, A. (2002) *Introduction to Cognitive Analytic Therapy; Principles and Practice*. Chichester: John Wiley & Sons, Ltd.

Safran, J.D. and McMain, S. (1992) 'A cognitive interpersonal approach to the treatment of personality disorders', *Journal of Cognitive Psychotherapy*, 6(1): 59–68.

Safran, J.D. and Segal, Z.V. (1990) *Interpersonal Processes in Cognitive Therapy*. New York: Basic Books.

Salkovskis, P. (ed.) (1996) *Frontiers of Cognitive Therapy*. New York: Guildford Press.

Sanders, D. (1996) *Counselling for Psychosomatic Problems*. London: Sage.

Schacht, T.E., Binder, J.L. and Strupp, H.H (1984) 'The dynamic focus', in H.H. Strupp and J. L. Binder (eds), *Psychotherapy in a New Key*. New York: Basic Books.

Schafer, N.D. (1982) 'Multi-dimensional measures of therapist behaviour as a predictor of outcome', *Psychological Bulletin*, 92: 670–81.

Scharff, J.S. (1992) *Projective and Introjective Identification and the use of the Therapist's Self*. New York: Aronson

Schön, D.A. (1983) *The Reflective Practitioner: How Professionals Think in Action*. New York: Basic Books.

Schön, D.A. (1987) *Educating the Reflective Practitioner*. San Francisco: Jossey-Bass.

Segal, Z.V., Williams, J.M.G. and Teasdale, J.D. (2001) *Mindfulness-based Cognitive Therapy for Depression*. New York: Guilford Press.

Shafer, D. (1976) *A New Language for Psychoanalysis*. London: Yale University Press.

Shapiro, D. (1987) 'Prescriptive vs exploratory psychotherapy: outcome of the Sheffield Psychotherapy Project', *British Journal of Psychiatry*, 151: 790–9.

Sharpe, C. (2008) 'Theory of mind and conduct problems in children: deficits in reading the "emotion of the eyes"', *Cognition and Emotion*, 22(6): 1149–58.

Shefler, G. (2001) *Time Limited Psychotherapy in Practice*. London: Brunner Routledge.

Shipton, G. and Smith, E. (1998) *Long Term Counselling*. London: Sage.

Sifneos, P. (1972) *Short-Term Psychotherapy and Emotional Crisis*. Cambridge, MA: Harvard University Press.

Sifneos, P. (1979) *Short-Term Dynamic Psychotherapy*. New York: Plenum Press.

Silberschatz, P.E. and Curtis, J.T. (1986) 'Clinical implications of research on brief dynamic psychotherapy. How the therapist helps or hinders psychotherapeutic progress', *Psychoanalytic Psychology*, 3: 27–38.

Sledge, W.H., Moras, K., Hartley, D. and Levine, M. (1990) 'Effect of time limited psychotherapy on patient drop out rates', *American Journal of Psychiatry*, 147: 1341–7.

Small, R. and Barnhill, L. (1998) *Practicing in the New Mental Health Marketplace: Ethical, Legal and Moral Issues*. Washington, DC: American Psychological Association.

Smith, J.D (2005) 'Time and again: intermittent brief dynamic therapy', *Psychodynamic Practice*, 11(3): 269–82.

Smith, J.D (2006) 'Form and forming a focus in brief dynamic therapy', *Psychodynamic Practice*, 12(3): 261–7.

Smith, M,L., Glass, G.V. and Miller, T.I. (1980) *The Benefits of Psychotherapy*. Baltimore, MD: Johns Hopkins University Press.

Spence, D.P. (1982) *Narrative Truth and Historical Truth: Meaning and Interpretation in Psychoanalysis*. New York: Norton.

Stadter, M. (2004) *Object Relations Brief Therapy: The Therapeutic Relationship in Short-Term Work*. Northvale, NJ: Jason Aronson.

Stanton, M. (1990) *Sandor Ferenczi: Reconsidering Active Intervention*. London: Free Association Books.

Stern, D. (1985) *The Interpersonal World of the Infant*. New York: Basic Books.

Stern, D. (2004) *The Present Moment in Psychotherapy and Everyday Life*. New York: W.W. Norton.

Stiles, W., Barkham, M., Mellor-Clark, J. and Connell, J. (2007) 'Effectiveness of cognitive-behavioural, person centred and psychodynamic therapies in UK primary care routine practice: replication in a larger sample', *Psychological Medicine*, 38:677–88.

Strasser, F. and Strasser, A. (1997) *Existential Time Limited Therapy: The Wheel of Existence*. Chichester: John Wiley & Sons, Ltd.

Strupp, H.H. and Binder, J.L. (1984) *Psychotherapy in a New Key: A Guide to Time Limited Dynamic Psychotherapy*. New York: Basic Books.

Sugarman, L. (1996) 'Narratives of theory and practice: the psychology of life span development', in R. Woolf and W. Dryden (eds), *Handbook of Counselling Psychology*. London: Sage.

Talmon, M. (1993) *Single Session Solutions*. Reading, MA: Addison-Wesley.

Tantum, D. (1995) 'Why assess?' in C. Mace (ed.), *The Art and Science of Assessment in Psychotherapy*. London: Routledge.

Terry, P. (2008) *Counselling and Psychotherapy with Older People*. Basingstoke: Palgrave

Towler, J. (1997) 'Managing the counselling process in organisations', in M. Carroll and M/ Walton (eds), *Handbook of Counselling in Organisations*. London: Sage.

Trevarthan, C. (1980) 'The foundations of intersubjectivity: development of interpersonal and cooperative understanding in infants', in D.R. Olson (ed.), *The Social Foundation of Language and Thought: Essays in Honour of Jerome Brunner*. New York: W.W. Norton.

Tudor, K. (2001) *Transactional Analysis Approaches to Brief Therapy: What Do You Say Between Saying Hello and Goodbye?* London: Sage.

Tudor, K. (2008) *Brief Person Centered Therapies*. London: Sage.

Walter, B. (1947) *Theme and Variations*. London: Hamish Hamilton.

Walter, J.L. and Peller, J.E. (1992) *Becoming Solution Focussed in Brief Therapy*. New York: Brunner/Mazel.

Weiss, J. and Sampson, J. (1986) *The Psychoanalytic Process: Theory, Clinical Observation and Clinical Research*. New York: Guildford Press.

Wells, A. (2008) *Metacognitive Therapy for Anxiety and Depression*. New York: Guilford Press.

Wheeler, S. (2006) *Difference and Diversity in Counselling: Contemporary Psychodynamic Perspectives*. Basingstoke: Palgrave.

White, M. and Epston, D. (1990) *Narrative Means to Therapeutic Ends*. New York: W.W. Norton.

Wiener, J. and Sher, M. (1998) *Counselling and Psychotherapy in Primary Health Care*. London: Macmillan.

Wilkinson, P. (2008) 'Review of *Clinician's Quick Guide to Interpersonal Psychotherapy* by M. Weissman, J. Markowitz. and J. Klerman', *Psychological Medicine*, 38: 900–1.

Wills, F. and Sanders, D. (1997) *Cognitive Therapy: Transforming the Image*. London: Sage.

Winnicott, D.W. (1971) *Therapeutic Consultations in Child Psychiatry*. London: The Hogarth Press.

Winnicott, D.W. (1990) *The Maturational Process and the Facilitating Environment*. London: Hogarth Press.

Winokur, M. and Dasberg, H. (1983) 'Teaching and learning short-term psychotherapy: techniques and resistances', *Bulletin of the Menninger Clinic*, 47(1): 36–52.

Wolberg, L.R. (1980) *Handbook of Short-Term Psychotherapy*. New York: Thieme-Stratton.

Young, J.E. (1994) *Cognitive Therapy for Personality Disorders: A Schema-Focussed Approach*. Sarasota, FL: Personal Resource Exchange.

INDEX

organisational issues 203–4
Osimo, F. 218
outcome *see* therapeutic outcome
outcome vs. process research 206

paradox 45
paradoxical injunction 60
part objects 43, 106
personal construct theory 46
personal idiom/s 65, 66–7, 71, 72, 74,
 81, 84, 88, 93, 95, 96, 97–8, 144, 168,
 170, 197, 198, 200, 224
personal schemas 37, 45, 64
Peterfreund, E. 36
Pingitore, D. 213
post traumatic stress disorder (PTSD)
 38, 200
primary care 189–93
 case study (Henrietta) 190–3
principle of flexibility 18, 19
process *see* therapeutic process
process vs. outcome research 206
projection/s 20, 28, 29, 35, 116, 120, 130
propaganda 58
psychiatric services 200
psychoanalysis 64, 78, 83, 103, 108,
 109–10, 123, 149, 158, 171, 172, 173,
 180, 188, 217, 221, 223, 225
 history of short-term therapy in the
  development of 7–33
psychoanalytic theory 87, 158, 172,
 174, 201, 204, 224
 application in contemporary time-
  limited therapies 34–62
psychodynamic interpersonal therapy
 (PIT) 40–1, 113
psychological mindedness 111, 114,
 115, 200, 202
psychosis/psychotic 26, 60, 117, 124, 207
public sector 1, 124, 177, 188

Rado, S. 148
Rank, O. 11–13, 16, 19, 20
rational-emotive therapy 43
reciprocal relationships 46, 64
recurrent interpersonal patterns 140
recurring motifs 65, 70, 71, 74, 77
reflection in action 180–1, 187
reflection on action 180, 181, 187

reflective practice/practitioners 181,
 185–6, 187
reflective self-function 33
reformulation/s 47–8, 155
reframing 59, 106, 108
 symptoms 9
regression 19, 103, 120, 148, 158
relatedness 12, 16
relational, the 216, 222, 225
relational approaches 11, 34–5, 37, 38,
 50, 87, 92, 108, 119
relational difficulties 39, 135
 core 140–1, 147, 152, 165–6, 219
relational focus 158
relational history 119, 142, 188, 200
relational models 17, 119, 143 *see also*
 object relations model
relational school of psychoanalysis 53
relational style 44, 121, 208
relational templates 65, 88, 91
relational skills 183
religious difference *see* difference
repetitive patterns 26, 64, 139
resistance/s 8, 10, 11, 12, 23, 28, 29, 30,
 33, 55, 80, 108, 123, 152–4, 155, 159,
 174, 190, 218
 case study (Jason) 153–4
 to short-term therapy 33, 173, 174,
  176, 186
 systemic 50
rigour 10, 219, 220, 221
ripple effect 21, 59, 61, 81, 101, 103, 117,
 134, 163, 182
role transitions 41
Ross, P. 45
Roth, A. 177, 206, 207, 216
Ryle, A. 46–9

'sacred moments' 58, 64, 65, 103, 138
Sampson, J. 64
Scharff, J.S. 157
schema-focused cognitive therapy
 44–5, 78
schemas *see* personal schemas
schematic representations 37, 64
schizoid 55, 105
 borderline/schizoid personality
  129–30
Schön, D. 180

triangle of persons/triangle of insight
(TCP)   25, 26, 27, 29, 72–3, 97, 118,
155, 163, 170, 194, 223
triangle of therapy *see* therapeutic
triangle
trust   23, 40, 80, 86, 94, 137, 144, 145, 209

Vanderbilt Group   36–7

Walter, Bruno   8
Walton, Tony   67

Warren, C.   79, 124, 127, 135, 143, 174–5,
176, 220
Weiss, J.   64
Wiener, J.   117
Winnicott, D.   56–9, 64, 67, 100, 103, 138,
157, 165, 186, 219
Wolberg, L.   49, 219
working alliance   78, 79, 80, 208
working through   10, 19, 55, 101, 162–4,
170